Essentials of Applied Econometrics

ESSENTIALS OF APPLIED ECONOMETRICS

Aaron Smith

J. Edward Taylor

UNIVERSITY OF CALIFORNIA PRESS

University of California Press, one of the most distinguished
university presses in the United States, enriches lives around
the world by advancing scholarship in the humanities, social
sciences, and natural sciences. Its activities are supported by the
UC Press Foundation and by philanthropic contributions from
individuals and institutions. For more information, visit
www.ucpress.edu.

University of California Press
Oakland, California

Library of Congress Cataloging-in-Publication Data
Names: Smith, Aaron, author. | Taylor, J. Edward, author.
Title: Essentials of applied econometrics / Aaron Smith,
    J. Edward Taylor.
Description: Oakland, California : University of California Press,
    [2017] | Includes index. | Description based on print version
    record and CIP data provided by publisher; resource not viewed.
Identifiers: LCCN 2016018912 (print) | LCCN 2016018067 (ebook) |
    ISBN 9780520963290 (ebook) | ISBN 9780520288331 (pbk. : alk.
    paper)
Subjects: LCSH: Econometrics—Textbooks.
Classification: LCC HB139 (print) | LCC HB139 .S6255 2017 (ebook) |
    DDC 330.01/5195—dc23
LC record available at https://lccn.loc.gov/2016018912

Manufactured in the United States of America

25 24 23 22 21 20 19 18 17 16

10 9 8 7 6 5 4 3 2 1

Contents

Preface

This book was designed to give students the tools they need to carry out econometric analysis in the modern world. Most textbooks assume that the purpose of econometrics is to formulate a true mathematical model of a piece of the economy or to estimate whether a change in one variable causes change in another. Many students are unsure what to do if they cannot justify the often unrealistic assumptions required of a true model or a causal effect. If the model is misspecified, does this mean it is useless? If we cannot convincingly justify causality, are we wasting our time?

Much work in practice does not have such grand goals. Google does not usually care about doing airtight tests of whether one variable *causes* another. It is more interested in using (often very large) data sets to find correlations and predict people's behavior. Estimating correlations and performing predictions are very different goals to formulating true models and establishing causality. We believe our book is unique among intermediate econometrics texts at making this distinction clear.

Traditional econometrics textbooks also confound two distinct sets of assumptions that econometricians make. Some of these assumptions address how your data sample represents the whole population (sampling theory) and some of these assumptions address how economic variables relate to each other (causal analysis). Most textbooks lump these assumptions together, which makes it unclear where one ends and the other begins. However, if your goal is correlation or prediction, then you need

the sampling theory assumptions but not the causal analysis assumptions.

Our book begins with sampling theory: how to use a sample to make inferences about a whole population. We address causality as a distinct topic in the last two chapters of the book. In between, we cover the critical topics that are an essential part of any econometrics course, including properties of estimators, hypothesis testing, dealing with nonlinear relationships, heteroskedasticity, correlated errors, and sampling bias. These are essentials of applied econometrics regardless of whether the goal of your research concerns correlation, prediction, or causation.

The book covers essential econometric theory but with an emphasis on the best practices for estimating econometric models. It stresses the importance of being explicit about the purpose of the analysis, i.e., the population we want our analysis to inform us about and whether our goal is to establish correlation, predict outcomes, or demonstrate causation. Real-world examples are used throughout to illuminate the concepts presented while stimulating student interest in putting econometric tools to use.

THE GENESIS OF REBELTEXT

It was Winter Quarter 2012. The memory of student protests and pepper spray still permeated the air above the UC Davis quad. Ed gritted his teeth and told the campus bookstore to order up 125 copies of an undergraduate econometrics textbook at \$150 a shot. (That's a gross of \$18,750 just from one class.)

Over dinner that night, Ed's 20-year-old son, Sebastian, just back from occupying the Port of Oakland, said he spent \$180 on a new edition calculus text required for his course. Sebastian's little brother, Julian, exclaimed: "That's obscene." Sebastian responded, "You're right. Basic calculus hasn't changed in decades. You don't need new editions to learn calculus."

Before dinner was over, Ed's two kids had ambushed him and made him promise never, ever, to assign an expensive textbook to his students again.

"So, what do you want me to do then, write one?" Ed asked them.

"Exactly," they answered in unison.

"And get a good title for it," Ed's wife, Peri, added.

The next day, RebelText was born. What's RebelText?

First, it's affordable. It costs as little as one-fifth the price of a normal textbook. Second, it's concise. It covers what one can hope to get through in a quarter- or semester-long course. Third, it's more compact than most textbooks. Being both affordable and compact, you can carry it around with you. Write in it. Don't worry about keeping the pages clean, because at this price there's no need to resell it after the class is through (or worry about whether there will still be a market for your edition). This RebelText will naturally evolve as needed to keep pace with the field, but there will never, ever, be a new edition just for profits' sake.

WHO SHOULD USE THIS BOOK AND HOW

When we sat down to write *Essentials of Applied Econometrics*, we wanted a compact book for an upper-division undergraduate econometrics class. That is primarily what this is. The knowledge in this book should prime any undergraduate for further study or to venture out into the real world with an appreciation for the essential concepts and tools of econometrics. More than a textbook, this can be a helpful basic reference in applied econometrics for any graduate student, researcher, or practitioner.

RebelText was created to make learning and teaching as efficient as possible. We need to learn the essentials of the subject. We do not want to wade through thick textbooks in order to locate what we need to know, constantly wondering what will and won't be on the next test. We especially do not want to pay for a big textbook that we don't come close to finishing in the course! Because it is concise, there is no reason not to read and study every word of *Essentials of Applied Econometrics*. All of it could be on the test. Master it, and you will be conversant enough to strike up a conversation with anyone who does econometrics, and you'll have the basic tools to do high-quality applied econometric work. Think of this book as presenting the "best practices" and state-of-the-art methods for doing econometrics. By mastering it, you'll also have the conceptual and intuitive grounding you need in order to move on to higher-level econometrics courses. You'll probably find yourself referring back to it from time to time, so keep it on your shelf!

STUDENT RESOURCES ONLINE

Essentials of Applied Econometrics is intended to be used interactively with online content. We encourage you to visit our living website, http://www.ucpress.edu/go/appliedeconometrics, where you will find an "Econometrics Rosetta Stone" showing how to use some of the most popular software packages to do econometric analysis. You will also find a variety of interesting data sets, study questions, and online appendices for our book. We welcome your suggestions for other online content you discover on your own! When we use the textbook, the website becomes a center of class activity.

INSTRUCTOR RESOURCES ONLINE

A set of instructor resources including test questions and images for lecture presentations are available for download with permission of the publisher. If you are teaching with *Essentials of Applied Econometrics*, consider contributing your ideas about novel uses of the book and website, interesting data sets, programs, and projects to the RebelText movement. To find out how, visit rebeltext.org and click on "contributing to RebelText."

Acknowledgments

This book would not have happened without our families and students. Ed gives special thanks to Sebastian and Julian, who shamed him into launching the RebelText project; to his wife Peri Fletcher, who believed in this project from the start; to Laika, who managed to eat only a couple early drafts of our manuscript; and to UC Davis undergraduate Quantitative Methods (ARE 106) students, who were our guinea pigs and cheerleaders while this book was being written. Aaron thanks his wife Heather and daughter Hayley for their enduring patience and inspiration while he labored on this book. He also thanks Heather for teaching him about California school finance and thereby providing us with the main example we use in the book. Abbie Turiansky was instrumental in helping us put together the very first draft of many of the chapters in this book. Michael Castelhano, Justin Kagin, Dale Manning, and Karen Thome provided valuable research assistance at various stages of this project. We are greatly indebted to Jan Camp at Arc Light Books, who helped us launch the first RebelTexts as print-on-demand books.

Aaron Smith and J. Edward Taylor
Davis, California, 2016

About the Authors

Aaron Smith's first real job was teaching econometrics (not counting working on the family farm in New Zealand where he grew up). In 1994, just before heading off to graduate school, he taught an econometrics class much like the one you're probably taking with this book. It was a scary and invigorating experience—he must have enjoyed it because he's still doing it all these years later! He is currently a professor of Agricultural and Resource Economics at UC Davis, where he has been since 2001 after earning his PhD in Economics from UC San Diego. When not teaching, he does research on policy, prices, and trading in agricultural, energy, and financial markets. Recent project topics include identifying which traders in commodity futures markets seem to know where prices are headed, estimating how the recent growth in the use of ethanol made from corn as an ingredient in gasoline has affected food and gas prices, and understanding commodity booms and busts. His research has won the Quality of Communication, Quality of Research Discovery, and Outstanding *American Journal of Agricultural Economics* Article Awards from the Agricultural and Applied Economics Association. You can learn more about Aaron at his website: asmith.ucdavis.edu.

J. Edward Taylor loves teaching economics, especially econometrics, microeconomics, and economic development. He's been doing it for about 25 years now at UC Davis, where he is a professor in the Agricultural and Resource Economics Department. He's also done a lot of economic research. At last count, he had published about 150 articles, book chapters, and books on topics ranging from labor economics, international trade, immigration, biodiversity, and poverty—and more than 20,000 citations on Google Scholar. He's in *Who's Who in Economics*, the list of the world's most cited economists; a Fellow of the Agricultural and Applied Economics Association (AAEA), and recent editor of the *American Journal of Agricultural Economics (AJAE)*. Nearly everything Ed does involves applied econometrics. He has presented his findings to the US Congress, the United Nations, the World Bank, and governments around the world, and he is published in journals ranging from *The American Economic Review* to *Science*. His recent book, *Beyond Experiments in Development Economics: Local Economy-Wide Impact Evaluation* (Oxford University Press, 2014), won the AAEA Quality of Communication Award. You can learn more about Ed at his website: jetaylor.ucdavis.edu.

Introduction to Econometrics

It is interesting that people try to find meaningful patterns in things that are essentially random.

—Data, Star Trek

LEARNING OBJECTIVES

Upon completing the work in this chapter, you will be able to:

▶ Define and describe the basics of econometrics
▶ Describe how to do an econometric study

Jaime Escalante was born in Bolivia in 1930. He immigrated to the United States in the 1960s, hoping for a better life. After teaching himself English and working his way through college, he became a teacher at Garfield High School in East Los Angeles. Jaime believed strongly that higher math was crucial for building a successful career, but most of the students at Garfield High, many of whom came from poor backgrounds, had very weak math skills. He worked tirelessly to transform these kids into math whizzes. Incredibly, more than a quarter of all the Mexican-American high school students who passed the AP calculus test in 1987 were taught by Jaime.

Hollywood made a movie of Jaime's story called "Stand and Deliver." If you haven't seen that movie, you've probably seen one of the other dozens with a similar plot. An inspiring and unconventional teacher gets thrown into an unfamiliar environment filled with struggling or troubled kids. The teacher figures out how to reach the kids, they perform well in school, and their lives change forever.

We all have stories of an inspiring teacher we once had. Or a terrible teacher we once had. Meanwhile, school boards everywhere struggle with the question of how to teach kids and turn them into economically productive adults. Do good teachers really make all the difference in our lives? Or do they merely leave us with happy memories? Not every school can have a Jaime Escalante. Is more funding for public schools the answer? Smaller class sizes? Better incentives for teachers? Technology?

Econometrics can provide answers to big questions like these.

WHAT IS ECONOMETRICS?

Humans have been trying to make sense of the world around them for as long as anyone knows. Data bombard our senses: movements in the night sky, the weather, migrations of prey, growth of crops, spread of pestilence. We have evolved to have an innate curiosity about these things, to seek patterns in the chaos (empirics), then explanations for the patterns (theories). Much of what we see around us *is* random, but some of it is not. Sometimes our lives have depended on getting this right: predicting where to find fish in the sea (and being smart enough to get off the sea when a brisk nor'easter wind starts to blow), figuring out the best time to plant a crop, or intervening to arrest the spread of a plague. A more complex world gives us ever more data we have to make sense of, from climate change to Google searches to the ups and downs of the economy.

Econometrics is about making sense of economic data (literally, it means "economy measurement"). Often, it is defined as the application of statistics to economic data, but it is more than that. To make sense of economic data, we usually need to understand something about the unseen processes that create these data. For example, we see differences in people's earnings and education (years of completed schooling). Econometric studies consistently find that there is a positive relationship between the two variables. Can we use people's schooling to predict their earnings? And if we *increase* people's schooling, can we say that their earnings will increase?

These are two different questions, and they get at the hardest part of econometrics—distilling causation from correlation. We may use an econometric model to learn that people with a college degree earn more than those without one. That is a predictive, or correlative, relationship. We don't know whether college graduates earn more because of useful things they learned in college—that is, whether college *causes* higher earnings. College graduates tend to have high IQ, and they might have earned a lot regardless of whether or not they went to college. Mark Twain (who was not educated beyond elementary school) once said: "I've never let my school interfere with my education." He might have had a point.

Often, an econometrician's goal is to determine whether some variable, X, causes an outcome, Y. But not all of econometrics is about causation. Sometimes we want to generate predictions and other times test a theory. Clearly defining the purpose of an econometrics research project is the first step toward getting credible and useful results. The second step is to formulate your research design and specify your econometric model, and the final step is to apply statistical theory to answer the question posed in step 1.

Most of your first econometrics course focuses on step 3, but don't forget steps 1 and 2! Throughout the book, we will remind you of these steps. Next, we discuss each of the three steps to put the rest of the book in context.

STEP 1: WHAT DO YOU WANT TO DO?

The first step in doing econometrics is to define the purpose of the modeling. It is easy to skip this step, but doing so means your analysis is unlikely to be useful.

Your purpose should be concrete and concise. "I want to build a model of the economy" is not enough. What part of the economy? What do you want to learn from such a model? Often, if you can state your purpose in the form of a question, you will see whether you have defined it adequately.

Here are some examples.

Do Good Teachers Produce Better Student Outcomes?

To estimate whether good teachers improve life outcomes, we first need to measure teacher quality. In a 2014 study, Raj Chetty, John Friedman, and Jonah Rockoff constructed measures of how much an above-average teacher improves students' test scores over what they would have been with an average teacher. These are called "value-added" (VA) measures of teacher quality and were estimated using detailed data on elementary school records from a large urban school district. This research was deemed so important that it was presented in not one but two papers in the most prestigious journal in economics, the *American Economic Review*.[1]

Chetty and his coauthors used econometrics with their VA measures to show that replacing an average teacher with a teacher whose VA is in the top 5% would increase students' earnings later in life by 2.8%. This might seem small, but the average 12-year-old in the United States can expect lifetime earnings of $522,000,[2] so a 2.8% earnings bump is worth about $14,500 per student. Multiply that by 20 kids per classroom and an excellent teacher starts to look really valuable. It works the other way too—teachers with low VA potentially have large negative effects on lifetime earnings.

Does the Law of Demand Hold for Electricity?

In microeconomic theory, the law of demand predicts that when the price of a good rises, demand for the good falls. Does this theoretical prediction hold up in the real world? Is the own-price elasticity of demand really negative? How large is it? Finding a negative correlation between price and demand is consistent with economic theory; finding the opposite is not.

Katrina Jessoe and David Rapson asked this question using data on residential electricity consumption.[3] They conducted an experiment in which they divided homes randomly into three groups. The first group faced electricity prices that jumped by 200–600% on certain days of the year. The second group faced the same price rises but also were given an electronic device that told them in real time how much electricity they were using. The third group was the control group: they experienced no change in their electricity prices.

Jessoe and Rapson used econometrics to estimate that consumers in the first group did not change their consumption significantly compared with the control group—they had a price elasticity of demand close to zero. However, the second group had a price elasticity of demand of −0.14. Conclusion: the law of demand holds for electricity, but only if consumers know how much electricity they are using in real time. Without this knowledge, they don't know how much electricity is used when they run the air conditioner or switch on a light, so they don't respond to a price change.

Is It Possible to Forecast Stock Returns?

Lots of people think they can make money in the stock market. We often receive emails informing us of the next greatest stock tip. Business TV channels are full of people yelling about how to make money in the stock market. Every time the market crashes, there's a great story about the genius investor who saw it all coming and made money during the crash.[4] But if it's so easy to make money in the stock market, why isn't everyone doing it?

Based on the theory of efficient financial markets, many economists cast a skeptical eye on claims that the stock market is highly predictable. If everyone knew the market was going to go up, then it would have already done so. However, economic theory also predicts that financial investments should have returns in proportion to risk. Riskier investments should have higher returns on average. So, if you can measure risk in the stock market, then you should be able to predict returns to some extent.

Ivo Welch and Amit Goyal took a large number of variables that people claimed could predict stock returns and used econometrics to test whether any of them actually could.[5] They conclude that there is little, if any, statistical evidence of stock return predictability. So next time you hear a prognosticator claiming that the stock market is about to crash because it crashed the last seven times the president went skiing on a Tuesday . . . or something . . .., change the channel!

STEP 2: FORMULATE YOUR RESEARCH DESIGN AND SPECIFY THE ECONOMETRIC MODEL

This step typically requires some economic theory, common sense, and a little cleverness. It is where you take your abstract objective from step 1 and convert it into an econometric model with data that can answer your questions.

Making a good choice about what data to collect and use determines whether you will be able to meet your objective. Let's look again at the three studies we highlighted above.

Do Good Teachers Produce Better Student Outcomes?

Microeconomic theory of the firm provides us with a theory of how a teacher might affect earnings. It's called human capital theory.[6] Human capital theory predicts that workers are paid the marginal value product of their labor (MVPL). A firm will not hire a worker unless the additional value she produces (her MVPL) is at least as large as what the firm will have to pay the worker (i.e., the wage). Characteristics that raise workers' productivity, like intelligence, ability to concentrate and willingness to work hard, should be associated with higher wages. Having had a good teacher is one characteristic that may raise productivity.

One possible research design would be to build an econometric model of the determinants of test scores. If students in teacher A's class get better than average test scores, then teacher A must be a good teacher. There is a big problem with that approach. Classes with a lot of students from disadvantaged backgrounds will tend to get lower-than-average scores no matter how good the teacher is (unless the teacher is the subject of a Hollywood movie).

This is why Chetty and his coauthors developed their VA measures.[7] Their method first predicts test scores for thousands of students based on variables such as last year's test score and family socioeconomic characteristics. Next, they look at how well each student does relative to the prediction. If the students in a class tend to do better than predicted, then Chetty and coauthors assign a high VA score to the teacher. They conduct a series of tests of their VA measure. For example, they look at what happens when an average teacher leaves a school and is replaced by a teacher with a higher VA. They find that test scores jump up from the previous year, which validates their method.

Does the Law of Demand Hold for Electricity?

Microeconomic theory posits that the price and quantity in a market are determined at the point where supply equals demand. When some exogenous shock (like a new invention) shifts the supply outward, the price drops to convince consumers to buy more. When demand increases, the price rises to convince suppliers to produce more. When testing the law of demand, an econometrician wants to see how much consumers respond when a supplier changes the price. The problem is that often in the real world the price is high because consumers really like the product.

When the weather gets hot, consumers turn on their air conditioners and their electricity consumption goes up. This weather-induced increase in demand could cause electricity prices to go up.[8] It would generate a positive correlation between consumption and price. Should we conclude, then, that the law of demand is false? Of course not, because the positive correlation comes from high demand causing high prices, not high prices causing more demand.

One way to think about whether you have a good research design is to imagine what experiment you would run if you could. Jessoe and Rapson went one better and actually ran it. They convinced an electric utility to let them raise prices for a random set of customers on hot days and keep prices the same for other customers. Because they were controlling prices themselves, and because they randomly assigned who got the high prices rather than cherry picking receptive customers, they could be confident they were really measuring consumer responses. This is an example of experimental economics.

Even if you can't run the experiment, thinking about how you would conduct that experiment can help you figure out whether you have data that can answer your research question.

Is It Possible to Forecast Stock Returns?

Finance theory says that stock returns should be higher when investors are more risk averse. (A higher return is needed to incentivize these investors to take on more risk and invest.) Researchers have proposed many measures of risk – often referred to as systematic risk factors. For example, if you have a high chance of losing your job, you are likely to be more risk averse than otherwise. You would only want to put your money in something risky like stocks if the price were low enough and the future expected gains high enough to make it worth the risk.

Welch and Goyal used this theory and the research from past studies to come up with a list of predictors to test. Without theoretical guidance on which predictors to consider, the possibilities would be endless.

Even with a theoretically motivated group of predictors, demonstrating whether a predictor works is hard because we don't *really* know how the predictor was chosen. A previous researcher may have engaged in data snooping, which means they searched repeatedly until they found a variable that correlated significantly with stock returns and then made up an economic story about why it measures risk aversion. If you search hard enough, you will find a significant looking but meaningless correlation. Welch and Goyal account for this possibility using what is called an *out-of-sample test*. They fit econometric models using data prior to 1965, and then they see whether the predictors that perform well prior to 1965 continue to work after 1965.

In each of these studies, the researchers applied some economic theory, some common sense, and a little cleverness. The best sources of theoretical insights are the intermediate theory courses that most likely were a prerequisite for this econometrics course. Throughout this book, we will refer to what we learned in our theory courses as a useful resource in building econometric models.

The researchers each thought about mathematical form of their models. Does Y increase linearly with X? Is this relationship likely to be quadratic instead of linear? Logarithmic? Which control variables should be included in the equation? We can use econometrics to test whether the relationship between X and Y is linear or nonlinear, and what mathematical form is best to predict an outcome of interest. For example, we might find that there is a significant relationship between X and Y that is evident using a nonlinear model but not a linear one. In short, we need both economic theory and mathematics—plus a little experimentation with functional forms—to come up with the model we want to estimate.

STEP 3: APPLY STATISTICAL THEORY

Statistical theory helps us fill the gap between the numbers we compute from our data and the broader world. There is a gap because no econometric model can perfectly predict every data point and because we usually only observe data from a sample of the population.

Suppose you are trying to predict earnings of individuals for a population of 100,000 people. Now, imagine you get really lucky: someone hands you data on earnings and years of education for the *whole* population. That's right, 100,000 people. (It sounds like a lot of data, but Aaron and Ed work with *samples* a lot larger than this sometimes, and it's puny compared to what Google works with!) We said "really lucky" because we almost never have data on whole populations.

With data on the whole population, you could fit a regression model using the methods we'll learn in Chapter 2. This model would produce the predicted income for each individual based on his or her education level. Suppose you find, with this population model, that the expected earnings for a person with 16 years of schooling is $50,000.

But not every person with 16 years of education will earn exactly $50,000. Some will earn more, and others will earn less. We cannot expect, using only information on education, to predict everyone's income perfectly. The model has an error. To be precise, let's call this the population error.

Perfect prediction is usually not a realistic goal for our analysis. So it's OK that the model has an error. However, the error creates another problem. In the real world, we typically observe only a sample of the population. You might only have 1,000 observations with which to make predictions about a population of 100,000. You know your sample model will have an error, but how much of the error comes from differences between the sample and population and how much is due to the population error?

This is where statistics comes in. Statistics is the science of using sample data to make statements about a whole population.

How do we do this? The first thing you should worry about is how the sample of 1,000 got chosen from the population of 100,000. To be able to say something about the whole population, the sample you used to estimate the model has to be representative of the whole population. If your sample is not representative of the population, the errors in your predictions will reflect that lack of representativeness. "Representative" means "as if drawn randomly from the population." For example, if your sample includes mostly low-ability people, it is not representative of a population that includes both low- and high-ability individuals. The representativeness of the sample is so important that we devote a chapter to it later in this book (Chapter 10).

Given a representative sample, we need to make some assumptions about what the population errors look like in order to use our sample data to make statements of probability about the whole population. Once we learn the basic econometric regression model, most of the rest of this book will be dedicated to testing whether those assumptions about the population error are correct, and what to do about it if they are not.

What generates errors in the population model? The answer is that anything that explains earnings and is not in the model gets reflected in the error. That "anything" could include variables that we think should be in the model, because theory, experience, or intuition tell us so, but for which we do not have information. The effects of innate intelligence, drive, willingness to take risks, and other variables that might systematically influence earnings fall into the error if we do not include them explicitly in our model.

Missing and unobserved variables, we shall see, can cause problems, particularly when we want to estimate a *causal* relationship between X and Y. That is what Chapters 11 and 12 are about. There we will see that if X is exogenous, like if education levels were assigned randomly at birth, then we can estimate the causal relationship between X and Y even if other relevant variables are not in the model. Often, though, the right-hand-side variables in our model are not exogenous, like when people decide how much education to get, and unseen variables like ability explain both education and earnings. Then it becomes difficult—sometimes impossibly so—to isolate the effect of the included variable (education) from the effect of the omitted one (ability).

Even when relevant variables are left out of the model, the model might be useful for predicting Y using information on X. Knowing how much education someone has allows us to get better predictions of someone's earnings. Including additional relevant variables in our model might improve our predictive power.

We cannot control for everything. There is a stochastic or random component of the error, which is often referred to as "white noise." Albert Einstein wrote: "God does not play dice with the universe." But when it comes to statistics, the relationship we see between X and Y has an error thrown in, like rolling dice.

AN ILLUSTRATION WITH THE POPULATION MEAN

Here's a simple illustration of the population error. Suppose we have reliable data on income (Y) for *everyone* in a population. We could use these data to calculate the population's true mean income, which we could designate as μ (the Greek letter "mu"). You know how to calculate it: take the sum of everyone's income and divide it by the size of the population.

We already pointed out that we almost never have data on the entire population—only a sample of it. Instead of gathering income data on everyone in the population (which may be prohibitively expensive and infeasible), we can collect data from a random sample of size N from the population. Assume the sampling is truly random, which makes the sample representative of the whole population. We can use these data to estimate the sample mean, using the estimator $\bar{Y} = \frac{1}{N}\sum_{i=1}^{N} Y_i$. Unless we are impossibly lucky, this will not equal μ. What we get will depend on the "luck of the draw" that gave us the sample.

We could go out and survey a different random sample of the population, and we'd get a different estimate of μ. We could repeat this process another 9,998 times, and we'd have 10,000 different estimates of μ. Sometimes we will get an estimate that is high, and sometimes it will be low. Every now and then it will be *very* high or *very* low.

If we were to pick one of the 10,000 estimates at random, we would have no reason to expect it to be too high or too low. Formally, this means that the sample mean is unbiased as an estimate of the population mean. With this knowledge and a little more—including an estimate of the population variance—statistics lets us make statements of probability about the true population mean using data from a single sample. That, in a nutshell, is the power of statistics. In Chapters 4–6, we will learn how to make similar kinds of statements of probability using econometric models.

Econometrics is challenging because it integrates all three of these fields—economics, mathematics, and statistics—into one.

PUTTING IT TOGETHER: POVERTY AND TEST SCORES

We started this chapter with a story about how a good teacher can improve student test scores. Many other variables also affect test scores. Like poverty. Some schools are located in poor neighborhoods, while others are in rich ones. Children who grow up in poor households might not have the same opportunities to learn and expand their minds through travel, the internet, or other means, as children in rich households. They may be consumed with worry about where the next meal will come from rather than focusing on school. Schools in poor neighborhoods might have poorer facilities, fewer extracurricular activities, less access to advanced placement courses, and less overall funding per pupil than schools in rich neighborhoods.

How does poverty relate to student performance? To answer this question, we first need to measure "student performance" and "poverty."

The government of California measures school performance using a single number, the academic performance index (API), constructed from students' scores on statewide standardized tests. The API ranges from a low of 200 to a high of 1,000. We can use the API as our measure of average student performance at each California school.

Measuring poverty is more problematic. We do not know the household per capita incomes for each student at each school, so we cannot measure poverty directly. However, we do have an indirect measure or proxy for poverty. The US National School Lunch Program provides free or reduced-price lunches to schoolchildren from low-income households. We know the share of students eligible for free or reduced-price lunches at each school in California. We can use free-lunch eligibility (FLE) as an indicator of the share of students from households with incomes below the poverty line at each school.

Table 1.1 presents the API and FLE at 20 randomly chosen California schools in 2013—from a total population of 5,765 schools. Our first challenge will be to figure out the relationship between FLE and API, using these data. In the next chapter, we will learn how to use econometric tools to predict schools' API based on their FLE. In chapter 3, we will take this a step further by asking what other variables can be used to predict API and how to include these other variables in our econometric model. In Chapters 4 and 5, we will learn how to use findings from samples of schools like this one to make statements about FLE and API in *all* schools in California. Subsequent chapters will address the problems that frequently appear when using econometric findings from a sample of data to generalize to populations outside the sample. Most of these problems have to do with the error term.

We'll see that we can learn a great deal by using econometrics to estimate the correlations between variables like FLE and API. As we've already pointed out, making statements about causation is more complicated. In the present example, suppose we find that high FLE predicts low API. Does this mean that

Table 1.1   Academic Performance Index (API) and Free Lunch Eligibility (FLE) at 20 California Elementary Schools in 2013

School	County	API	FLE
Joe A. Gonsalves Elementary	Los Angeles	960	16
Old River Elementary	Kern	849	0
Sierra Vista Elementary	Kern	722	96
West Portal Elementary	San Francisco	914	44
Isabelle Jackson Elementary	Sacramento	754	83
Rio Vista Elementary	Orange	796	90
Poplar Avenue Elementary	Butte	802	80
Cloverly Elementary	Los Angeles	903	46
Creative Arts Charter	San Francisco	844	33
Carolyn A. Clark Elementary	Santa Clara	963	6
Raymond Elementary	Orange	824	69
Fernangeles Elementary	Los Angeles	730	100
Rainbow Ridge Elementary	Riverside	826	90
Cyrus J. Morris Elementary	Los Angeles	882	29
Benjamin Franklin Elementary	Riverside	882	36
Salvador Elementary	Napa	736	65
Bowers Elementary	Santa Clara	788	59
Vintage Parkway Elementary	Contra Costa	830	54
Balboa Magnet Elementary	Los Angeles	981	22
Selby Lane Elementary	San Mateo	730	80
	Mean	835.80	54.90
	Std. deviation	81.14	31.00

SOURCE: California Department of Education (http://www.cde.ca.gov/ta/ac/ap/apidatafiles.asp).

if the government increased funding for free school lunches by, say, 10%, API would decrease?

You're probably thinking, "Wait a minute, that's a different question!" If so, you're right. Our motivation for using FLE to predict API was that FLE reflects, or is a proxy for, poverty. If the state provided more funding for school lunches, there's no reason to think poverty would go up. On the contrary, more poor students might become well nourished, and their school performance might improve, so increased funding for free lunches could increase API! Clearly, correlation and causation are very different matters in this case. FLE might be a good predictor of (lower) API, but that doesn't mean that a government program that increases FLE will decrease API.

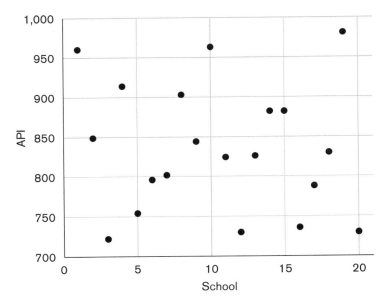

Figure 1.1 2013 API in 20 California elementary schools. Academic performance varies widely across these 20 schools.

We could think of other possible interventions to increase API. What if welfare payments to poor households with school-age children increased? Or the state provided new funding to decrease class sizes in schools? Would API increase? Addressing these sorts of cause-and-effect questions is a focus of what many econometricians do, so we include them in this book (Chapter 11)—after we master the classical econometric regression model.

FROM STATISTICS TO ECONOMETRICS

Before we get into the econometrics, let's get some mileage out of the statistics courses you've taken. We can plot student performance across schools (figure 1.1). In figure 1.1, each of the 20 schools is lined up, in no particular order, along the horizontal axis, and the schools' APIs are measured along the vertical axis.

This figure shows that academic performance varies widely across these 20 schools, from less than 750 to over 950. The average is 835.80, and the standard deviation is 81.14. (You can use a spreadsheet program like EXCEL to verify this.)

What if we use the average API to predict the API of any given school? That would mean using a model like this one, from your introductory statistics course, in which the API of school i is denoted by Y_i:

$$Y_i = \mu + \varepsilon_i.$$

In this statistical model, we imagine that the APIs we see for different schools are generated by taking the population mean API (which we call μ, a constant) and then throwing in an error, ε_i, which we hope is random. The sum of μ and ε_i gives us the observed school performance outcome for school i, Y_i.

If we used our sample mean to predict the API at Sierra Vista Elementary in Kern County, it would do a lousy job. This school has an API of 722, which is much lower than the mean of 835.80.

What is it about Sierra Vista Elementary, and many other schools in these data, that makes the mean for *all* schools a poor predictor of API for a *particular* school? If we could find some variable, X_i, that helped explain differences in APIs across schools, we could use it to construct a new (hopefully better) prediction model. In the new model, Y_i might be a simple linear function of X_i:

$$Y_i = \beta_0 + \beta_1 X_i + \varepsilon_i.$$

Notice what we've done here. We've replaced μ with $\mu_i = \beta_0 + \beta_1 X_i$. A school's expected API is no longer constant; it depends on X_i. X_i could be poverty. It could be that schools in poor neighborhoods perform more poorly, on average, than schools in rich neighborhoods. Sierra Vista Elementary is only one school among many in California, but it is striking that 96% of kids at this school receive free school lunches, compared to only 22% at the school with the highest API score in Table 1.1 (Balboa Magnet Elementary in Los Angeles; API = 981).

A Theoretical Foundation for an Econometric Model of Academic Performance

What kind of economic theory would predict an impact of poverty on API? We need a model of how schools achieve a high API. Call it an "API production function."

You studied production functions in microeconomic theory courses. Firms combine labor, capital, and other inputs to produce an output. The production function describes the technology that turns inputs into output. Do schools have a production function that turns inputs into API? What would those inputs be?

Classrooms, teachers, teaching aids, specialists, books, art supplies, computers, electricity to run everything—all of these are inputs in our API production function, and all of them cost money. Schools face budget constraints, and

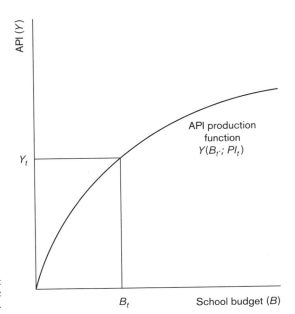

Figure 1.2 Schools convert budgets per pupil into academic performance, indexed by the API.

despite some states' best efforts to equalize spending per pupil, significant inequalities remain. Schools in high-income districts can pass bond measures and run successful fundraising campaigns to support extracurricular activities, build new facilities, and hire teaching specialists. Schools in poor districts have a tough time keeping up.

Schools with larger budgets per pupil (B) can buy more inputs, which in turn help them achieve a higher API, as shown in figure 1.2. This figure assumes that the impact of B on API is positive, but at high levels of per-pupil budget diminishing marginal returns eventually set in, like in a conventional production function.

The other critical input in the API production function, of course, is students. Students come from households, which face their own budget constraints. Households take their limited budgets (BH) and allocate them to goods and services that directly benefit their children ("child investments"), as well as to other goods and services. Nutritious foods, clothing, medical care, books, the internet, parents' time spent nurturing their children's minds, travel—all of these are examples of private investments that can prepare children to do well in school. Poor households face severe constraints on the investments they can make in their children. For a disproportionate share of children in poor US households, English is a second language. This makes the school's job more challenging. As household incomes rise, so do private investments per student (PI), as shown in figure 1.3.

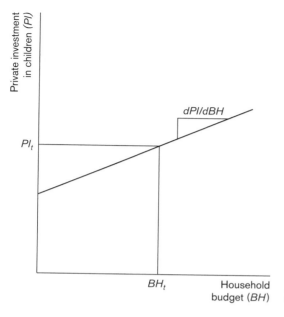

Figure 1.3 Private investments per student (PI) increase with household budgets (*BH*), assuming they are a normal good.

You will notice that we included PI in the API production function in figure 1.2. There is no axis in the diagram for PI because PI is an exogenous "shifter" in the API production function. Schools in neighborhoods where PI is high have a head start in turning *B* into API (upward shift in the API production function) compared with schools in poor neighborhoods, as illustrated in figure 1.4.

The model depicted in figures 1.2–1.4 provides a theoretical grounding for an econometric analysis of the relationship between poverty (proxied by FLE) and children's academic performance (measured by the API). Our theoretical model predicts that there is a negative relationship between poverty and academic performance: as school lunch eligibility increases, academic performance declines. This theory is particularly useful because it gives reasons why poverty might not only be *correlated* with lower school performance, but also actually *cause* it. It is also useful because it offers some insights into what other variables we might need to have in our model, besides poverty. We'll return to these two points in Chapters 2 and 3.

We can begin by plotting API against FLE, as in figure 1.5.

It looks like there's a negative relationship. The next step is to use econometrics to estimate it for these 20 schools. Let's see what we can learn from FLE to help us predict API. We'll begin by estimating a linear model in which FLE is the only variable explaining API, that is,

$$Y_i = b_0 + b_1 X_i + e_i,$$

where Y denotes API and X denotes FLE.

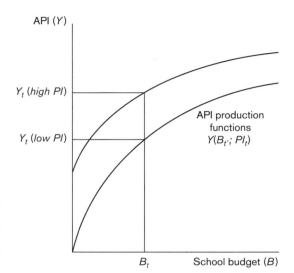

Figure 1.4 Private investments per pupil (PI) shift the API-production function upward; the same per-pupil school budget produces a higher average student performance.

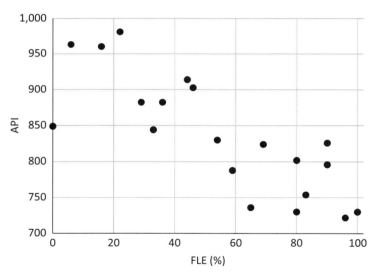

Figure 1.5 API and free lunch eligibility (FLE) for 20 California elementary schools. Academic performance appears to decrease with free lunch eligibility.

In this model, b_1 measures the relationship between free school lunches and schools' academic performance in our sample of 20 schools, b_0 is the intercept (literally, the API corresponding to zero FLE), e_i is an error term that will be much of the focus of this book, and the subscript i denotes school. (Econometricians often use t instead of i as a subscript. We can use any subscript we wish, as long as we're consistent. Often, econometricians use t to refer to time and i to individuals.)

We now use Roman letters like b instead of Greek letters like β to indicate that we are going to estimate this equation from sample data. This is just like using $\bar{X}$ to denote the sample mean estimated from a population with mean μ.

We want to use our data to estimate this simple regression model. Before we can do that, though, we need formulas to compute b_0 and b_1; that is, we have to derive our estimators. That's the subject of the next chapter.

What We Learned in This Chapter

- Econometrics is about making sense of economic data.
- Three steps to conducting econometric analysis.
  1. State the purpose of the analysis.
  2. Formulate the research design and specify the econometric model.
  3. Apply statistical theory.

Simple Regression

Everything should be made as simple as possible, but not simpler.

—Albert Einstein

LEARNING OBJECTIVES

Upon completing the work in this chapter, you will be able to:

► Explain what a simple regression model is
► Fit a simple regression model using the least-squares criterion
► Interpret the results from a simple regression model
► Compute R^2 to measure how well the model fits the data

This chapter introduces the simple linear regression model. We will learn to fit a model with only a single right-hand-side variable, like this:

$$Y_i = b_0 + b_1 X_i + e_i.$$

Y_i is a *dependent or outcome variable*, that is, a variable that we hope to explain in relation to a right-hand-side variable, X_i. (X_i is also commonly referred to as a *regressor, explanatory variable*, or *independent variable*.) This model has two parts: a prediction part, $b_0 + b_1 X_i$, which describes a line, and an error part, e_i, which is the difference between the prediction and the outcome. If you plot your data, with your dependent variable on the Y axis and your right-hand-side variable on the X axis, $b_0 + b_1 X_i$ describes a straight line running through your scatter of data points, while each data point has an error term describing the vertical distance from that point to the line. The error is what makes this a statistical or econometric relationship, instead of a mathematical one.

Our first job is to find a line that is the best predictor of Y given different levels of X. We'll discuss what we mean by "best predictor" below. This will be our estimated regression line, and the vertical distance between it and each data point will be the prediction error, or residual. We can use the regression line to predict the values of Y in our sample of data.

The power of econometrics is that we can do much more: under many conditions, we can use our estimated regression line to say something about a population that exists outside of our data. We will have to think clearly about what that population is and how well our sample data represent it—that is, the process that gave us those data from the whole population. Then, we may use the model to predict the values of Y in a future year. Or, we may ask the question of *why* X and Y are correlated (if they are). That is, what is the process that generates Y from X? In the real world, X and Y might move together because X is *exogenous* or given, and it causes Y. Alternatively, X and Y might cause each other, in which case we say the relationship between X and Y is simultaneous. Or both might be affected by another variable not included in our model, in which case we say that there are omitted variables.

All these questions and possibilities make econometrics interesting and powerful, but let's put off addressing them until Chapter 4. First, we need to learn how to compute b_0 and b_1 using our sample data.

Like in most econometrics books, we will use Greek letters to denote the parameters in a hypothetical population model and Roman letters to denote things we can compute with our data. In your statistics courses, μ might have been used to denote the population mean, and $\overline{X}$ the formula used to estimate the mean, or the estimated mean, itself. In our study of econometric regression models, $\beta_0 + \beta_1 X_i$ might be used to denote the relationship between X_i and Y_i in the whole population, which we generally do not know, while $b_0 + b_1 X_i$ represents the relationship we estimate using the sample data. We also use e_i as the sample error to differentiate it from the population error, ε_i, which we do not know. It is important to keep the difference between the Roman and the Greek letters straight.

We're choosing to fit a linear model, so for starters, we'll hope that using a line is a good way to predict Y from X. We'll move on to more complicated models soon enough; in Chapter 3 ("Multiple Regression"), we'll let it be a plane (two right-hand-side variables) or a hyperplane (more than two), and in Chapter 7 ("Predicting in a Nonlinear World") we'll let it be all sorts of things.

Another requirement of our data is that we have variation in our variables. Since two different points are required to define a line, X must take on at least two different values. If all the people in our sample have the same education level, naturally we cannot estimate the correlation between education and earnings. There has to be some variation in the X direction.

THE LEAST-SQUARES CRITERION

Consider the scatter plot of school performance (measured by the academic performance index, API) and poverty (measured by free-lunch eligibility, FLE) in Chapter 1 (figure 1.5). Our goal is to find the line that best fits these data. It

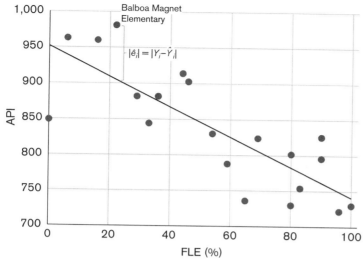

Figure 2.1 API and free lunch eligibility (FLE) for 20 California elementary schools. The regression line minimizes the sum of squared errors, $\sum_{i=1}^{N}(\hat{e}_i)^2$.

will be our best estimate of the relationship between FLE and API. We could let X denote FLE and Y, API, and write the regression equation in terms of X and Y like the one at the beginning of this chapter. Or, alternatively, we could write it like this:

$$API_i = b_0 + b_1 FLE_i + e_i.$$

As we figure out how to estimate this regression line, we'll mostly use X and Y, to keep it short and simple. Notice that we don't use Greek letters here. We do not know the population parameters, β_0 and β_1. We are not even thinking about them yet. We are working with quantities we can compute from our sample: b_0 and b_1.

Our task is illustrated in figure 2.1. You might think that the line in this figure fits the data pretty well. By that you probably mean that it follows the flow of the scatterplot, angled and placed so that it minimizes the distance between it and the data points. If so, you're close: the line in this figure minimizes the sum of squared distances—what econometricians call the *sum of squared errors* or *SSE* for short. Squaring the errors gives us a number that is always positive. It also makes the magnitude of big deviations large.

It turns out that there are many different ways to estimate the relationship between X and Y. We need a criterion for choosing the best estimator. The one most commonly used in econometrics is the *least-squares criterion*. According to this criterion, the best line is the one that minimizes the *SSE*. For each data point, the difference between the observed Y and the level of Y predicted by the model we will estimate, or the vertical distance between each data point and the regression line, is called the regression error, or residual (e_i). It is the amount by which you "miss" if you use your regression line to predict Y for different levels of X. The line we estimate will minimize the sum of these misses squared.

The SSE is calculated by squaring each residual and then adding them all together. Assuming N observations or data points,

$$SSE = \sum_{i=1}^{N}(e_i)^2 = \sum_{i=1}^{N}(Y_i - b_0 - b_1 X_i)^2.$$

Our goal, then, is to find the b_0 and b_1 that minimize this SSE; that is,

$$\min_{b_0, b_1} SSE = \sum_{i=1}^{N}(Y_i - b_0 - b_1 X_i)^2.$$

This is not hard to do using calculus. (If you have not had calculus, don't worry—do your best to capture the intuition behind what follows, but learn the key formulas that come out of it by heart!)

First, we take the partial derivatives with respect to b_0 and b_1 and set each equal to 0 (to get the minimum, since the slope of any continuous function at its minimum is zero):

$$b_0 : \sum_{i=1}^{N} 2(Y_i - b_0 - b_1 X_i)(-1) = 0,$$

$$b_1 : \sum_{i=1}^{N} 2(Y_i - b_0 - b_1 X_i)(-X_i) = 0.$$

In calculus, the equations that minimize the sum of squared differences are called *normal* equations. (In case you've only had single-variable calculus, taking the partial derivative of a function of more than one variable [here b_0 and b_1] with respect to only one variable is just like taking a simple derivative, while holding the other variable constant.) You can verify that the second derivatives are both positive, a condition for getting the minimum.

Now at this point, you might be wondering whether we've gotten things backward. In calculus, don't we usually take derivatives of functions with respect to variables? Didn't we just take derivatives with respect to parameters (b_0 and b_1), instead?

This is a different use of calculus than you're accustomed to, because we're trying to find the parameter values that minimize our *SSE* function, taking X_i and Y_i as given.

Deriving the two normal equations is the easy part of getting our estimators. The more tedious part is algebraically solving the two normal equations for the two unknowns, b_0 and b_1. The first equation gives us b_0 as a function of b_1:

$$\sum_{i=1}^{N}(Y_i - b_0 - b_1 X_i) = 0,$$

$$\sum_{i=1}^{N}(Y_i) - \sum_{i=1}^{N}(b_0) - \sum_{i=1}^{N}(b_1 X_i) = 0,$$

$$\sum_{i=1}^{N}(Y_i) - N b_0 - b_1 \sum_{i=1}^{N} X_i = 0,$$

$$b_0 = \overline{Y} - b_1 \overline{X}.$$

(We got the last equation by dividing by N and rearranging.)

We can substitute this in for b_0 in the second equation, and after some algebraic manipulation, we get the formula for b_1:

$$\sum_{i=1}^{N}(Y_i - (\overline{Y} - b_1 \overline{X}) - b_1 X_i)(-X_i) = 0,$$

$$\sum_{i=1}^{N}\left[(Y_i - \overline{Y}) - b_1(X_i - \overline{X})\right](X_i) = 0,$$

$$\sum_{i=1}^{N}\left[X_i(Y_i - \overline{Y}) - b_1 X_i(X_i - \overline{X})\right] = 0,$$

$$b_1 = \frac{\sum_{i=1}^{N} X_i y_i}{\sum_{i=1}^{N} X_i x_i},$$

where x and y are the deviations of X_i and Y_i from their means: $x_i = X_i - \overline{X}$ and $y_i = Y_i - \overline{Y}$. It turns out that we can use deviations all around:

$$b_1 = \frac{\sum_{i=1}^{N} x_i y_i}{\sum_{i=1}^{N} x_i^2}.$$

Box 2.1 shows why this is true. These formulas are what we call the *ordinary least-squares (OLS)* formulas for a *simple regression model*—that is, a model having only one right-hand-side variable. Let's use them to estimate our school performance model.

BOX 2.1　　　**The OLS Formula in Terms of Deviations from the Mean**

Showing that

$$b_1 = \frac{\sum_{i=1}^{N} X_i y_i}{\sum_{i=1}^{N} X_i x_i} = \frac{\sum_{i=1}^{N} x_i y_i}{\sum_{i=1}^{N} x_i x_i}$$

is not hard, if you follow these steps.

To get the formula on the right from the one on the left, we have to replace X_i with $X_i - \bar{X}$:

$$\frac{\sum_{i=1}^{N} x_i y_i}{\sum_{i=1}^{N} x_i x_i} = \frac{\sum_{i=1}^{N} (X_i - \bar{X}) y_i}{\sum_{i=1}^{N} (X_i - \bar{X}) x_i}.$$

We want to show that this is the same as

$$\frac{\sum_{i=1}^{N} X_i y_i}{\sum_{i=1}^{N} X_i x_i}.$$

That means the terms involving $\bar{X}$ somehow have to disappear. Let's see why they do.

First, distribute

$$\frac{\sum_{i=1}^{N} (X_i - \bar{X}) y_i}{\sum_{i=1}^{N} (X_i - \bar{X}) x_i} = \frac{\sum_{i=1}^{N} (X_i y_i - \bar{X} y_i)}{\sum_{i=1}^{N} (X_i x_i - \bar{X} x_i)}.$$

Now, $\bar{X}$ is a constant, so we can bring it outside the summation and rewrite the right-hand-side expression as follows:

$$\frac{\sum_{i=1}^{N} X_i y_i - \bar{X} \sum_{i=1}^{N} y_i}{\sum_{i=1}^{N} X_i x_i - \bar{X} \sum_{i=1}^{N} x_i}.$$

Next, recall from your statistics courses that the sum of a variable's deviations from its mean is always zero. For example, suppose X_i takes on three values: 3, 4, and 5. Its mean is 4, so x_i has the values −1, 0, and 1. Summing these, we get zero

$(\sum_{i=1}^{N} x_i = 0)$. Since this is true for y_i, too, the terms involving sums of deviations vanish, and we're left with

$$\frac{\sum_{i=1}^{N} X_i y_i}{\sum_{i=1}^{N} X_i x_i}.$$

That proves that

$$\frac{\sum_{i=1}^{N} X_i y_i}{\sum_{i=1}^{N} X_i x_i} = \frac{\sum_{i=1}^{N} x_i y_i}{\sum_{i=1}^{N} x_i^2}.$$

Q.E.D.

ESTIMATING A SIMPLE REGRESSION MODEL OF ACADEMIC PERFORMANCE

Let's see how to do this using the sample data on academic performance and school lunch eligibility. (You should make sure you can derive the OLS estimates using EXCEL; the EXCEL version of the data are available online in the Exercise Folder for Chapter 2.) First of all, we need to transform both variables into deviations from means; see columns D and E of Table 2.1. Then we need $\sum_{i=1}^{N} x_i y_i$ and $\sum_{i=1}^{N} x_i^2$. These are in columns F and G, respectively.

The OLS estimate of b_1 is the sum of column F divided by the sum of column G, or $-38,610.4/18,261.8 = -2.11$. Sometimes econometricians use hats "^" to indicate something they've actually estimated; for example, β_1 is the (unknown) population parameter, b_1 is the OLS formula used to estimate it, and $\hat{b}_1$ is the actual value we get when we use real data with this formula (here, $\hat{b}_1 = -2.11$). We'll keep things simple by using b_1 to represent both the formula and the value it takes when we evaluate it with sample data. The most important thing to keep in mind is the difference between b_1, the sample estimate, and β_1, the population parameter.

According to our estimates, a one-percentage point increase in FLE is associated with a 2.11 point decrease in API. That's a pretty big association. The intercept estimate is $b_0 = 835.8 - (-2.11)(54.9) = 951.64$. This is what our model

Table 2.1   Estimation of a Simple Ordinary Least-Squares Regression Model for School Performance

A	B	C	D	E	F	G
School (*t*)	API	FLE	*y*	*x*	*xy*	x^2
Joe A. Gonsalves Elementary	960	16	124.2	−38.9	−4,831.38	1,513.21
Old River Elementary	849	0	13.2	−54.9	−724.68	3,014.01
Sierra Vista Elementary	722	96	−113.8	41.1	−4,677.18	1,689.21
West Portal Elementary	914	44	78.2	−10.9	−852.38	118.81
Isabelle Jackson Elementary	754	83	−81.8	28.1	−2,298.58	789.61
Rio Vista Elementary	796	90	−39.8	35.1	−1,396.98	1,232.01
Poplar Avenue Elementary	802	80	−33.8	25.1	−848.38	630.01
Cloverly Elementary	903	46	67.2	−8.9	−598.08	79.21
Creative Arts Charter	844	33	8.2	−21.9	−179.58	479.61
Carolyn A. Clark Elementary	963	6	127.2	−48.9	−6,220.08	2,391.21
Raymond Elementary	824	69	−11.8	14.1	−166.38	198.81
Fernangeles Elementary	730	100	−105.8	45.1	−4,771.58	2,034.01
Rainbow Ridge Elementary	826	90	−9.8	35.1	−343.98	1,232.01
Cyrus J. Morris Elementary	882	29	46.2	−25.9	−1,196.58	670.81
Benjamin Franklin Elementary	882	36	46.2	−18.9	−873.18	357.21
Salvador Elementary	736	65	−99.8	10.1	−1,007.98	102.01
Bowers Elementary	788	59	−47.8	4.1	−195.98	16.81
Vintage Parkway Elementary	830	54	−5.8	−0.9	5.22	0.81
Balboa Magnet Elementary	981	22	145.2	−32.9	−4,777.08	1,082.41
Selby Lane Elementary	730	80	−105.8	25.1	−2,655.58	630.01
Average:	**835.8**	**54.9**		*Sums:*	**−38,610.40**	**18,261.80**
Variance:	**6,584.17**			b_1:	**−2.11**	
				b_0:	**951.64**	

predicts the API to be at a school in which no students are eligible for free lunches ($X = 0$).

In short, our estimated regression equation is

$$\hat{Y}_i = 951.64 - 2.11X_i.$$

THE R^2

How good is our simple regression model at predicting schools' APIs? The goal of our regression is to explain some of the variation in our dependent variable,

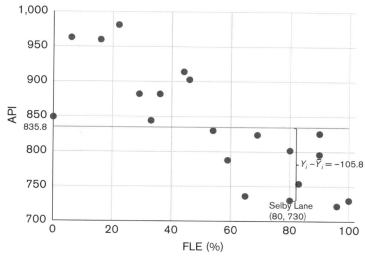

Figure 2.2 API and free lunch eligibility (FLE) for 20 California elementary schools. The mean API does a poor job of predicting the API for Selby Lane Elementary (and most other schools).

Y, using the information provided by the independent variable, X. One way to measure how well our model fits the data points is to determine how much of the variation in Y our model is explaining. This is what the R^2 statistic tells us.

Let's start by considering the variation in the dependent variable, Y. If we take all the deviations of Y from its mean, which we have called y, square them (so that we have all positive numbers), and add them up, we get the *total sum of squares* (*TSS*):

$$TSS = \sum_{i=1}^{N} y_i^2.$$

You'll recognize *TSS*: it's just the numerator in the formula for the sample variance of Y (the denominator is $N - 1$). The *TSS* is unit sensitive. If Y is income, its *TSS* will be a thousand times bigger if we express income in dollars rather than in thousands of dollars. In this sense, it isn't very useful by itself. However, since y_i is the deviation of Y_i from its mean, it is the part of the variation in Y that is *not* explained by the mean. This will be useful to us later on, because our regression model is "good" if it helps explain an important share of the variation in Y around its mean.

Figure 2.2 shows the variation in Y around its mean using our API and FLE example.

As you can see, the values of Y vary quite a bit, and none of them are equal to the mean value. Take Selby Lane Elementary, whose data point is identified in the figure. It corresponds to $(X,Y) = (80, 730)$. We can see that this observed

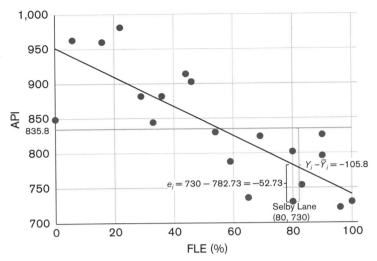

Figure 2.3 API and free lunch eligibility (FLE) for 20 California elementary schools. We do a much better job predicting API at Selby Lane Elementary by using the regression line instead of the mean—missing by 52.73 instead of 105.80 points.

value of Y corresponding to $X = 80$ is far below the mean—the deviation is $730 - 835.8 = -105.8$. Without a regression model, we would only have the mean to work with, and it would not be a very good predictor of Y.

Now bring in our regression line (see figure 2.3).

By plugging in 80 for X in our estimated regression equation, we get a predicted API at Selby Lane Elementary of 782.73. You can see that our regression does a much better job of predicting Y given $X = 80$ than if we tried to predict Y using only the mean value for all schools. The estimated regression error, or residual, is 52.73 points. This is our "miss" using the regression equation to predict this school's performance. It is less than half of the "miss" using the sample mean, that is, Selby Hill Elementary's deviation from the mean API for all schools.

Table 2.2 adds two new columns to the ones in Table 2.1.[1] Column H gives the predicted API for each school, using our regression model. Column I shows the residual, or difference between the observed and predicted API. You can compare these residuals to the deviations of each school's API from the mean for all schools (Column D) to see how well the regression model does compared to predicting with the mean. Almost all of the data points in this example lie closer to the regression line than to the mean of Y; $|e_i|$ is almost always smaller than $|y_i|$.

If we square all the residuals (Column K) and add them up, we get the *SSE* (in this regression, 43,466). You'll recall that this is what we minimized to

Table 2.2   Calculating the R^2 to Measure the Model's Goodness of Fit

A	B	C	D	H	I	J	K
School (*t*)	API	FLE	*y*	$\hat{y}$	*e*	y^2	e^2
Joe A. Gonsalves Elementary	960	16	124.20	918.05	41.95	15,425.64	1,760.21
Old River Elementary	849	0	13.20	951.87	−102.87	174.24	10,582.96
Sierra Vista Elementary	722	96	−113.80	748.90	−26.90	12,950.44	723.80
West Portal Elementary	914	44	78.20	858.85	55.15	6,115.24	3,042.01
Isabelle Jackson Elementary	754	83	−81.80	776.39	−22.39	6,691.24	501.27
Rio Vista Elementary	796	90	−39.80	761.59	34.41	1,584.04	1,184.11
Poplar Avenue Elementary	802	80	−33.80	782.73	19.27	1,142.44	371.26
Cloverly Elementary	903	46	67.20	854.62	48.38	4,515.84	2,340.91
Creative Arts Charter	844	33	8.20	882.10	−38.10	67.24	1,451.80
Carolyn A. Clark Elementary	963	6	127.20	939.19	23.81	16,179.84	567.02
Raymond Elementary	824	69	−11.80	805.99	18.01	139.24	324.40
Fernangeles Elementary	730	100	−105.80	740.45	−10.45	11,193.64	109.13
Rainbow Ridge Elementary	826	90	−9.80	761.59	64.41	96.04	4,148.77
Cyrus J. Morris Elementary	882	29	46.20	890.56	−8.56	2,134.44	73.27
Benjamin Franklin Elementary	882	36	46.20	875.76	6.24	2,134.44	38.94
Salvador Elementary	736	65	−99.80	814.45	−78.45	9,960.04	6,153.75
Bowers Elementary	788	59	−47.80	827.13	−39.13	2,284.84	1,531.27
Vintage Parkway Elementary	830	54	−5.80	837.70	−7.70	33.64	59.33
Balboa Magnet Elementary	981	22	145.20	905.36	75.64	21,083.04	5,721.48
Selby Lane Elementary	730	80	−105.80	782.73	−52.73	11,193.64	2,780.64
Average:	**835.8**	**54.9**			*Sums:*	**125,099.20**	**43,466.34**
Variance:	**6,584.17**				R^2		**0.65**

derive the OLS estimators in the first place. The *SSE* is the variation in *Y* that is *not* explained by our regression. By dividing it by the total sum of squares (*TSS*, which measures the *total* variation of *Y* around its mean, or the sum of deviations-squared), we get the *share* of variation not explained by the regression. (In our data, the *TSS* = 125,099.) Subtract this from 1.0 and we get the share that *is* explained by our regression, or the R^2:

$$R^2 = 1 - \frac{SSE}{TSS} = 1 - \frac{\sum_{i=1}^{N} \hat{e}_i^2}{\sum_{i=1}^{N} y_i^2}.$$

The R^2 statistic is our measure of goodness of fit, that is, how good a job our regression does at explaining the variation in Y around its mean. If the regression explains little of this variation, our model is not very useful for prediction; the SSE will be close in value to the TSS, and R^2 will be close to zero. If the regression explains a lot of the variation in Y around its mean, the SSE will be small, and R^2 will be closer to 1. Because the R^2 is a proportion, it will always be the case that $0 \le R^2 \le 1$.

Why R^2? The R here is the correlation between Y and X. If you compute the correlation between Y and X and square it, then you get the R^2.

So what's a big R^2? That depends. Some outcomes are harder to model than others. We usually get a higher R^2 from time series regressions than from cross-section regressions. There are typically a lot of differences we can't observe across people or whatever it is we are modeling in the cross section, so we won't be able to explain much of the variation in the dependent variable using the right-hand-side variables. In this case, an R^2 lower than 0.10 or 0.20 might not be unreasonable. If we are modeling the same actor (for example, an individual school in the API example) over time, we are likely to do a better job of explaining variations in the dependent variable.

Think of it this way: compare your demand for rice over 52 weeks to 52 people's demand for rice this week. Those 52 people will have all sorts of characteristics you won't be able to observe that might affect their demand for rice. On the other hand, you are you (with the same taste or distaste for rice, etc.) no matter what week it is. Even though we still can't observe all of the characteristics that affect your rice demand, for the most part, they don't change over time, so we don't have to worry about them. It is likely that we'll be able to explain your variations in rice demand better than the variations in rice demand of many different people.

We can calculate the R^2 for our simple OLS regression of API on FLE:

$$R^2 = 1 - \frac{SSE}{TSS} = 1 - \frac{43,466}{125,099} = 0.65 .$$

Our simple regression succeeds in explaining 65% of the variation of school APIs around their mean for this sample of schools. Not too shabby, especially for a cross-section analysis. Clearly, we are better off with the regression model than without it if our goal is to predict APIs.

A note of caution: don't think that your model is better just because it has a high R^2. Remember that *Step 1* in an econometric study is to define the purpose of the modeling. What do you want to do? If your answer is that you want to predict Y accurately, then maximizing R^2 is a good objective—up to a point. We say "up to a point" because, if you think about it, adding another right-hand-side variable to your model logically will never reduce the R^2, and usually it will increase R^2 by at least a little, whether the variable belongs in the model or not. We have to draw the line on what variables are in the model somewhere.

Suppose, however, that your goal is to estimate how much sales will decrease if a firm raises its prices. There are many things that may affect sales, and you cannot account for all of them. So, you may not get an accurate prediction of next year's sales (low R^2), which is OK because your objective is not to estimate how much the firm will sell next year, but how much *less* it will sell at higher prices than if it had kept prices constant.

R^2 is a useful characteristic of your model, but maximizing R^2 is often not the objective of your analysis.

BEYOND SIMPLE REGRESSION

What explains the other 35% of the variation? Remember that our theoretical model in the last chapter predicted that academic performance depends on variables shaping both public and private investments in kids. The FLE variable is a proxy for families' ability to invest in their children. Parents' willingness to invest time and energy into their children's education also matter. So do the resources schools have at their disposal, which affect things like classroom size, the quality of teachers, technology, books, supplies, etc.

Considering how many different variables potentially affect academic performance, it is quite remarkable that we can predict so much of the variation in API across schools using only FLE. Nevertheless, by including variables that we left out of this simple regression model, we might be able to explain more of the variation in academic performance. We might also improve our estimate of the relationship between FLE on API, as we shall see. In the next chapter, we will consider what happens when we include more than one right-hand-side variable in the equation. Then, in Chapters 4 and 5, we'll test the statistical significance of our findings and set up confidence intervals around them. In the meantime, you might just want to hold off presenting these findings to the school board!

What We Learned

- How to solve the least-squares problem to fit a simple regression model.
- How to apply the least-squares formula using a spreadsheet.
- R^2 is a useful characteristic of your model, but maximizing R^2 is often not the objective of your analysis.

Multiple Regression

3

I think there is a world market for about five computers.

—Thomas J. Watson, CEO of IBM, 1958

LEARNING OBJECTIVES

Upon completing the work in this chapter, you will be able to:

▶ Derive the ordinary least-squares estimators of the regression coefficients when there are two or more right-hand-side variables in the model

▶ Fit a multiple regression model using the least-squares criterion

▶ Identify the conditions under which a multiple regression estimate is the same as the simple regression estimate

▶ Explain the consequences of omitting relevant right-hand-side variables from the model

So far we have been working with a simple regression model—a model with only a single right-hand-side variable. For example, we modeled schools' academic performance index (API) as a function only of poverty, proxied by free-lunch eligibility (FLE). You should not feel satisfied with this; our microeconomic theory suggests that other variables in addition to poverty are likely to explain school performance. This means that we might be able to predict the outcome of interest better by including some additional right-hand-side variables in our model.

There are two major problems with leaving relevant variables out of a regression model. First, we obviously cannot estimate how they relate to the outcome of interest if we do not include them. How well does parents' education (PE) level or school quality predict children's academic performance? We do not know this unless we put these variables (or good proxies for them) in our model.

But even if we only care about the effect of income or poverty on API, there is another serious concern about leaving relevant variables out of our model. We shall see below that adding new variables to the model almost always changes our estimate of the coefficient on the variables that are *already* in the model. A multiple regression model—one with more than one right-hand-side variable—enables us to "net out" the correlations of individual right-hand-side variables with the dependent variable.

In the example we've been working with, we do not know why API is so strongly correlated with FLE. Our theory suggests that it could be because school quality is lower in poor districts. But it could also be because private investments in children are lower in poor districts, because poor parents have less time and money to invest in their children, and they are also less likely to be highly educated than rich parents. So which is it that explains API: school quality or private investments in kids?

If our only goal is to predict schools' APIs, then having only FLE in our model might be alright (though adding other relevant variables could improve our predictive power). We have seen that information about FLE gives good predictions of the API at 20 different elementary schools in California. Whether that's because poverty explains API and FLE is a good indicator of poverty, or because FLE is correlated with a whole set of other variables (including parents' schooling and school funding) that explain API, we do not know.

If our goal is to *isolate* or *identify* how poverty affects API, then we have more work to do. Omitting potentially relevant variables from the model will almost certainly bias our estimated effect of poverty (proxied by FLE) on API. Based on a simple regression, we might think that poverty causes low test scores, when in fact a variable that was omitted from the model is the true cause. Shortly, we shall see what happens when we introduce a new variable—PE—into our model of school performance.

THE MULTIPLE REGRESSION MODEL

The multiple regression model with $K + 1$ parameters (that is, K parameters multiplying the right-hand-side variables plus an intercept) looks like this:

$$Y_i = b_0 + b_1 X_{1i} + b_2 X_{1i} + \ldots + b_K X_{Ki} + e_i.$$

In theory, we can include as many right-hand-side variables in our model as we have observations, though as we shall see later on, there is a cost to including variables that should not be there—that is, irrelevant variables—as well as to omitting relevant variables. At a minimum, we must have one data point with which to estimate each parameter of the model; that is, our sample size, N, must at least equal $K + 1$, the number of parameters we wish to estimate. This was true for the simple regression model with two parameters: estimating a line required having at least two points. (In statistics, estimating the mean—a single parameter—in theory requires at least one data point.)

If we have two right-hand-side variables, our model looks like this:

$$Y_i = b_0 + b_1 X_{1i} + b_2 X_{2i} + e_i.$$

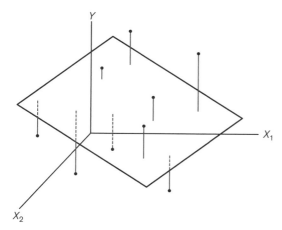

Figure 3.1 Illustration of a regression plane for a model with two explanatory variables, X_1 and X_2.

From a geometric point of view, we do not have a regression line anymore. We have a regression plane in (X_1, X_2, Y) space, as depicted in figure 3.1.

With three right-hand-side variables this picture becomes impossible to draw, but you could imagine there being a third variable (X_3), the different values of which shift this plane around, perhaps linearly (e.g., up and down in a fashion that is linear with respect to X_3) or perhaps nonlinearly (e.g., small changes in X_3 shift this plane a lot when the value of X_3 is small, but less when X_3 is large). Beyond three right-hand-side variables we start having trouble visualizing the model. Graphically, the model would be what we call a *hyperplane* in a $K + 1$ space.

Now let's see how to derive the least-squares estimators of a multiple regression model. This derivation uses the same criterion as the simple regression model (finding the values of $b_0, b_1, b_2, ..., b_K$ that minimize the sum of squared errors, or SSE):

$$\min_{b_k, k=0,1,...,K} SSE = \sum_{i=1}^{N} e_i^2 = \sum_{i=1}^{N} (Y_i - b_0 - b_1 X_{1i} - ... - b_K X_{Ki})^2.$$

We derive the estimators the same way, using calculus to get normal equations by taking the (partial) derivative of the SSE with respect to each of the parameters in the model and setting these derivatives equal to zero. In the general case of a model with K right-hand-side variables, this is what the normal equations will look like:

$$b_0 : \sum_{i=1}^{N} (Y_i - b_0 - b_1 X_{1i} - ... - b_K X_{Ki})(-1) = 0,$$

$$b_1 : \sum_{i=1}^{N} (Y_i - b_0 - b_1 X_{1i} - ... - b_K X_{Ki})(-X_{1i}) = 0,$$

$$b_2 : \sum_{i=1}^{N} (Y_i - b_0 - b_1 X_{1i} - ... - b_K X_{Ki})(-X_{2i}) = 0 ,$$

$$...$$

$$b_K : \sum_{i=1}^{N} (Y_i - b_0 - b_1 X_{1i} - ... - b_K X_{Ki})(-X_{Ki}) = 0 .$$

The only difference between this and the simple regression model is that, instead of having only two normal equations (one for the intercept and one for the slope), we have one for each parameter in the model.

Like before, we have as many normal equations as unknowns ($K + 1$ of each), so this system of equations can be solved to get our least-squares estimators, or formulas, $b_0, b_1, b_2, ..., b_K$. We can then plug our data into these formulas to estimate the model's parameters. Econometricians sometimes use a hat ("^") to indicate when they are talking about actual estimates, that is, numerical values obtained for the parameters: $\hat{b}_0, \hat{b}_1, \hat{b}_2, ..., \hat{b}_K$. Some authors do not do this, though—they let $b_0, b_1, b_2, ..., b_K$ refer to both the formulas and the values they take on. That's the tack we will use here. It's easier not having so many hats flying around.

The Two Right-Hand-Side Variables Case

Suppose we have two right-hand-side variables, X_1 and X_2. Then this is what our normal equations look like:

$$b_0 : \sum_{i=1}^{N} (Y_i - b_0 - b_1 X_{1i} - b_2 X_{2i})(-1) = 0 ,$$

$$b_1 : \sum_{i=1}^{N} (Y_i - b_0 - b_1 X_{1i} - b_2 X_{2i})(-X_{1i}) = 0 ,$$

$$b_2 : \sum_{i=1}^{N} (Y_i - b_0 - b_1 X_{1i} - b_2 X_{2i})(-X_{2i}) = 0 .$$

Solving the first of these for b_0 gives a formula for the constant term in our model that looks a lot like the one from our simple regression model:

$$b_0 = \overline{Y} - b_1 \overline{X_1} - b_2 \overline{X_2} .$$

Deriving the least-squares formulas for the two slope parameters is more tedious. You can try this: first, substitute in for b_1 in the other two normal equations (this will get rid of b_1 in those equations); then solve the two equations for b_2 and b_3. Doing this, you should end up with the following formulas:

$$b_1 = \frac{\displaystyle\sum_{i=1}^{N} x_{1i} y_i \sum_{i=1}^{N} x_{2i}^2 - \sum_{i=1}^{N} x_{1i} x_{2i} \sum_{i=1}^{N} x_{2i} y_i}{\displaystyle\sum_{i=1}^{N} x_{1i}^2 \sum_{i=1}^{N} x_{2i}^2 - \left(\sum_{i=1}^{N} x_{1i} x_{2i}\right)^2}$$

and

$$b_2 = \frac{\displaystyle\sum_{i=1}^{N} x_{2i} y_i \sum_{i=1}^{N} x_{1i}^2 - \sum_{i=1}^{N} x_{1i} x_{2i} \sum_{i=1}^{N} x_{1i} y_i}{\displaystyle\sum_{i=1}^{N} x_{1i}^2 \sum_{i=1}^{N} x_{2i}^2 - \left(\sum_{i=1}^{N} x_{1i} x_{2i}\right)^2}.$$

The lower-case x_{1i}, x_{2i}, and y_i are deviations from means. (Notice that the denominators are the same; only the numerators are different.)

WHEN DOES THE MR ESTIMATOR COLLAPSE TO THE SR ESTIMATOR?

You can see that these multiple regression (MR, hereinafter) estimators for the two- right-hand-side-variable case look quite different (and more complicated) than the simple OLS formulas in Chapter 2. That is because we are now using two right-hand-side variables (e.g., FLE and PE) to predict the dependent variable (API), so the formulas for our estimators have to include both variables.

But what if you really are only interested in b_1, the association between FLE and API? Do you need to include PE in your model? To answer this question, we can think about what conditions would have to hold in order for b_1 from a simple model with only FLE to be the same as b_1 from an MR model including both FLE and PE.

If you look closely (or not so closely, because we've circled it here), you can find the simple OLS formula for b_1 hidden within the MR one for b_1:

$$b_1 = \frac{\displaystyle\sum_{i=1}^{N} x_{1i} y_i \sum_{i=1}^{N} x_{2i}^2 - \sum_{i=1}^{N} x_{1i} x_{2i} \sum_{i=1}^{N} x_{2i} y_i}{\displaystyle\sum_{i=1}^{N} x_{1i}^2 \sum_{i=1}^{N} x_{2i}^2 - \left(\sum_{i=1}^{N} x_{1i} x_{2i}\right)^2}.$$

Similarly, you can find the simple OLS formula for b_2 hidden within the MR one for b_2. Is there some condition under which the multiple OLS estimator of b_1 "collapses" to the simple OLS estimator? If so, then estimating the model with and without the second right-hand-side variable, X_2, would give the same coefficient on X_1.

What if $\sum_{i=1}^{N} x_{1i}x_{2i} = 0$? You should be able to verify that this would eliminate the second term in both the numerator and the denominator of the MR formula for b_1. After canceling the $\sum_{i=1}^{N} x_{2i}^2$ terms, we would be left with the simple OLS estimator for the association between X_1 and Y, which we'll call b_1^s:

$$b_1^s = \frac{\sum_{i=1}^{N} x_{1i}y_i}{\sum_{i=1}^{N} x_{1i}^2}.$$

So, when does $\sum_{i=1}^{N} x_{1i}x_{2i} = 0$? You might recognize this expression from your statistics classes: it is the numerator in the formula for the sample correlation between X_1 and X_2. Divide it by N and it is the covariance between the two right-hand-side variables in our new model (e.g., between FLE and PE). If this covariance is zero, we can use the simple formula to isolate the effect of X_1 on Y.

That's a really big "if," though. It is highly likely that the two right-hand-side variables are correlated, positively or negatively. We are not saying that one *causes* the other, only that they tend to move together in some way. In general, if we leave out a relevant variable, X_2, the value of b_1 will be different. This difference may be large, depending on the covariance between X_1 and X_2 and also the covariance between X_2 and Y, which you will find in the numerator of the MR formula for b_1. This is an important point to keep in mind when deciding which variables to include in your model.

BACK TO API AND FLE (AND PE, TOO)

Let's see how including a new variable, PE, affects our simple API–FLE example. Our school data set also contains information on the percentage of parents with a college degree for each school. For example, if 43% of kids at a school have a parent with a college degree, $PE = 43$. In Table 3.1, Columns B, C, and L show the three variables in our model. The rest of the data columns reproduce the calculations needed to plug into the two-right-hand-side-variable MR formulas. These data are all available in the online Exercise Folder for Chapter 3.

Let's retrieve the important totals we need from this table. They include the following:

$$\sum_{i=1}^{N} x_{1i}^2 = 18,262 \text{ and } \sum_{i=1}^{N} x_{1i}y_i = -38,610.$$

Table 3.1 Calculations for a Two-Right-Hand-Side Variable Regression Model

A	B	C	D	E	F	G	L	M	N	O	P
School (t)	API	FLE	y	x_1	$x_1 y$	x_1^2	PE	x_2	x_2^2	$x_2 y$	$x_1 x_2$
Joe A. Gonsalves Elementary	960	16	124.2	−38.9	−4,831.38	1,513.21	81	43.9	1,927	5,452.38	−1,707.71
Old River Elementary	849	0	13.2	−54.9	−724.68	3,014.01	24	−13.1	172	−172.92	719.19
Sierra Vista Elementary	722	96	−113.8	41.1	−4,677.18	1,689.21	6	−31.1	967	3,539.18	−1,278.21
West Portal Elementary	914	44	78.2	−10.9	−852.38	118.81	63	25.9	671	2,025.38	−282.31
Isabelle Jackson Elementary	754	83	−81.8	28.1	−2,298.58	789.61	20	−17.1	292	1,398.78	−480.51
Rio Vista Elementary	796	90	−39.8	35.1	−1,396.98	1,232.01	20	−17.1	292	680.58	−600.21
Poplar Avenue Elementary	802	80	−33.8	25.1	−848.38	630.01	18	−19.1	365	645.58	−479.41
Cloverly Elementary	903	46	67.2	−8.9	−598.08	79.21	53	15.9	253	1,068.48	−141.51
Creative Arts Charter	844	33	8.2	−21.9	−179.58	479.61	60	22.9	524	187.78	−501.51
Carolyn A. Clark Elementary	963	6	127.2	−48.9	−6,220.08	2,391.21	84	46.9	2,200	5,965.68	−2,293.41
Raymond Elementary	824	69	−11.8	14.1	−166.38	198.81	25	−12.1	146	142.78	−170.61
Fernangeles Elementary	730	100	−105.8	45.1	−4,771.58	2,034.01	7	−30.1	906	3,184.58	−1,357.51
Rainbow Ridge Elementary	826	90	−9.8	35.1	−343.98	1,232.01	14	−23.1	534	226.38	−810.81
Cyrus J. Morris Elementary	882	29	46.2	−25.9	−1,196.58	670.81	61	23.9	571	1,104.18	−619.01
Benjamin Franklin Elementary	882	36	46.2	−18.9	−873.18	357.21	40	2.9	8	133.98	−54.81
Salvador Elementary	736	65	−99.8	10.1	−1,007.98	102.01	20	−17.1	292	1,706.58	−172.71
Bowers Elementary	788	59	−47.8	4.1	−195.98	16.81	31	−6.1	37	291.58	−25.01
Vintage Parkway Elementary	830	54	−5.8	−0.9	5.22	0.81	26	−11.1	123	64.38	9.99
Balboa Magnet Elementary	981	22	145.2	−32.9	−4,777.08	1,082.41	83	45.9	2,107	6,664.68	−1,510.11
Selby Lane Elementary	730	80	−105.8	25.1	−2,655.58	630.01	6	−31.1	967	3,290.38	−780.61
Average:	836	55		*Sums:*	−38,610.40	18,261.80	*Sums:* 37		13,356	37,600.40	−12,536.80
Variance:	6,584					*Average:*				b_1:	−0.51
										b_2:	2.34
										b_0:	777.17

Table 3.2   Comparison of Coefficient Estimates and R^2 from Simple and Multiple Regression Models of School Performance

Estimated Coefficient	Model Specification	
	Simple (only FLE)	Multiple (FLE and PE)
b_0	*951.87*	777.17
b_1	*–2.11*	–0.51
b_2		2.34
TSS	125,099.20	
SSE	43,466.34	17,550.31
R^2	0.65	0.86
Sample size	20	

(These come from the table in Chapter 2, but we now use X_{1i} instead of X_i to refer to FLE.) According to our formulas for b_1 and b_2, we need three other sums: $\sum_{i=1}^{N} x_{2i}^2 = 13,356$, $\sum_{i=1}^{N} x_{2i} y_i = 37,600$ and $\sum_{i=1}^{N} x_{1i} x_{2i} = -12,537$. These are the sums of the last three columns in Table 3.1.

If we plug these sums into the formulas for the two-regressor model, above, we get (give or take a little rounding error)

$$b_1 = \frac{(-38,610)(13,356) - (-12,537)(37,600)}{(18,262)(13,356) - (-12,537)^2} = -0.51,$$

$$b_2 = \frac{(37,600)(18,262) - (-12,537)(-38,610)}{(18,262)(13,356) - (-12,537)^2} = 2.34,$$

and

$$b_0 = 836 - (-0.51)(55) - (2.34)(37) = 777.17.$$

Table 3.2 compares the coefficients in the new model (right-hand-side data column) to those in the original model (left-hand-side data column).

Including PE dramatically changes our estimate of the association between FLE and API. The coefficient estimate b_1 falls (in absolute value) from –2.11 to –0.51. We say that controlling for PE, API decreases at a rate of 0.51 points per percentage-point increase in FLE. This is the *association between FLE and API net of PE*.

What happened here? API is lower in schools with high FLE, but PE is also lower in schools with high FLE. Parents with less education have lower income, and their children therefore are more likely to qualify for FLE. So is it high FLE or low PE that explains poor school performance? Our regression analysis reveals that part of what appeared to be a negative association between FLE and API in the simple regression is better explained by the fact that PE is lower in the schools where FLE is higher.

Our simple regression did not account for the negative correlation between FLE and PE while it estimated the association between FLE and API. It attributed *all* of the differences in API across schools to differences in FLE. Once we net out the negative correlation between FLE and PE, we find that the simple regression model estimated an association between FLE on API that was much more negative. If FLE is a good proxy for poverty, the simple regression made it look like there is a stronger negative association between poverty and API than there really is.

You will notice that the intercept estimate also changes dramatically. Usually, our main interest in MR is in the slope parameters, not the intercept. Intercepts often become difficult to interpret when there are many right-hand-side variables in a model, particularly when one of the variables is a price (in most markets, the price is never zero). The intercept in our 2-variable model does have a mathematical interpretation: the predicted API at schools where no students qualify for free lunches and at which no parents have a college degree is 777.17 points.

Our new model gives us an estimated association between PE and API: for every percentage-point increase in parents with college degrees, API increases by 2.34 points. That's a big association. If PE is a good proxy for how much parents value education, then our new findings might offer hope that helping parents value education more could improve API, even at schools whose students come from poor families. But let's not get ahead of ourselves. There is a lot we need to learn before we are ready to use our estimates to make policy recommendations or strong claims about causality.

Is our new model better than the simple regression model at explaining the variation of API around its mean? We can answer this question by comparing the R^2 from the two models. First, we use the MR equation to predict API using what we know about schools' FLE *and* PE. The prediction equation from the MR model is

$$\hat{Y}_i = 777.17 - 0.51X_{1i} + 2.34X_{2i} .$$

In any regression model, the residual is $e_i = Y_i - \hat{Y}_i$, no matter how many right-hand-side variables are in the model.

Table 3.3 shows the predicted APIs, errors, and R^2 calculations from the simple regression and MR model.

You should be able to verify that including PE increases the R^2 from 0.65 to 0.86. Our model now explains 86% of the variation in Y around its mean. That is an improvement! (Soon we will learn to test whether the improvement is statistically significant; for now, we'll have to be content knowing it looks big.)

Table 3.3   Comparison of Goodness of Fit of Simple and Multiple Regression Models

A	H	I	J	K	Q	R	S
School (t)	$\hat{y}$	e	y^2	e^2	$\hat{y}(MR)$	$e(MR)$	$e^2(MR)$
Joe A. Gonsalves Elementary	918.05	41.95	15,425.64	1,760.21	958.21	1.79	3.19
Old River Elementary	951.87	−102.87	174.24	10,582.96	833.23	15.77	248.68
Sierra Vista Elementary	748.90	−26.90	12,950.44	723.80	742.16	−20.16	406.62
West Portal Elementary	858.85	55.15	6,115.24	3,042.01	901.87	12.13	147.19
Isabelle Jackson Elementary	776.39	−22.39	6,691.24	501.27	781.51	−27.51	756.61
Rio Vista Elementary	761.59	34.41	1,584.04	1,184.11	777.93	18.07	326.44
Poplar Avenue Elementary	782.73	19.27	1,142.44	371.26	778.37	23.63	558.55
Cloverly Elementary	854.62	48.38	4,515.84	2,340.91	877.49	25.51	650.93
Creative Arts Charter	882.10	−38.10	67.24	1,451.80	900.48	−56.48	3,189.59
Carolyn A. Clark Elementary	939.19	23.81	16,179.84	567.02	970.33	−7.33	53.68
Raymond Elementary	805.99	18.01	139.24	324.40	800.33	23.67	560.03
Fernangeles Elementary	740.45	−10.45	11,193.64	109.13	742.46	−12.46	155.21
Rainbow Ridge Elementary	761.59	64.41	96.04	4,148.77	763.92	62.08	3,854.37
Cyrus J. Morris Elementary	890.56	−8.56	2,134.44	73.27	904.85	−22.85	522.35
Benjamin Franklin Elementary	875.76	6.24	2,134.44	38.94	852.22	29.78	886.57
Salvador Elementary	814.45	−78.45	9,960.04	6,153.75	790.70	−54.70	2,991.80
Bowers Elementary	827.13	−39.13	2,284.84	1,531.27	819.46	−31.46	989.54
Vintage Parkway Elementary	837.70	−7.70	33.64	59.33	810.33	19.67	386.91
Balboa Magnet Elementary	905.36	75.64	21,083.04	5,721.48	959.82	21.18	448.55
Selby Lane Elementary	782.73	−52.73	11,193.64	2,780.64	750.33	−20.33	413.49
		Sums:	125,099.20	43,466.34		Sum:	17,550.31
			R^2	0.65		R^2	0.86

You might wonder what would happen if we had only PE in our model, and not FLE. A good exercise is to estimate a simple regression model with API as a function only of PE. If you do that, you will find that the estimated coefficient on PE rises to 2.82, and the R^2 is 0.85. Thus, PE turns out to be a *better* predictor of API than FLE is in this sample.

You could probably come up with a long list of variables that *might* be correlated with kids' school performance (or any other outcome you wished to model): the weather, unemployment rates, etc. But as we saw above, if these variables are not correlated with the variables that are included in the regression, excluding them will not bias your results.

This means that, if your goal is to identify the impacts of particular variables on the outcome of interest, you don't have to be worried about *every* possible variable that could affect the outcome you are modeling, only those that you think will be correlated with the included right-hand-side variables. This is important, because as we will see, we can run into problems if we include too many right-hand-side variables in our model, just like we can if we include too few. On the other hand, if your goal is to predict well, you do not want to leave out variables that may improve your prediction—even if they are not correlated with other variables in your model.

FROM TWO TO MANY RIGHT-HAND-SIDE VARIABLES

When we went from one to two right-hand-side variables, our OLS formulas became more complicated because of the correlation between X_1 and X_2. Imagine how much more complicated things get when there are three, four, or many more right-hand-side variables in the model! As we add variables to the model, we need to move from a manual computation to a multiple regression routine in EXCEL or, more convenient still, in a specialized econometrics software package, which will let us estimate more complex models with several right-hand-side variables and many observations.

Economists use many different econometrics programs to estimate MR models. With the unimaginable advances in computer technology that have occurred over the past few decades, even the most complicated linear regression models can be estimated almost instantaneously with the click of a mouse, just as easily as simple regression models. At the online website for this book, you will find an Exercise Folder that we've called the Econometrics Rosetta Stone. It will show you how to to run all the models in this book using a variety of econometrics packages, including one that is available free online (Shazam) as well as the open-source statistics package R and the most commonly used and versatile (but expensive) econometrics package (Stata). In most programs, all you need is a single command to run a regression involving many right-hand-side variables. You will see that in most cases the programs are quite similar—and simple. In fact, they're so simple it's dangerous. The most important thing you can do while using econometrics packages is to make sure you understand exactly what's going on "inside the black box" of your laptop every step of the way!

The goal of this section is to give you a feel for what the programs are doing when they estimate a MR model.

To begin with, remember the problem we have when adding a new variable to a simple regression model: the new variable is almost certainly correlated in some way with the one that's already in the model. Unless we control for this correlation, our estimate of the net correlation between each variable and the outcome of interest will be biased. In our example, we had to control for the correlation between FLE and PE ($\sum_{i=1}^{N} x_{1i}x_{2i}$) in order to estimate the net association between either one and API.

But what if we could "remove" or "purge" the correlation between X_1 and X_2? Purging this correlation from X_1 would leave us with the part of X_1 that is *not correlated with* X_2. Remember that adding PE to our model changed the coefficient on FLE. If we could somehow remove this correlation, then we'd be able to use a simple regression with only the part of X_1 that is not correlated with X_2, without worrying about bias. We could call what's left v_1. We could do the same thing for X_2, and we would be left with v_2, the part of X_2 that is *not correlated with* X_1.

Sounds like science fiction, right? Run both variables through a Star Trek transporter that rematerializes only the part of each variable that is *not* correlated with the other variable?

Actually, we don't need a transporter to do this—it turns out not to be so hard. The v_1 is just the error from a regression of X_1 on X_2. Let's write down the regression equation

$$X_{1i} = c_0 + c_1 X_{2i} + v_{1i}.$$

(We use c_0 and c_1 rather than b_0 and b_1 to avoid confusion between the coefficients in this auxiliary regression and the ones in our main model.) In this simple regression, the error tells you the part of X_1 *not explained by* (that is, *not correlated with*) X_2. Simply estimate a regression of X_1 on X_2 and calculate the errors. This is exactly what we want our Star Trek transporter to do for us. Then do a regression of Y on those errors. If we used v_1 instead of x_1 in our simple regression formula, like this:

$$b_1 = \frac{\sum_{i=1}^{N} v_{1i} y_i}{\sum_{i=1}^{N} v_{1i}^2},$$

we'd get the right value of b_1. We could do the same thing for b_2, using v_2, the error from a regression of X_2 on X_1. (Since the mean of OLS residuals is always zero, we don't have to distinguish between a big and little v here—they're both the same because big V has zero mean.) You might try doing this as an exercise using the API, FLE, and PE data in the online Exercise Folder for Chapter 3.

If there were many right-hand-side variables in our model, we'd have to purge each one of its correlations with *all* of the other variables in the model. For each right-hand-side variable X_{ki}, we'd end up with v_{ki}, the part of X_{ki} not correlated with any other variable in the model. Then we could write the MR least-squares parameter estimates as

$$b_k = \frac{\sum_{i=1}^{N} v_{ki} y_i}{\sum_{i=1}^{N} v_{ki}^2}.$$

You might think it would be incredibly cumbersome and tedious to purge each variable of all its correlations with all the other variables, especially if you've got a model with a lot of right-hand-side variables. Doing it one variable at a time would be very tedious, but we can do it all in one swoop using matrix algebra, even in EXCEL. Knowing matrix algebra is not a prerequisite for reading this book, but in case you are interested, we summarize the procedure at the end of this chapter. Whether you're into matrix algebra or not, these little ν thingies will prove useful for thinking about how to interpret our MR estimates.

PERFECT MULTICOLLINEARITY

This is a good moment to point out a serious problem that can arise in regression analysis involving two or more right-hand-side variables: perfect multicollinearity. We have learned that if we leave out a relevant right-hand-side variable, we are okay only if that variable is uncorrelated with the included variable or variables. At the other extreme, we might try to include a variable that is perfectly correlated with one of the right-hand-side variables. It is possible—though unlikely—that PE is perfectly correlated with FLE. In this case, it would be impossible to separate out the correlations of PE from FLE when modeling API outcomes.

Here's a more blatant (and somewhat silly) example. Suppose, in a model to predict people's wage earnings, we included both days worked (X_1) and hours worked (X_2) as right-hand-side variables. If everyone works 8-hour days, then $X_2 = X_1 * 8$. Your gut should tell you that the second variable adds no new information to our model, and you would be right. That's perfect multicollinearity.

What happens to our estimator? More generally, what happens if $X_2 = cX_1$, where c is some constant? Let's substitute cX_1 for X_2 in our MR least-squares formula for b_1 in a model with two right-hand variables and see what happens:

$$
\begin{aligned}
b_1 &= \frac{\displaystyle\sum_{i=1}^{N} x_{1i} y_i \sum_{i=1}^{N} (cx_{1i})^2 - \sum_{i=1}^{N} x_{1i} cx_{1i} \sum_{i=1}^{N} cx_{1i} y_i}{\displaystyle\sum_{i=1}^{N} x_{1i}^2 \sum_{i=1}^{N} (cx_{1i})^2 - \left(\sum_{i=1}^{N} x_{1i} cx_{1i}\right)^2} \\[2em]
&= \frac{c^2 \left(\displaystyle\sum_{i=1}^{N} x_{1i} y_i \sum_{i=1}^{N} x_{1i}^2 - \sum_{i=1}^{N} x_{1i}^2 \sum_{i=1}^{N} x_{1i} y_i\right)}{c^2 \left(\displaystyle\sum_{i=1}^{N} x_{1i}^2 \sum_{i=1}^{N} x_{1i}^2 - \left(\sum_{i=1}^{N} x_{1i}^2\right)^2\right)} \\[2em]
&= 0/0.
\end{aligned}
$$

Our least-squares estimator is not defined. When there's perfect multicollinearity, the OLS estimator degenerates into something whose numerator and, more problematically, denominator are zero.

Perfect multicollinearity usually happens because of an error in logic: it simply does not make sense to include one of the variables in the model, because it adds no new information.

You might be wondering why we even bother mentioning this silly problem. We are all high-level logical thinkers, so multicollinearity would never happen to us. Actually, something approaching it might happen. In many cases, the included variables are very highly, but not perfectly, correlated. This might be the result of bad luck rather than sloppy thinking.

Correlations between right-hand-side variables aren't usually a problem: our OLS method was designed to sort them out, and in most cases it does a good job of that. But *very* high correlations make it hard to sort out the correlations of two (or more) variables. If X_1 goes up every time X_2 goes up and vice versa, then you can't estimate what would happen if X_1 increased but X_2 stayed the same or went down. The more highly correlated the right-hand-side variables are, the more likely we are to have a multicollinearity problem.

We'll see in Chapter 5 that when two or more variables are (nearly) perfectly collinear, the variance of the coefficients on all the related variables (nearly) goes to infinity. This means that your coefficients could be pretty much any value. Mathematically, this happens because collinearity makes v_{ki} really small and $\sum_{i=1}^{N} v_{ki}^2$ appears in the denominator of the formula for b_k. When the denominator in a fraction is close to zero, even a small change in it can generate a large change in the fraction. In Chapter 5, we'll see how to estimate the variance of b_k. A telltale sign of a multicollinearity problem is if the estimated variance increases once a second variable is added.

INTERPRETING MR COEFFICIENTS

Our rationale for including FLE in the model is that it is a good proxy for (that is, it's highly correlated with) household income. Specifically, it is negatively correlated with income (or positively correlated with poverty). Because we do not have data on the incomes of families that send kids to each school, we used FLE instead.

Variables besides family income are likely to influence school performance, and FLE might be correlated with those, as well. Parents' education is an example. Few people would doubt that parents with high levels of schooling tend to instill in their children's minds the importance of doing well in school. Thus, we would expect schools whose students have highly educated parents to perform better, on average, than schools where kids have less-educated parents. Education is positively correlated with income. That means children from better-educated households are less likely to be eligible for school lunches than children from households where parents have little education.

In the last chapter, we estimated a negative relationship between FLE and API: a 1-percentage-point increase in FLE reduced API by 2.11 points. The model seemed to do a good job of predicting API in the data sample. But we do not know how much of the 2.11 drop in API was due to household poverty, and how much was due to omitted variables that are correlated with both poverty and school performance. If we want to identify or isolate the correlation of poverty from other variables, we need to include the other variables in our model. We did that in this chapter and got a coefficient on FLE of $b_1 = -0.51$ when we added PE to the model.

What do these estimates of b_1 *mean*?

Formulating the regression formula in terms of v_{1i} and v_{2i} gives an answer to this question. The coefficient b_1 is what you would get from a simple regression of API on the component of FLE not correlated with PE. Think of it as what we would get if we ran a simple regression of API on FLE using only schools with the same PE (assuming we had enough such schools).

Suppose we were to give you two random schools with the same PE, but school A has a FLE that is 1 percentage point higher than school B. Based on our regression findings, you would predict that school A has an API that is 0.51 points lower than school B's API. However, if we were to give you two random schools regardless of PE, but school C has a FLE 1 percentage point higher than school D, you would predict that school C has an API that is 2.11 points lower. You predict a bigger difference between C and D because you expect that if C has more FLE kids, then it probably also has more parents without a college education. When comparing A and B, you knew that they had the same parental education level, so you predicted a smaller difference in API outcome.

You may find this answer unsatisfying, especially if you want to know what causes kids to do well in school. Our answer tells you how much difference you can expect to see between pairs of schools, but it tiptoes around the deep questions of causality and whether or not we have a good model. We begin to address these questions in the next chapter.

USING MATRIX ALGEBRA TO ESTIMATE A MULTIPLE REGRESSION MODEL

Linear (also called "matrix") algebra is not required for this course, but if you are already familiar with linear algebra, MR estimators can be easier to compute using matrix notation. If you go on to take more advanced econometrics courses in the future, you will need linear algebra to understand more complex econometrics models, but for this course you should only read this section if it makes understanding MR models easier for you.

For each observation in our sample,

$$Y_i = b_0 + b_1 X_{1i} + b_2 X_{2i} + \ldots + b_K X_{Ki} + e_i.$$

With N observations that means we have N equations:

$$Y_1 = b_0 + b_1 X_{11} + b_2 X_{21} + \ldots + b_K X_{K1} + e_1,$$

$$Y_2 = b_0 + b_1 X_{12} + b_2 X_{22} + \ldots + b_K X_{K2} + e_2,$$

$$\ldots$$

$$Y_N = b_0 + b_1 X_{1N} + b_2 X_{2N} + \ldots + b_K X_{KN} + e_N.$$

We can stack these N equations and represent them using matrix notation:

$$\begin{bmatrix} Y_1 \\ Y_2 \\ \vdots \\ Y_N \end{bmatrix} = \begin{bmatrix} 1 & X_{11} & \cdots & X_{K1} \\ 1 & X_{12} & \cdots & X_{K2} \\ 1 & \vdots & \ddots & \vdots \\ 1 & X_{1N} & \cdots & X_{KN} \end{bmatrix} \begin{bmatrix} b_0 \\ b_1 \\ \vdots \\ b_K \end{bmatrix} + \begin{bmatrix} e_1 \\ e_2 \\ \vdots \\ e_N \end{bmatrix}$$

or, more simply

$$Y = Xb + e,$$

where Y is an $N \times 1$ vector of the dependent variable, X is an $N \times (K + 1)$ matrix of the X values for all observations, b is a $(K + 1) \times 1$ vector of parameter values, and ε is an $N \times 1$ vector of error terms. Note that we've added a column of 1s to the X matrix. These are multiplied by b_0 to give us the intercept in our regression.

To derive the least-squares estimators of a MR model, we want to find the vector $b = (b_0, b_1, b_2, \ldots, b_K)$ that minimizes the SSE. To write out the SSE in matrix notation, let's define $e = (e_1, e_2, \ldots, e_N)$ as the vector of residuals. Remember that to add up the squares of each term in a vector, you pre-multiply the vector by its transpose:

$$\sum_{i=1}^{N} e_i^2 = \begin{bmatrix} e_1 & e_2 & \cdots & e_N \end{bmatrix} \begin{bmatrix} e_1 \\ e_2 \\ \vdots \\ e_N \end{bmatrix} = e'e.$$

Our minimization problem can then be represented simply as

$$\min_b SSE = e'e = (Y - Xb)'(Y - Xb).$$

We can then use matrix calculus to take the (partial) derivative of the SSE with respect to the vector b and set this derivative equal to a vector of zeros. In the general case of a K-parameter model, we get

$$\frac{\partial SSE}{\partial b'} = -2X'(Y - Xb) = 0 .$$

which we can rearrange and solve for b:

$$2X'Y = 2X'Xb ,$$

$$b = (X'X)^{-1}X'Y .$$

If you put this back into summation notation and multiply everything out, you'll see that this is precisely the same as the estimates we derived earlier in the chapter, but it requires a lot less ink! You'll also notice a striking similarity with our simple regression estimator b_1, which we could rewrite as

$$b_1 = \left(\sum_{i=1}^{N} x_{1i}x_{1i} \right)^{-1} \sum_{i=1}^{N} x_{1i}y_i .$$

What We Learned

- How to solve the least-squares problem to fit a MR model.
- MR estimates differ from simple regression estimates if the right-hand-side variables are correlated with each other.
- How to apply the MR least-squares formula using a spreadsheet.

CHAPTER

Generalizing from a Sample

4

There are three kinds of lies: lies, damned lies, and statistics.

—Mark Twain

LEARNING OBJECTIVES

Upon completing the work in this chapter, you will be able to:

▶ Articulate the difference between sample coefficients (b) and population coefficients (β)
▶ Develop the three steps to generalize from a sample to a population
▶ Explain the classical regression assumptions
▶ Connect the data type to potential assumption failures and potential relevant populations

We do econometrics with a purpose in mind, and that purpose is to claim something about a population that exists beyond the data. But making such claims correctly is perhaps the hardest thing to do in econometrics.

The regression coefficients we learned to compute in Chapters 2 and 3 are examples of statistics. Other examples of statistics include the proportion of people in a political poll who support a candidate and the average grade on an exam in an econometrics class. In this chapter, we cover the necessary steps to generalize from sample statistics to a population. We want to avoid people like Mark Twain lumping us in with "liars and damned liars."

THREE STEPS TO GENERALIZING FROM A SAMPLE

Our sample regression equation is

$$Y_i = b_0 + b_1 X_{1i} + b_2 X_{2i} + \ldots + b_K X_{Ki} + e_i.$$

With this equation, you take the X variables and estimate the b_k values that give the best prediction of Y.

The corresponding population equation that we wish to make inferences about is

$$Y_i = \beta_0 + \beta_1 X_{1i} + \beta_2 X_{2i} + \ldots + \beta_K X_{Ki} + \varepsilon_i, \qquad \text{cov}[X_{1i}, \varepsilon_i] = \ldots = \text{cov}[X_{Ki}, \varepsilon_i] = 0 .$$

You should note two things in these equations. First, we use Greek letters to describe the population coefficients β and the population errors ε. We use Roman letters to denote the sample coefficients b and the sample errors e. Be sure that you understand the difference between β and b.

Second, in our population model the Xs have zero covariance with the error terms, expressed mathematically as $\text{cov}[X_{ji}, \varepsilon_i] = 0$ for each variable j. This means that our population model is the best linear prediction of Y using the Xs. The model leaves no information about X in the error because it uses all the information in X to predict Y. Sometimes, an econometrician's main goal is not to get the best prediction of Y given X. We study that case in Chapter 11.

Next, we describe the three steps to generalize from a sample to a population. First, define your population. Second, make assumptions about your population and how your sample was generated. Finally, compute statistics from your sample that describe how accurately your sample represents the population.

STEP 1: DEFINE YOUR POPULATION AND RESEARCH GOAL

To interpret the results from an econometric model, the first step is to define the population of interest. Using the example in Chapters 2 and 3, do we want to predict 2013 test scores for the other 5,700 elementary schools in California? Is our goal to make inference about schools throughout the United States? Do we want to predict 2014 test scores for our 20 schools? Are we interested in what would happen to test scores if the free-lunch program were to change?

This step seems easy, but it is often the most difficult part of an econometric study. To see why, let's look more closely at our schools example. The multiple regression model in Chapter 3 implies that schools with 1% more students on free lunch have test scores that are 0.51 points lower. Does this mean that we would expect test scores to improve if we enacted a *policy* that makes fewer students eligible for free lunch? Or does it merely mean that we *predict* that schools with fewer free-lunch students have higher test scores? Answering yes to the first question implies that a change in the free-lunch program *causes* a change in test scores, whereas an affirmative answer to the second implies a *correlation* between free lunch and test scores, without necessarily saying anything about *causation*.

In the United States, free-lunch eligibility is determined by parental wealth. Students from relatively poor families are eligible for a free or reduced-price lunch, whereas students from richer families are not. So, are the students in schools with more free-lunch-eligible students doing worse because of the lunches (could they be unhealthful?) or are they doing worse because their families provide them with fewer resources to succeed in school? If our policy reduces free lunches but doesn't change the wealth distribution in the school population, then it may have no effect on test scores. It is generally accepted that students do worse when they are hungry, so this policy could even exacerbate the gap between rich and poor.

We focused on the free-lunch coefficient here because you don't need to know econometrics to understand that eliminating the free-lunch program would not cause test scores to rise. A free lunch is not causing these students to perform poorly; free-lunch eligibility is correlated with underlying features of these students' background that lead them to perform poorly.

Whether we can claim causation from an econometric model depends on how the X variables in the sample were generated compared to how they are generated in the population. Free lunch is assigned in our sample based on income, and we see a negative correlation between free lunch and test scores. If we plan to assign free lunches in a different way in the future, our sample relationship may not be informative about that future population. In short, if the X variables are going to be assigned in a different way in our population than they were in our sample, then what we learn from our sample may not be informative about that population.

Often in econometrics, we are not trying to establish causation. Our goal may be to predict 2014 test scores for California elementary schools. If the school lunch program is operated in the same way in 2014 as in 2013, we may be able to use our regression to make such a prediction.

The best way to decide on the relevant population for your analysis is to ask yourself questions like those in the preceding paragraphs. After answering these questions, you should be able to state the following about your population:

- *Scope.* For example, all individuals in a state, all countries in the world, all companies in a country, all houses in a county.
- *Time.* For example, next year, any future year, the same year as my sample.
- *Assignment of X variables.* For example, exactly as in my sample, through a new government policy or project, an experiment, or a different state of nature (like weather).

At the end of this chapter, we will discuss common data types in econometrics and what kinds of populations they may generalize to.

STEP 2: MAKE ASSUMPTIONS ABOUT YOUR POPULATION (AND HOW YOUR SAMPLE REPRESENTS IT)

Every econometrics student has not just to memorize but *internalize* four classical assumptions about the population model. Understanding each assumption and its implications is fundamental, because our ability to generalize from our econometric estimates depends on them. Much of the effort we put into econometric research involves recognizing whether these assumptions hold, what happens to the properties of our estimators if they do not, and if there is a problem, what to do about it. The assumptions are as follows:

- *CR1: Representative sample.* Our sample is representative of the population we want to say something about. If we were to select a random sample from the population, it would have the same distribution as our sample. Without this assumption, we cannot expect our sample to be informative about the population.
- *CR2: Homoskedastic errors.* $Var[\varepsilon_i] = \sigma^2$. The variance of the error is constant over all of our data, that is, the error isn't likely to be larger or smaller for higher values of X than for lower values. In this case, we say the error is *homoskedastic*; if it's *heteroskedastic* we've got a problem.
- *CR3: Uncorrelated errors.* $Cov[\varepsilon_i, \varepsilon_j] = 0$ for $i \neq j$. The errors are uncorrelated across observations. We want the errors to be random, and for the error term from one observation to be unrelated with the error terms from other observations. For example, if we overpredict test scores in one of our schools in Chapter 2, we don't want to see overpredictions of test scores in all of the nearby schools.
- *CR4: Normally distributed errors.* This assumption is only required for small samples. There is no hard and fast definition of a small sample. The sample of 20 that we used in Chapters 2 and 3 is certainly small. A sample over 100 would typically be considered large enough that we don't need to make this normality assumption. For samples in between 20 and 100, it matters how close to normal the data are.

We will refer to these assumptions as CR1, CR2, CR3, and CR4 (Classical Regression Assumptions 1, 2, and so on). CR1–CR4 imply that the population errors are normal and independently and identically distributed (iid), which we write as $\varepsilon_i \sim iidN(0, \sigma^2)$. The squiggle sign ($\sim$) means "is distributed as." If we were to be more formal, we would write $\varepsilon_i \mid X \sim iidN(0, \sigma^2)$, where the slash mark "$\mid$" means "given," to make explicit that our analysis conditions on X; that is, our model predicts Y given X. We can think about these assumptions by imagining each error term as drawn randomly and independently from the same (or an identical) population.

We will usually drop CR4 because typically we will not be working with small samples. In large samples, we only have to assume that the errors are uncorrelated with each other and share the same distribution with a mean of zero and a constant variance of σ^2.

CR1–CR3 are often referred to as the "Gauss-Markov" assumptions. That's because, given these assumptions, the Gauss-Markov theorem ensures that our ordinary least-squares (OLS) estimators are the Best Linear Unbiased Estimators, or BLUE. What does it mean to be BLUE? We answer this question in Chapter 5.

When we have a large enough sample to drop CR4, we apply the central limit theorem (CLT). The CLT is a powerful mathematical principle that implies that, in large samples, $b_0, b_1, \ldots, b_K$ are approximately normally distributed even if the errors are not. We will learn about the CLT in Chapter 6.

Assumptions CR2–CR4 are testable. Using our sample, we can assess whether they hold and modify our analysis accordingly. We will explain this in Chapters 8 and 9.

CR1 says that we can use our sample to generalize to the population. We cannot test whether this assumption holds without getting more data. That's why defining our population is so hard. It's also why it is so important to state what our population *is* explicitly. We address these questions further in Chapter 10.

Most econometrics textbooks add a fifth assumption to this list:

- *CR5*: The values of the right-hand-side variable are exogenous, or given (there are no errors in the X-direction).

Assumption CR5 is critical if our goal is to test whether right-hand-side variables *cause* the outcome we are modeling. This assumption is so deeply embedded in many economists' minds that often we see the terms "right-hand-side," "explanatory," "exogenous," and "independent" variables used interchangeably.

However, if our goal is to use econometrics to estimate correlations and use right-hand-side variables to predict outcomes, we do not need to make assumption CR5. In Chapters 2 and 3, we did not have to assume that free school lunch eligibility is exogenous in order to use this variable to predict schools' academic performance. Similarly, X could be internet searches for "influenza" or "flu," and Y could be the number of cases of flu in an area. A regression model can predict the number of flu cases based on the number of internet searches, even though internet searches do not cause flu outbreaks.

In fact, Google currently does this using its Google Flu Trends regression model. In 2009, a new strain of influenza known colloquially as swine flu spread quickly around the world. Most flu strains disproportionately affect people over 60 but, like the 1918 flu pandemic, older people were more immune to swine flu than were younger people. This difference caused widespread fear and made it important to quickly identify outbreaks. In February 2010, the Centers for Disease Control announced a spike in swine flu cases in the Mid-Atlantic region of United States. Google Flu Trends had identified the outbreak two weeks earlier (see https://www.google.org/flutrends/).

Usually, when econometricians use assumption CR5, they have in mind a specific example of CR1. To see this, consider the Google Flu Trends example. Google used a sample to estimate that high internet searches predict high flu incidence. Now suppose we confused prediction with causation and decided to ban internet searches for "flu" and related words. It would be like the old Russian folk tale described in *Freakonomics*, in which the Tsar discovers that the province with the highest disease rate also has the most doctors, so he orders all the doctors killed.[1]

Can we use the Google Flu Trends regression model to predict the incidence of flu after searching for "flu" on the internet has been banned? Obviously, we cannot. The regression model would predict zero flu cases when there are zero searches, but we know that banning internet searches will not reduce the spread of flu. What have we done? By banning flu searches, we have changed the way X is generated, so the sample used to get the regression estimates (in which people can search freely) is not representative of future population (in which people cannot search freely). Assumption CR1 then has failed.

Other times when econometricians invoke assumption CR5, they do not necessarily want the best prediction of Y given the Xs. They are more interested in knowing what *changes* Y. For example, you might theorize that people could use the information from Google Flu Trends to change their behavior and slow the spread of flu. If people notice lots of internet searches for "flu" on a particular day, they could take extra precautions to avoid getting sick. You might specify an econometric model to measure whether more internet searches in a region *cause* lower flu incidence than if people did not have information about the internet searches of others. It is still true that increased internet searches predict increased flu, but you aren't so interested in that. You want a more complicated model that lets internet searches be *endogenous*.

What do we mean by "let internet searches be *endogenous*"? Let's think about it in diagrams, in which the symbol "→" means "leads to or results in".

The Google Prediction Model: More Google searches on "flu" → prediction of more flu. Of course, the whole model is based on the assumption that more cases of flu lead to more searches. Google doesn't care which causes which as long as they are correlated and it can see one of them (searches) and use it to predict the other (flu). We can predict the incidence of flu at time $t + 1$ with information on flu searches at time t, using a regression equation like this one:

$$FLU_{t+1} = b_0 + b_1 SEARCHES_t + e_{t+1}.$$

Based on this model, we predict that the number of flu cases will rise by an amount equal to b_1 for every one-unit increase in the number of searches.

"Using Searches to Fight the Flu": More flu → more Google searches on "flu" → Google Flu Trends reports more searches on "flu" → less flu (because people take precautions). Of course, the story doesn't end here, because less flu → fewer Google searches on "flu," and so on.

The basic model still looks like this:

$$FLU_{t+1} = b_0 + b_1 SEARCHES_t + e_{t+1}.$$

But now, we recognize that both *SEARCHES* and *FLU* are endogenous outcomes—they each cause each other. You can probably see that simply regressing *FLU* on *SEARCHES* will not get us what we want if our aim is to test whether information on searches affects the spread of flu.

We will revisit assumption CR5, endogeneity, and nonpredictive population models in Chapter 11 (Identifying Causation). In the meantime, we will refer to the *X* variables as "right-hand-side" or "predictive" but not necessarily "explanatory," "exogenous," or "independent."

STEP 3: COMPUTE STATISTICS TO MEASURE OLS ACCURACY

We have defined our population and made some assumptions about it. If these assumptions hold, then OLS is BLUE; it gets us estimated coefficients that are as close to the population coefficients as we could expect from any estimator. But how close are they? OLS is best, but is it good?

Let's think about the statistical problem of estimating household income. Imagine that we have answers from a group (sample) of households to the question: "how much money did your household earn last year?" The average of these numbers is our estimate of average household income.

To generalize from our sample, we first define the population: all households in the United States. According to the US Census Bureau, a household consists of all people who occupy a housing unit regardless of relationship. Next, we make our assumptions about the population, CR1–CR3. We would not want to impose CR4 in this problem because income data are notorious for not being normally distributed—the United States, like the world, has many more people with income below the mean than above it, whereas a normal distribution is symmetric around the mean.

How close is our sample average to the population mean? What if your sample has only two households in it? You probably won't be very confident that your estimate is close to the target. If your sample has thousands of households, you might be very confident. How likely is it that one observation could significantly affect your estimate? If you happen to get Mark Zuckerberg or LeBron James in your sample, then you might overestimate the population mean unless you have enough people from the rest of the income distribution to counterbalance them. On the other hand, if you were sampling in a country with fewer extremely wealthy people, you might not need a large sample to be confident that no single observation will skew your results. These same considerations are relevant when we are estimating things other than the mean—the correlation between X and Y in a population, for example.

It turns out that our assumptions can help us estimate how close our sample estimate is likely to be to the population value. The previous paragraph gives some ideas about the relevant factors. If we have more data, then we expect our estimate to be closer to the target. If our population is less variable, we also expect to be closer to the target.

To measure closeness, we use the standard error, which is the square root of the variance. Remember from your statistics class that the variance is a measure of the expected (squared) distance between a statistic and its mean. The variance of the OLS estimator b_j is

$$V[b_j] = E\left[(b_j - \beta_j)^2\right].$$

A small standard error means an estimator is accurate; it is expected to be close to the population value.

In the next chapter, we derive formulas you can use to estimate the standard error of your estimator.

DATA TYPES

While thinking about the classical regression assumptions, this is a good time to stop and consider the data we use for econometric research. Econometric studies use several different kinds of data. Each has advantages and disadvantages, and each raises different concerns about the population that we can generalize to. Here are the most important categories of econometric data we use:

- Cross-section
- Time-series
- Panel

Cross-section data sets provide information on different units of observation (i.e., individuals) at a given point in time. For example, we might have data on consumption spending (C_i) and income (Y_i) for N households and use this information to estimate the marginal propensity to consume from a model like this (often called estimating "Engel curves"):

$$C_i = \beta_0 + \beta_1 Y_i + \varepsilon_i.$$

Here, we can use the subscript "i" to indicate that the data we have are on individuals. Most individual-level (or household-level) data are cross-sectional.

An obvious advantage of cross-section data is that they can be gathered in a single survey and analyzed immediately. The single most important disadvantage is that there are many characteristics of individuals that we cannot easily observe but that are likely to affect the outcomes we are modeling. Cross-section data do not permit us to control for these individual-level unobservables because we only have one data point for each individual or household.

It is also common to encounter the problem of heteroskedastic errors (failure of CR2) with cross-section data (Chapter 8). For example, it is common for spending on food to vary widely among high-income households but less among low-income households.

Occasionally, correlated errors might also be a concern, especially when there is a possibility of spatially correlated errors (for example, "neighborhood effects"). Error correlation is the subject of Chapter 9.

Because there tend to be so many unseen variables affecting individuals' economic behavior, usually it is more difficult to explain a significant amount of the variation in the dependent or outcome variable using cross-section data. Data sets rich in information on many different variables can overcome some of these concerns.

Many possible populations may be compatible with a cross-section data set. In any analysis, you need to define the scope, time, and assignment of the X variables in your population. Think of the schools example in Chapters 2 and 3. We may want to make inference about all other California schools in the same year, or perhaps all other US schools in the same year (scope). We may want to make inference about schools in a future year (time). Or we may be interested in predicting the effects of a policy that changes the assignment of the X variables.

Time-series data give information on the same unit of observation at different points in time. Often, time-series data are aggregated across units. For example, we might have information on total consumption spending in the United States over a period of N years and use these data to estimate a time-series consumption model, like this one:

$$C_t = \beta_0 + \beta_1 Y_t + \varepsilon_t.$$

The subscript "t" is often used to indicate we are working with time-series data.

An advantage of time-series analyses is that it can provide insights into dynamics, that is, changes in economic behavior over time. A disadvantage is that aggregate time-series data hide differences in behavior across individuals.

Generally, it is not possible to go out and create a time-series data set, unless the data already exist. Most time-series studies rely on existing, secondary data.

Whenever working with time-series data, there is a strong likelihood of encountering serially correlated errors, that is, errors from one time period being correlated with errors from the next time period, which violate the third of our classical assumptions (Chapter 9). Economic outcomes generally vary less for the same unit over time than across units, so time-series studies tend to explain more of the variation in the outcome variable than do cross-section studies. (See the discussion of the R^2 in Chapter 2. The R^2 tends to be higher in time-series analyses.)

With a time-series data set, there may be two populations of interest. Sometimes, an econometrician wants to predict the future. Given a sample of, say, macroeconomic growth over the past 40 years, the econometrician forecasts the next year. Other times, a time-series analyst performs a counterfactual analysis, asking questions like: if the Federal Reserve had not raised interest rates in 2001, what would have been the level of inflation in 2002–2003? In the first case, the population of interest is future days, months, or years. In the second case, the population of interest is an alternate reality that we would have observed if the X variables were different.

Panel data sets provide the best of both worlds: information on multiple units of observation over time. Matched panels provide this information for *the same* units of observation over time. A consumption model using panel data might look like this:

$$C_{i,t} = \beta_{0,i} + \beta_1 Y_{i,t} + \varepsilon_{i,t}.$$

In a household panel, the subscript "i,t" indicates "household i at time t."

A big advantage of matched panel data is that they can make it possible to control for unobserved individual characteristics that might otherwise confound our analysis, like natural ability that may be correlated with both education and earnings in our Chapter 2 example. (This issue is also discussed in Chapter 11, Identifying Causation.) Notice the "$0,i$" subscript on the intercept in this regression equation. It indicates time-invariant "fixed effects," or unobserved characteristics of individuals affecting the outcome we are modeling. In effect, we can now have a different intercept for each individual in the sample, capturing characteristics that vary across individuals but remain constant over time for each individual (again, like natural ability in an earnings model, or household tastes in a consumption model).

Panel data make it possible to model changes in economic behavior over time as well as differences in behavior across individuals. Micro panel data (especially matched data) are not easy to come by: it is rare to have multiple survey rounds collect information from the same individuals or households. Aggregate panel data are more common. For example, in the equation above, i might refer to counties, states, or counties, and t to time.

Whenever using panel data, it is important to pay attention to problems of both heteroskedasticity and correlated errors. For all their advantages and challenges, panel econometrics requires a particular set of skills; many of these are beyond the scope of this book, but some are touched upon in Chapter 11 (Identifying Causation).

Aggregate and Micro

Another way of categorizing data, alluded to above, is by their level of *aggregation*. Some data, particularly survey information, are on individuals or households; other data are highly aggregated. There are many cross-section and panel econometric studies in which the unit of observation is a country, state, or county. There can even be studies in which the unit of observation is the world, but they, naturally, would have to be based on time-series data. Aggregate data are most available from secondary sources, because governments and international agencies compile a large array of aggregate information that can be useful for econometric research. Often, these data are constructed from micro data that are more difficult to get one's hands on for a number of reasons that may include confidentiality concerns. Those who invest the resources in collecting micro data often are less than willing to make these data available to other researchers, though increasingly there are publicly available micro and even panel data sets. (Examples include public-use micro data from the United States Census and living standards measurement survey data from the World Bank.) Whenever using aggregate data, heteroskedastity is a major concern, because the process of aggregating information is likely to result in violating the assumption of constant error variance (see Chapter 8).

Secondary, Primary, and Experimental

Most data used in econometric work are *secondary*, that is, information gathered and made available by public agencies, international development organizations, and other entities. Examples include census data, information on economic indicators, or stock prices.

Micro-econometricians frequently work with *primary* data, mostly gathered in surveys of individuals, households, or firms. Theory guides the need for primary data collection. Testing new theories often requires gathering new data. In some fields, particularly development economics, secondary data often are not available to carry out the research we wish to do; thus, part of doing econometric work can involve data collection.

In the past couple of decades, economists have become increasingly interested in using *experiments* as a way of generating primary data for econometric studies. A randomized experiment—say, giving cash transfers to a randomly selected "treatment group" of poor households and comparing those individuals with another randomly selected "control group" that did not receive the transfers—can provide important information allowing us to identify the average effect of a treatment. In this case, researchers are not only collecting primary data but actually creating experimental conditions for data to be generated. Researchers like experimental data, because they can control who gets treatment and who doesn't. This can reduce the chance that omitted variables are causing the observed results, if the omitted variables are randomly distributed between the treatment and control groups. Data from carefully designed laboratory experiments, in which subjects participate in risk games, hypothetical or real auctions, or other activities, can be used to elicit important information about people's economic behavior.

The diversity of data available for econometric analysis has grown enormously over time.

Quantitative and Qualitative

Usually when we think about econometric research, we imagine working with *quantitative* information: dollars spent on consumption, income, years of schooling or work experience, prices. Often, these data can be thought of as being continuous and covering such a wide range of possible values that we do not have to think much about the end points of this range. There are exceptions, though. For example, nominal prices generally are assumed to be positive, that is, censored at zero. (This is not the case for real prices—nominal prices adjusted for inflation, like the real interest rate. On August 4, 2011, the *nominal* interest rate on short-dated US Treasury bills went to −0.01%, so anything's possible!) A lot of data are not continuous. Some are *categorical*, either because it is naturally lumpy (e.g., people's educational attainment is measured in years, not days) or because of how they are collected (respondents check the box corresponding to their income category: "Less than $10,000/year," "Between $10,000 and $19,999," etc.).

A great many effects we try to quantify in econometrics are *qualitative*, not quantitative. A few examples include the following: differences in earnings between men and women or ethnic groups (gender, ethnicity); differences in cost of living across space (location); seasonal differences in sales (seasons); the impacts of government policies on economic behavior (policies); or the effects of choosing different production technologies on profits (technology choice). Some of these variables, like many continuous variables, are exogenous (for example, gender or season). We can create categorical or "dummy" variables to estimate the impacts of these qualitative variables on outcomes of interest.

Other qualitative variables are endogenous outcomes that might easily appear as dependent variables in an econometric model (for example, technology choice). We can use econometric methods (largely beyond the scope of this book) to model endogenous qualitative outcomes or outcome variables that are limited in some way. Some examples include the following: which technology a firm chooses (where the dependent variable can take on a limited number of values, for each possible technology they can choose, rather than being a continuous variable); wages (which we observe only for people who are in the workforce); whether or not people decide to work (where the dependent variable is simply yes or no); remittances (observed only for households that send migrants abroad); or spending on cars (which we see only for people who chose to purchase a car).

It is generally easier to deal with endogenous continuous variables than endogenous qualitative or limited variables in econometric models. Including *exogenous* qualitative or limited variables in econometric models usually is straightforward, though, as we shall see in Chapter 7.

What We Learned

- Three steps to generalizing from a sample:
  1. Define your population and research goal.
  2. Make assumptions about your population (and how your sample represents it).
  3. Compute statistics to measure OLS accuracy.

- When defining the population, consider scope, time period, and how the X variables are determined.

- Three critical assumptions are required to generalize to a population:
  - CR1: representative sample
  - CR2: homoskedastic errors
  - CR3: uncorrelated errors

- A fourth assumption matters only in small samples:
  - CR4: Normally distributed errors

- A fifth assumption is only relevant if doing causality analysis (wait until Chapter 11):
  - CR5: The values of the right-hand-side variables are exogenous

- Knowing your data type tells you which assumptions are likely to fail and which populations are potentially relevant.

Properties of Our Estimators

Fast is fine, but accuracy is everything.

—Wyatt Earp

LEARNING OBJECTIVES

Upon completing the work in this chapter, you will be able to:

▶ Demonstrate the concept of sampling error

▶ Derive the *best, linear,* and *unbiased* properties of the ordinary least-squares (OLS) estimator

▶ Develop the formula for the standard error of the OLS coefficient

▶ Describe the consistency property of the OLS estimator

How accurately do our sample estimates represent the population of interest? This chapter answers this question by covering the statistical properties of the OLS estimator when the assumptions CR1–CR3 (and sometimes CR4) hold.

We look at the properties of two estimators: the sample mean (from statistics) and the ordinary least squares (OLS) estimator (from econometrics). Comparing the two can help us understand the properties of estimators and the power of econometrics in enabling us to make general statements about the world and attach confidence to those statements.

AN EXPERIMENT IN RANDOM SAMPLING

In Chapter 2, we learned that schools with a higher share of students eligible for free lunch had lower test scores. Suppose we wish to generalize these findings to the population of all California elementary schools in 2013?

Our 20 schools constitute a sample of data. We calculate some statistics from those data and then use those statistics to infer something about the population we are interested in. To do this, we imagine that our sample of data is but one of many possible samples that we could have observed out of this population.

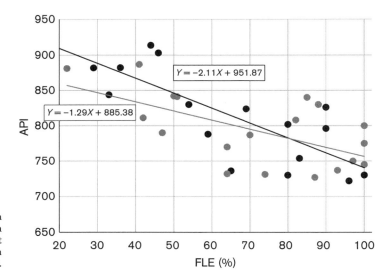

Figure 5.1 API and free lunch eligibility (FLE) for 20 California elementary schools. A different sample means a different regression line.

There were 5,765 elementary schools in California in 2013. The regressions in Chapters 2 and 3 used a sample of 20 randomly chosen schools. What if we randomly choose another set of 20 schools?

Figure 5.1 shows a different set of 20 randomly chosen schools as well as the original sample. The regression line for the new sample has a slope coefficient of –1.29, which is less than the value of –2.11 we obtained with the original sample. If we were to choose another sample, we would obtain another different result. Each different sample tells us a little more about the population of California schools in 2013.

In a typical econometric analysis, we perform computations on a sample and use the results to make inferences about the population, but we never see the whole population. If we observed the population, then we wouldn't need any statistical theory to help us leap from our sample to the population.

The schools example provides a nice opportunity to understand how econometric and statistical inference works, because we observe data on the population of 5,765 schools in 2013. We can use the population data to conduct econometric experiments. We can assign a random sample of 20 schools to econometricians and see how accurately they can make predictions about the population if they only have access to those 20 schools.

We wrote a computer program to conduct 10,000 such experiments. The program randomly selects 20 schools, runs a regression of academic performance index (API) on free-lunch eligibility (FLE), and records the results. After it

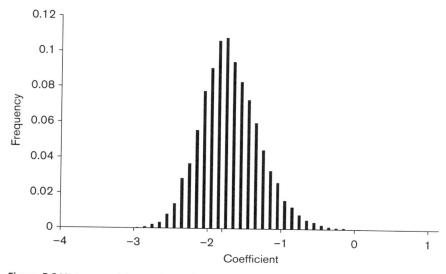

Figure 5.2 Histogram of slope estimates from 10,000 random samples of 20 schools.

runs, we have 10,000 different estimates of the slope coefficient. Each estimate is a value that an econometrician would have gotten if he or she had been assigned that sample.

Figure 5.2 plots a histogram of the 10,000 slope estimates. The average is −1.80 and the standard deviation is 0.41. This means that, if we are going to pick a sample randomly from the population, our best guess is that the slope coefficient in that sample would be −1.80. However, we may get a coefficient quite different from the average. Based on our simulation, there's a 10% chance of getting a value less than −2.29. There's also a 10% chance of getting a value greater than −1.27.

Can you guess what slope coefficient we would obtain if we ran a regression with all 5,765 schools? The answer is −1.80. This is the value of the slope coefficient in the population; it is what we are trying to estimate when we run a regression with a given sample of 20 schools. It is also exactly equal to the average across our 10,000 samples.

We have just seen the econometric property of *unbiasedness* in action. Choosing a sample of 20 schools and running a regression gives us an unbiased estimate of the population coefficient because the average estimate across samples of 20 equals the population value. If our estimator is unbiased, we are not systematically overestimating or underestimating the value of the parameter; that is, the expected value of our estimate is the population parameter value.

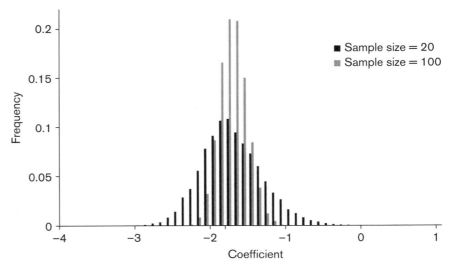

Figure 5.3 Comparison of histograms of slope estimates from 10,000 random samples of size 20 (black bars) and 100 (gray bars) schools.

Figure 5.2 also shows us how close we can expect a sample estimate to be to the population parameter, −1.80. The smaller the standard deviation is across samples, the more accurate a given sample estimate is likely to be. The standard deviation across samples is known as a standard error. We want to use statistical procedures that give us the smallest possible standard error.

One way to get a small standard error is to use a large sample. If we had used samples of 100 instead of 20 in our experiment, it turns out that we would have obtained a standard error of 0.18 instead of 0.41. Figure 5.3 compares the distribution of slope estimates from 10,000 random samples of 20 schools (same as figure 5.2) with 10,000 random samples of 100 schools (gray bars). Both are centered on the population parameter, −1.80. However, you can see that having larger random samples results in a much "tighter" distribution, reflecting a smaller standard deviation of the slope estimate around the population parameter.

Another way to get a small standard error is to use an efficient estimation procedure. We will learn in this chapter that OLS is the most efficient, or *best*, estimator because it has the smallest standard error. This property only holds if CR1–CR3 are true.

It is helpful to know that we are using the best estimator, but we also want to know the standard error so that we can characterize how close our estimate is likely to be to the population value. The only way to know the standard error for sure is to have data on the whole population and conduct a sampling experiment like we used to generate figures 5.2 and 5.3. Even though we almost *never* have data on the whole population, all is not lost. We have enough information in our sample to estimate the standard error. This is a powerful insight. Using only the information in our sample, we can get an idea of how close our estimate is likely to be to the population value.

BLUE ESTIMATORS

By the formulas in Chapters 2 and 3, we know we have a *L*inear *E*stimator. Given CR1, we can show that our OLS regression estimators, like the familiar estimator of the sample mean from statistics, are *U*nbiased *L*inear *E*stimators of the population parameters. This is important, but it turns out that there are many different unbiased estimators out there. If CR2 and CR3 also hold, we can show that OLS is the *B*est among all unbiased linear estimators. In short (brilliantly reorganizing the underlined letters in the last three sentences), we say that our least-squares estimators are BLUE. With the addition of CR4, our OLS estimator is BUE; it is better than any linear or nonlinear unbiased estimator. In the sections that follow, we derive the BLUE property and we derive formulas for estimating the standard error.

We will consider two estimators: the sample mean (which you already know) and the OLS estimators. Both the sample mean and OLS estimators can be thought of as coming from econometric models, one in which there is only one parameter (μ), the other in which there are multiple parameters (β_0, β_1, β_2, and so on). You can think of the first model as one in which all but one of the parameters (β_0) is constrained to be zero (that is, we set the slope of our regression equation equal to zero, and the intercept is therefore the mean of the sample; in this case, β_0 and μ are the same thing).

THE SAMPLE MEAN

Consider a very simple model, in which

$$Y_i = \mu + \varepsilon_i.$$

That is, the potential data we could observe equal the population mean of Y (which we call μ) plus an error. Assuming we have a sample of size N and $\varepsilon_i \sim iid\,(0, \sigma^2)$, we can show that $\overline{Y} = \dfrac{1}{N}\sum_{i=1}^{N} Y_i$ is the best linear unbiased estimator (BLUE) of the population mean, μ.

First, notice that $\bar{Y}$ is an average of the Y_i, in which the weights attached to each of the Y_i are all the same: $1/N$. So, the estimator is linear. Second, the expected value of this estimator is

$$E[\bar{Y}] = E\left[\frac{1}{N}\sum_{i=1}^{N} Y_i\right] \qquad \text{(by definition)}$$

$$= \frac{1}{N}\sum_{i=1}^{N} E[Y_i] \qquad \text{(expectation of sum = sum of expectation)}$$

$$= \frac{1}{N}\sum_{i=1}^{N} \mu \qquad \text{(assume CR1)}$$

$$= \frac{N\mu}{N}$$

$$= \mu,$$

so our estimator is unbiased as well as linear. This derivation uses assumption CR1 because it assumes $E[Y_i] = \mu$. If our sample consisted only of the large values of Y_i, then the expected value of Y_i in our sample would be greater than μ, or if it consisted only of the small values of Y_i, it would be less than μ.

Now, the variance is

$$V[\bar{Y}] = V\left[\frac{1}{N}\sum_{i=1}^{N} Y_i\right] \qquad \text{(by definition)}$$

$$= \frac{1}{N^2}\sum_{i=1}^{N} V[Y_i] \qquad \text{(assume CR3)}$$

$$= \frac{1}{N^2}\sum_{i=1}^{N} \sigma^2 \qquad \text{(assume CR2)}$$

$$= \frac{1}{N^2} N\sigma^2$$

$$= \frac{\sigma^2}{N}.$$

The second line uses an implication of assumption CR3 that if the observations are uncorrelated across i, then the variance of a sum equals the sum of the variances. The third line uses assumption CR2 to impose a constant variance: $V[Y_i] = \sigma^2$.

The standard error, our measure of precision, is the square root of the variance:

$$s.e.(\bar{Y}) = \frac{\sigma}{\sqrt{N}}.$$

Notice the two components of the standard error. The larger the sample (N), the smaller the standard error, and the smaller the standard deviation (σ) of the data, the smaller the standard error.

If we also assume that the error is normally distributed, $\varepsilon_i \sim iidN(0, \sigma^2)$, then $\bar{Y}$ is also normally distributed. We know this is true because $\bar{Y}$ is just a sum of the normally distributed Y_i observations, and the sum of normal variables is also normally distributed. Mathematically, we can write

$$\bar{Y} \sim N\left(\mu, \frac{\sigma^2}{N}\right).$$

In Chapter 6, we will see how to use this result to construct confidence intervals and conduct hypothesis tests. There, we will also learn about how, through the magic of the central limit theorem, $\bar{Y}$ has an approximate normal distribution even if the underlying data come from a different distribution, provided that the sample is large enough.

This isn't quite practical yet. We don't know what σ^2 is, because it is a population parameter (a Greek letter). However, we can estimate it as

$$s_Y^2 = \frac{1}{N-1}\sum_{i=1}^{N}(Y_i - \bar{Y})^2 .$$

(This is, in fact, an unbiased estimator of the true population variance; that is, $E(s^2) = \sigma^2$.) We plug s_Y^2 into the formula for the standard error of $\bar{Y}$ to take the place of the unknown true variance σ^2. The estimated standard error is

$$est \ s.e.(\bar{Y}) = \frac{s_Y}{\sqrt{N}} .$$

THE OLS REGRESSION

Consider a slightly more complicated (but potentially much more interesting and useful) model:

$$Y_i = \beta_0 + \beta_1 X_i + \varepsilon_i .$$

Notice what we've done here: we've replaced μ with $\beta_0 + \beta_1 X_i$. Rather than just a sample mean of a variable of interest (Y), we're estimating a linear relationship between Y and some right-hand-side variable X.

Using assumptions CR1–CR3, we can show that b_1 is the BLUE of the population parameter β_1.

There are three steps to show this. You should learn them, because later on they will give us insights into what happens when one or another of our Gauss-Markov assumptions breaks down, which is what a great deal of econometrics is about.

Step 1: Linear

Recall from Chapter 2 that the OLS formula is

$$b_1 = \frac{\sum_{i=1}^{N} x_i Y_i}{\sum_{i=1}^{N} x_i^2}.$$

(We saw that we can use either a large or a small Y_i in the numerator—here we use a large one—and a large or a small X_i in the denominator—here we use a small one.)

Define a new variable

$$w_i = \frac{x_i}{\sum_{i=1}^{N} x_i^2}.$$

Then, we can write the OLS formula as $b_1 = \sum_{i=1}^{N} w_i Y_i$. Writing it this way, we see that b_1 is a weighted sum of Y_i with w_i being the weight applied to each observation. A weighted sum of Y_i is by definition a linear function as long as the weights do not include Y_i. So, we have a linear estimator.

Step 2: Unbiased

$$E[b_1] = E\left[\sum_{i=1}^{N} w_i Y_i \right]$$

$$= E\left[\sum_{i=1}^{N} w_i (\beta_0 + \beta_1 X_i + \varepsilon_i) \right] \qquad \text{(by definition of } Y_i\text{)}$$

$$= E\left[\beta_0 \sum_{i=1}^{N} w_i + \beta_1 \sum_{i=1}^{N} w_i X_i + \sum_{i=1}^{N} w_i \varepsilon_i \right].$$

The first two pieces in this expression simplify nicely. First, the sum of the weights is zero. We'll show an example soon, but here is the derivation:

$$\sum_{i=1}^{N} w_i = \frac{\sum_{i=1}^{N} x_i}{\sum_{i=1}^{N} x_i^2} = \frac{\sum_{i=1}^{N} (X_i - \overline{X})}{\sum_{i=1}^{N} x_i^2} = \frac{\sum_{i=1}^{N} X_i - N\overline{X}}{\sum_{i=1}^{N} x_i^2} = \frac{0}{\sum_{i=1}^{N} x_i^2}.$$

Second,

$$\sum_{i=1}^{N} w_i X_i = \frac{\sum_{i=1}^{N} x_i X_i}{\sum_{i=1}^{N} x_i^2} = \frac{\sum_{i=1}^{N} x_i x_i}{\sum_{i=1}^{N} x_i^2} = 1.$$

Now we have

$$E[b_1] = E\left[\beta_0 * 0 + \beta_1 * 1 + \sum_{i=1}^{N} w_i \varepsilon_i \right]$$

$$= E[\beta_1] + E\left[\sum_{i=1}^{N} w_i \varepsilon_i \right]$$

$$= \beta_1 + \sum_{i=1}^{N} E[w_i \varepsilon_i] \qquad \text{(expectation of sum = sum of expectation)}$$

$$= \beta_1$$

The parameter β_1 of course is a constant, so its expectation equals itself. The expectation $E[w_i \varepsilon_i]$ is another way of expressing the covariance between w_i and ε_i. (This is true because w_i has mean zero.) Remember that w_i equals x_i divided by a sum of squares, and remember that the covariance between x_i and ε_i equals zero in our population model. This is always true in a predictive population model. So, $\text{cov}[x_i, \varepsilon_i] = 0$ means that $\text{cov}[w_i, \varepsilon_i] = 0$, which leads us to the conclusion that b_1 is unbiased.

Step 3: Best

To show that OLS is best, i.e., has the smallest standard error, we first need to derive the standard error. Remember that the standard error equals the square root of the variance. The variance is

$$V[b_1] = V\left[\sum_{i=1}^{N} w_i Y_i \right] \qquad \text{(by definition of } b_1)$$

$$= \sum_{i=1}^{N} V[w_i Y_i] \qquad \text{(assume CR3)}$$

$$= \sum_{i=1}^{N} w_i^2 V[Y_i] \qquad \text{(we condition on } X, \text{ i.e., take it as given)}.$$

$$= \sum_{i=1}^{N} w_i^2 V[\varepsilon_i] \qquad \text{(we condition on } X, \text{ i.e., take it as given)}$$

$$= \sigma^2 \sum_{i=1}^{N} w_i^2 \qquad \text{(assume CR2)}$$

The fact that we condition on X is used twice in this derivation. First, conditioning on X means that w_i is a known constant for each i. It has no variance and can therefore be pulled out of the variance operator and squared. Second, conditioning on X means that the only part of Y with nonzero variance is the error term, so $V[Y_i] = V[\varepsilon_i]$.

We can simplify this expression a bit

$$V[b_1] = \sigma^2 \sum_{i=1}^{N} w_i^2$$

$$= \sigma^2 \frac{\sum_{i=1}^{N} x_i^2}{\left(\sum_{i=1}^{N} x_i^2\right)^2} \cdot$$

$$= \frac{\sigma^2}{\sum_{i=1}^{N} x_i^2}$$

So, the standard error is

$$s.e.[b_1] = \frac{\sigma}{\sqrt{\sum_{i=1}^{N} x_i^2}} \cdot$$

This formula has three components. The first component is the standard deviation of the errors, σ. The larger it is, the larger the standard error of b_1 is. If the errors tend to be larger (i.e., larger σ), then we get a less precise estimate of β_1. The second component is the sample size. The standard error is smaller when N is larger. Look at the denominator. It is a sum of numbers that are always positive (or zero) and N is the number of elements we sum. The more x^2 terms we add, the smaller is the standard error and the more precise is our estimate of β_1. The third component involves the differences between the X_is from their mean, $x_i = X_i - \bar{X}$. The larger these differences typically are, the smaller the standard error. The sum of squared x_is is larger when X has a larger variance. This makes good intuitive sense. If X varies only a little, it will be hard to get a precise estimate of slope of the regression line. In the extreme case, if X doesn't vary at all, we will not be able to say anything about this relationship.

Next, we show that, among all linear unbiased estimators of β_1, our OLS estimator b_1 has the lowest standard error, i.e., it is the "best." The logic behind the proof is basically this: take our estimator b_1, which we saw we can express as

$$b_1 = \sum_{i=1}^{N} w_i Y_i.$$

That is, it is a linear function of the Y_i, and we have shown that given our classical assumptions it is unbiased. Now take any other linear unbiased estimator:

$$\tilde{b}_1 = \sum_{i=1}^{N} k_i Y_i,$$

where $k_i = w_i + c_i$ and c_i is another constant. It takes a bit of work, but one can show that

$$V[\tilde{b}_1] = V[b_1] + \sigma^2 \sum_{i=1}^{N} c_i^2.$$

The second term is never negative because it is a product of two squared terms, which are always positive. It follows that $s.e.[\tilde{b}_1] \geq s.e.[b_1]$. The two variances are equal only if $c_i = 0$ for all the i—that is, if we are back to the OLS estimator. In other words, our OLS estimator has the lowest standard error of all linear unbiased estimators. Given assumptions CR1–CR3, it is BLUE. The Gauss-Markov theorem ensures this for b_0 as well.

Note that this does not mean that our OLS estimator has the lowest standard error of all estimators. Other estimators might have a lower standard error; however, if they do, they will not be LUE. One silly example would be an estimator that always sets $b_1 = 7$. This estimator has zero variance but obviously is not LUE. You can see, then, that we are putting a premium on having linear estimators that are unbiased.

If we also assume CR4, then we can show that

$$b_1 \sim N \left(\beta_1, \frac{\sigma^2}{\sum_{i=1}^{N} x_i^2} \right)$$

(This holds approximately for large samples, regardless of whether or not CR4 holds.) With a little math, we can rewrite this statement as

$$\frac{b_1 - \beta_1}{s.e.[b_1]} \sim N(0,1).$$

In this case, it turns out that OLS is BUE—it is better than all linear and non-linear estimators.

The only way to know the standard error with certainty is to have data on the whole population and conduct a sampling experiment like we used to generate figure 5.2. However, we can use our sample information to estimate the standard error. We can do that better now than in the first model, in which we only used the mean. Now we can use the residuals from our regression, which take into account the fact that part of the variation in Y is explained by X:

$$s^2 = \frac{1}{N-K-1} \sum_{i=1}^{N} (Y_i - \hat{Y}_i)^2 = \frac{SSE}{N-K-1},$$

where K is the number of slope parameters we estimate in our regression model (here, $K = 1$), and $\hat{Y}_i$ is the level of Y_i predicted by our model, $b_0 + b_1 X_i$. (Since we have to estimate the intercept as well as slope coefficients, $N - K - 1$ is the degrees of freedom when we estimate s^2. We "use up" $K + 1$ degrees of freedom estimating the parameters of the model, just like in the sample variance we use up one degree of freedom estimating $\bar{Y}$.) This is an unbiased estimator of the variance of ε_i, the error in the population model.

We plug s^2 in for σ^2 in the formula for the standard error of b_1:

$$est \ s.e.[b_1] = \frac{s}{\sqrt{\sum_{i=1}^{N} x_i^2}}.$$

Again, remember what we had to assume in order to derive the standard error formula. The errors in the population model have to have a constant variance (CR2); otherwise, we would not have been able to pull σ^2 out of the summation the way we did. And the errors cannot be correlated from one observation to the next (CR3); otherwise, $V\left[\sum_{i=1}^{N} w_i Y_i\right]$ would have a bunch of covariance terms between errors across observations.

Remember this: when assumptions CR2 and CR3 break down, the standard error formula is wrong.

Look at the "Experiment in Random Sampling" at the beginning of this chapter again. The variance of an estimated parameter comes from imagining that we draw repeated samples from the population and estimate the slope coefficient many times. If we've got that variance wrong, our hypothesis tests and confidence intervals for our OLS estimates (which we will talk about in the next chapter) won't be valid anymore, and we'll lose the "B" in "BLUE."

MULTIPLE REGRESSION

What if we have not one but many right-hand-side variables? It turns out that the Gauss-Markov theorem holds no matter how many right-hand-side variables our model has, as long as our classical assumptions are satisfied. To show that the OLS estimator is BLUE takes a little more algebra than we just saw for the simple regression case, but the logic and the results are the same. So if you know that the classical assumptions are satisfied, you know that your estimator is BLUE no matter how many variables you have on the right-hand side of your model.

There's one catch to deriving standard errors in a multiple regression model: the covariances between the estimators b_k, $k = 1, \ldots, K$, are not zero, unless the right-hand-side variables are uncorrelated with one another. Because of this, the standard-error formulas are quite a bit more complicated than in the simple regression case. Econometrics software programs take all the correlations among right-hand-side variables into account when they estimate covariance matrices for OLS estimates in multiple regression models. The standard errors shown in regression output tables are correct, in the sense that they reflect these correlations.

You might be wondering whether that "v method" we used in Chapter 3 might help here. Recall that we defined v_k as the part of variable X_k that is *not* correlated with any of the other right-hand-side variables. It is the residual from a regression of X_k on all the other right-hand-side variables.

If we have v_k instead of X_k, things become simple; the variance of b_k is just $\sigma^2 / \sum_{i=1}^{N} v_{ki}^2$. In general, then, we can say that if the assumptions CR1–CR3 hold,

$$E[b_k] = \beta_k \qquad \text{and} \qquad s.e.[b_k] = \frac{\sigma}{\sqrt{\sum_{i=1}^{N} v_{ki}^2}}.$$

BACK TO SCHOOLS AND FREE LUNCH

We can use the data on FLE and API from Chapter 2 to estimate the variance of our estimator of β_1. First we need the regression variance, s^2, which we do not have yet. Then we need to divide it by $\sum_{i=1}^{N} x_i^2$, which we already have because we used it in Chapter 2 to compute b_1.

To get s^2, we use our estimated model to predict the level of API (our Y variable) corresponding to each level of FLE (the X variable):

$$\hat{Y}_i = 951.87 - 2.11 X_i.$$

We subtract this from the observed sales to get the estimated residuals:

$$e_i = Y_i - \hat{Y}_i.$$

Then, we square the residuals, add them up, and divide by $N - 2 = 18$. In the process, we add new columns to Table 2.1. The relevant columns are presented in Table 5.1. We keep the letter headings in the corresponding EXCEL spreadsheet columns.

(You can reproduce this table using the data in the online appendix for Chapter 5.)

The regression variance is

$$s^2 = SSE / (N - K - 1) = 43,466 / 18 = 2,415.$$

(Notice that estimating the regression variance is about as easy to do in multiple regressions as in a simple regression. In multiple regressions, the predicted-API equation would just be a little longer, and K would equal however many right-hand-side variables you had.)

Table 5.1   Calculating the Variance of a Simple Least-Squares Estimator

A	B	C	G	H	I	K
School (t)	API	FLE	x^2	$\hat{y}$	e	e^2
Joe A. Gonsalves Elementary	960	16	1,513.21	918.05	41.95	1,760.21
Old River Elementary	849	0	3,014.01	951.87	−102.87	10,582.96
Sierra Vista Elementary	722	96	1,689.21	748.90	−26.90	723.80
West Portal Elementary	914	44	118.81	858.85	55.15	3,042.01
Isabelle Jackson Elementary	754	83	789.61	776.39	−22.39	501.27
Rio Vista Elementary	796	90	1,232.01	761.59	34.41	1,184.11
Poplar Avenue Elementary	802	80	630.01	782.73	19.27	371.26
Cloverly Elementary	903	46	79.21	854.62	48.38	2,340.91
Creative Arts Charter	844	33	479.61	882.10	−38.10	1,451.80
Carolyn A. Clark Elementary	963	6	2,391.21	939.19	23.81	567.02
Raymond Elementary	824	69	198.81	805.99	18.01	324.40
Fernangeles Elementary	730	100	2,034.01	740.45	−10.45	109.13
Rainbow Ridge Elementary	826	90	1,232.01	761.59	64.41	4,148.77
Cyrus J. Morris Elementary	882	29	670.81	890.56	−8.56	73.27
Benjamin Franklin Elementary	882	36	357.21	875.76	6.24	38.94
Salvador Elementary	736	65	102.01	814.45	−78.45	6,153.75
Bowers Elementary	788	59	16.81	827.13	−39.13	1,531.27
Vintage Parkway Elementary	830	54	0.81	837.70	−7.70	59.33
Balboa Magnet Elementary	981	22	1,082.41	905.36	75.64	5,721.48
Selby Lane Elementary	730	80	630.01	782.73	−52.73	2,780.64
		Sums:	**18,261.80**			**43,466.34**
					s^2	**2,414.80**
					est $V[b_1]$	**0.132**
					est s.e.$[b_1]$	**0.36**

We can now estimate the variance and standard error of b_1:

$$est\,V[b_1] = s^2 / \sum_{i=1}^{N} x_i^2 = 2,415 / 18,262 = 0.132 \text{ and } est\,s.e.(b_1) = \sqrt{est\,V[b_1]} = 0.36.$$

We will use these results in the next chapter to carry out hypothesis tests and construct confidence intervals around our estimated relationship between FLE and API.

Let's compare the estimated standard error to true standard error that we estimated in the experiment at the beginning of the chapter. There, we found that the population slope coefficient is −1.80 and the standard error is 0.41. Our sample of 20 schools produced a coefficient estimate of −2.11 and a standard error estimate of 0.36. So, based on this sample of 20, we get a slope estimate that is too large and we think this estimate is more precise than it really is.

Things improve if we increase the sample size. If we had a sample of size 100, the correct standard error would be 0.18. We randomly chose 100 schools from the population and got a coefficient estimate of −1.60 and a standard error of 0.16. This is just one sample, but not how 0.16 is much closer to 0.18 than 0.36 was to 0.41. As N gets larger, both b_1 and $est\ s.e.(b_1)$ are more likely to be close to their population counterparts.

CONSISTENT ESTIMATORS

Imagine using an estimator that would get the wrong answer even if you observed the whole population. Econometricians would call such an estimator "inconsistent." Never use an econometric estimator unless it is consistent.

You may ask how an inconsistent estimator can even exist. The formal definition of consistency is that the sample estimate becomes more likely to be close to the population parameter as the sample size increases. There are three ways this can fail.

First, you could use a silly estimator. Suppose you are trying to estimate average height and you count all the tall people twice.

Second, you could be working with a weird statistical distribution. For example, suppose you want to estimate the average hourly wage. You collect data on earnings and hours worked. For each person, you compute the hourly wage as the ratio of dollars earned to hours worked. Then you take the average. If you have some people in your sample who report working zero hours, you'll be dividing by zero and your average will be undefined no matter how large your sample is. Even if you drop the zeros, you may have a few outliers that are so large they dominate the average even in very large samples. A transformation of the data, or sensible dropping of uninformative outliers, often fixes this problem. (This example is related to problems we will look at in Chapter 8.)

Third, you could have a failure of CR1. No matter how large your sample is, it does not represent the population well. Increasing sample size will not improve your estimator if you are not using representative data. We address this point more in Chapter 10.

The definition of consistency may have raised a question in your mind about population size. In our schools example, the population was 5,765. So, once our sample gets to 5,765, we have no way of further increasing our sample size to improve our estimate. We have the whole population, yet the standard error given by the formula in this chapter would not be zero. Shouldn't the standard error be zero if we have the whole population? The answer is yes. The formulas in this chapter assume an infinite population. In the case of a finite population, you can adjust our formulas by multiplying the standard error by

$$\text{Finite population scale factor} = \sqrt{\frac{P-N}{P-K-1}},$$

where P is the population size. For our example with $N = 20$, $K = 1$, and $P = 5765$, this scale factor is 0.99, so it is not worth worrying about. Throughout the rest of the book, we will assume an infinite (or virtually infinite) population, so we will not use the finite population scale factor.

PROPERTIES OF THE REGRESSION LINE (OR PLANE, OR HYPERPLANE)

Assumptions CR1–CR3 (and sometimes CR4) are critical if we wish to use our regression to make statements about the whole population from which our data come. Even without these assumptions, our least-squares estimators have certain mathematical properties that will be important later on. They are a direct result of the least-squares method. These properties, which you can verify with the data in Table 5.1, are as follows:

1. The least-squares regression residuals sum to zero. In Column I of Table 5.1, all of the residuals are different from zero—estimated models almost never predict the observed Y_i exactly. However, our OLS procedure guarantees that, on average, the predicted and observed value of the dependent variable will be the same.
2. The actual and predicted values of Y_i have the same mean. This follows straight from the fact that we can rewrite the regression equation as

$$Y_i = \hat{Y}_i + \hat{e}_i .$$

   (The observed Y_i is just the predicted $\hat{Y}_i$ plus the residual, which has a mean of zero.) Given (1), then, the mean of Y_i must equal the mean of $\hat{Y}_i$.
3. The estimated residuals, e_i, are uncorrelated with the X_i: $\text{cov}(X_i, e_i) = 0$. This means there is nothing more in Y_i that can be explained by X_i or by a linear function of X_i.
4. The covariance between the predicted $\hat{Y}_i$ and the residuals, $\hat{e}_i$, is zero. This property follows from (3). It will come in handy when we deal with errors in variables in Chapter 11.

What We Learned

- An unbiased estimator gets the right answer in an average sample.
- Larger samples produce more accurate estimates (smaller standard error) than smaller samples.
- Under assumptions CR1–CR3, OLS is the best, linear unbiased estimator—it is BLUE.
- We can use our sample data to estimate the accuracy of our sample coefficient as an estimate of the population coefficient.
- Consistency means that the estimator gets closer to the population value as the sample size increases.

Hypothesis Testing and Confidence Intervals

LEARNING OBJECTIVES

Upon completing the work in this chapter, you will be able to:

▶ Test a hypothesis about a regression coefficient
▶ Form a confidence interval around a regression coefficient
▶ Show how the central limit theorem allows econometricians to ignore assumption CR4 in large samples
▶ Present results from a regression model

Now that we know the properties of our ordinary least-squares (OLS) estimator, we can test hypotheses and set up confidence intervals around our model's parameters. Using estimates from sample data to make statements about the whole population is what statistics is all about. Usually, we are most interested in the slope parameters (in our multiple regression model, β_1, β_2, etc.), because economists like to be able to say things about the correlation between one variable (say, income) and another (demand). These correlations are also ingredients of other interesting economic objects, such as *elasticities* and *causal effects*.

Our regression gave us an estimate of β_1 (or β_1, β_2, . . ., β_K in the case of multiple regression), but so far we don't know how confident we can be that what we estimated is close to the population parameter. That is where hypothesis testing and confidence intervals come in.

HYPOTHESIS TESTING

An econometric hypothesis is about a potential value of the population parameter. We want to determine whether that value seems reasonable given our data. We often want to test the hypothesis that our parameter value equals zero, that is, whether there is any relationship at all between the right-hand-side and dependent variables. But we can pick any hypothesis that is relevant to our analysis.

Suppose we are interested in the population parameter β_1. Let's call our hypothesized value of this parameter β_1^*. We want to test the null hypothesis $H_0 : \beta_1 = \beta_1^*$ versus the alternative hypothesis $H_a : \beta_1 \neq \beta_1^*$. We will compare our estimate b_1 to the hypothesized value β_1^* and draw conclusions based on how different they are.

The first step in doing any hypothesis test is creating the test statistic:

$$t = \frac{b_1 - \beta_1^*}{est\ s.e.[\mathrm{b}_1]}.$$

This is the standard formula for a test statistic. Whatever it is that we estimate (a slope, intercept, mean; we'll come across other things we'll want to estimate later in this book), just (i) take the difference between our estimate and the value it would assume under the null hypothesis, and then (ii) standardize it by dividing by the standard error of the parameter. This turns our estimate into the number of standard errors it is from the hypothesized value of the parameter.

If t is a large positive or negative number, then we reject the null hypothesis. We conclude that b_1 is too far from β_1^* for β_1^* to be a plausible value of the population parameter. If t is close to zero, then we cannot reject the null hypothesis. We conclude that β_1^* is a plausible value of the population parameter. Note that we do not say that we *accept* the null hypothesis—other values of β_1 may also be plausible.

How large should the t-statistic be before we reject the null hypothesis? To answer this question, we need some theory. We saw in Chapter 5 that if CR1–CR4 hold, then

$$\frac{b_1 - \beta_1}{s.e.[b_1]} \sim N(0,1).$$

This expression looks a lot like the t-statistic. It tells us that a statistic similar to the t-statistic is normally distributed. Notice that there are two differences between this normal statistic and the t-statistic formula. First, the normal statistic contains the population parameter β_1, whereas the t-statistic contains our hypothesized value β_1^*. Second, the denominator in the normal statistic is the standard error, whereas the denominator in the t-statistic is the estimate of the standard error that we compute from our sample.

To begin with, let's assume that we know the standard error. Later we'll see that, as long as we have a large enough sample, we can ignore the fact that we usually have to use a standard error estimated from our sample. We'll also see that we can dispense with CR4, which is the assumption of normally distributed errors. In large samples, we need only CR1–CR3 to do hypothesis testing.

Imagine that our null hypothesis is true, i.e., $\beta_1 = \beta_1^*$. Then, the numerators of the two expressions would be the same, and if we knew the standard error, we would know the distribution of our t-statistic. Knowing the distribution means that we know which values are likely and which are unlikely. In particular, from the normal table, we would know that getting a t-statistic larger than 1.96 only happens with probability 2.5%. The probability of getting a t-statistic less than −1.96 also only happens with probability 2.5%. (You can verify this by looking at the normal table or, alternatively, at the bottom row of the t-table.) Adding the two tails, there is a 5% chance that the t-statistic exceeds 1.96 in absolute value.

The value 1.96 is the most common benchmark in hypothesis testing. When the null hypothesis is true, it is rare to get a t-statistic larger than 1.96 in absolute value, so we take such a value as evidence against the null hypothesis.

Stated formally, we reject the null hypothesis at 5% significance if the t-statistic exceeds 1.96 in absolute value. The value 1.96 is known as the 5% two-sided critical value. If you want a 10% two-sided test, you use 1.64 as your critical value.

Hypothesis tests are two-sided when the null hypothesis is an equality and the alternative hypothesis is an inequality. If, on the other hand, the null hypothesis were $H_0: \beta_1 \leq \beta_1^*$ and the alternative hypothesis were $H_a: \beta_1 > \beta_1^*$, then we would perform a one-tailed test. We would compute the t-statistic using the same formula as for the two-sided test, but we would only look at the right tail of the distribution to find the critical value. (The 5% one-sided critical value is 1.64.) We would reject the null hypothesis for large positive t-statistics. Similarly, if we were testing $H_0: \beta_1 \geq \beta_1^*$ versus $H_a: \beta_1 < \beta_1^*$, then we would reject the null hypothesis for large negative t-statistics.

Let's put this into practice with our California schools data by testing $H_0: \beta_1 = 0$ (that free-lunch eligibility, FLE, is uncorrelated with academic performance index, API) versus $H_a: \beta_1 \neq 0$. In Chapter 2, we used 20 randomly chosen schools to get $b_1 = -2.11$ in a regression of API on FLE. Early in Chapter 5, we used data from the whole population to determine that the standard error equals 0.41.

The ideal t-statistic would use the standard error from the whole population, i.e.,

$$t = \frac{-2.11 - 0}{0.41} = -5.15 .$$

Because the absolute value of this test statistic 5.15 > 1.96, we reject the null hypothesis at 5% significance.

If our null hypothesis is true, then we would expect t to be small. The probability of getting a value as large as 5.15 is essentially zero. Put another way, if the population parameter really is zero, then it is almost impossible to draw a random sample that produces a slope coefficient as far from zero as −2.11.

Econometricians run into a lot of situations in which the standard error is unknown. Instead, we have to estimate it using our sample data. Sometimes we cannot even figure out a formula for it, so we have to use ingenious methods to estimate it. (One of these is called "bootstrapping.") In Chapter 5, we invoked CR2 and CR3 to come up with a formula that allowed us to estimate the standard error of b_1. We got 0.36. Our small sample misled us into thinking the standard error is smaller than it really is.

If we compute a t-statistic using the estimated standard error rather than the correct standard error, can we still use the normal distribution to determine the critical value? The answer is yes if the sample size is large. We'll explain why when we get to the magical central limit theorem (CLT) later in this chapter.

Why is the CLT magical? Well, for one thing it requires few assumptions. We only need CR1–CR3. This means that, with a large sample, you can do hypothesis testing using the normal critical values even if your errors have a non-normal distribution. That is really helpful because assuming normally distributed errors is often pretty unrealistic.

HYPOTHESIS TESTING WITH SMALL SAMPLES

We just told you that you can't use the normal critical values for hypothesis testing if you have a small sample and you estimate the standard error using your sample. So, what should you do if you have a small sample? The best thing would be to find more data. We're going to let you in on a little secret. Aaron and Ed would never do serious econometric analysis with only 20 observations like we have been doing in our schools example. We have been using this small sample because it allows students to easily do the calculations in Excel and see what is going on "under the hood of the car" when doing econometrics.

If you can't find more data, then you're stuck with CR4. You need to assume that your errors are normally distributed. But you still can't use the normal critical values because you have estimated a standard error based on a small sample of data, which has introduced additional error into your calculations. That estimated standard error may be quite wrong, as was the case with our 20 schools when we got 0.36 even though the true standard error was 0.41.

Instead of the normal critical values, you can use critical values from Student's t-distribution with $N - K - 1$ degrees of freedom. (The sample size is N and the number of slope coefficients in the model is K plus one for the intercept.) For our simple OLS schools example, $N - K - 1 = 18$ and the 5% critical value is 2.10. For even smaller values of $N - K - 1$, the critical value is larger than 2.10. As the degrees of freedom increase beyond 18, Student's t critical value decreases, getting closer and closer to 1.96, which is the critical value for a normally distributed error.

Our t-statistic using the estimated standard error is

$$t = \frac{-2.11 - 0}{0.36} = -5.86.$$

The t-statistic exceeds the critical value ($|-5.86| > 2.10$), so we still reject the null hypothesis. But remember that we had to assume CR4 in order to perform this hypothesis test. If there's any reason to think that the errors are not normally distributed (picture a nice bell curve), this analysis will be very hard to defend to your colleagues.

CONFIDENCE INTERVALS

A confidence interval around a parameter estimate gives us a range of values that we can reasonably expect the true population parameter to take on. We like to think of it as the set of null hypotheses that you cannot reject. In a large sample, this means that a 95% confidence interval is all the values of β_1^* for which

$$-1.96 \leq \frac{b_1 - \beta_1^*}{s.e.[b_1]} \leq 1.96.$$

A more common way to express the confidence interval is to say that the $1 - \alpha$ confidence interval is all the values in the range

$$b_1 \pm N_\alpha * s.e.[b_1],$$

where N_α is the critical value for an α% two-sided test. With a little algebra, you can prove to yourself that these are two ways of writing the same thing.

When constructing confidence intervals, we must use the critical value that would correspond to a 2-tailed test; thus, for a 95% confidence interval, look in the .975 column of your table (2.5% in each tail).

Remember that, if you have a large sample, you can construct the confidence interval using the normal critical value and $est\ s.e[b_1]$ computed from your data. (We still haven't told you what we mean by a large sample. We're getting there.) In a small sample, you can cross your fingers and hope CR4 holds along with CR1–CR3. Then you can construct the confidence interval using the Student's t critical value and $est\ s.e[b_1]$ computed from your data.

For our schools example, we have a small sample. Assuming that CR4 holds, we can use the Student's t critical value to get the 95% confidence interval:

$$-2.11 \pm 2.10 * 0.36 = -2.11 \pm 0.76.$$

Here it is in picture form:

$$-2.87 \qquad\qquad -2.11 \qquad\qquad -1.35$$

This means that there is a 95% chance that the confidence interval includes the population parameter β_1. Because we know the population value is -1.80 in this case, we can see that β_1 is inside this interval. If we were to take many random samples of size 20 and repeat this process, we expect that 95% of the samples would give us a confidence interval that includes -1.80.

But remember that our data gave us a standard error that was too low. If we'd gotten a better standard error estimate (closer to 0.41), which we would with more data, then our confidence interval would have been wider.

WHAT DETERMINES CONFIDENCE INTERVAL WIDTH?

It's worth asking what makes it harder or easier to reject the null hypothesis, and what determines how wide our confidence intervals are. What would we need in order to have a more convincing result?

Our test statistics would become larger and confidence intervals narrower if (a) the regression explained more of the variance in Y around its mean (that is, the sum of squared errors [SSE] were lower); (b) N were larger; and (c) there were more variation in X around its mean.

Points (a) and (b) should not surprise you. A low regression variance means we do a good job at explaining whatever it is we are modeling, so we can have more confidence in our econometric results. (Geometrically, this means that the regression line is close to most of the data points.) A big sample size lets us estimate things with more precision.

Point (c) deserves some explanation. We need variation in our right-hand-side variable if we want to obtain precise estimates of its correlation with the outcome of interest. In the extreme case where there is no variation in X around its mean, we cannot estimate anything, so our standard errors go to infinity, t-statistics go to infinity, and confidence intervals become infinitely wide. You can verify this by looking at the formula for the standard error. It's like trying to test the effect of fertilizer on plant growth by giving all your plants the same amount of fertilizer. If you really want to estimate the effect, mix up the fertilizer applications—the more variation here, the better.

When things go well—the SSE is low, N is large, and there's a lot of variation in X—our econometrics may let us estimate even very small effects very precisely—and give us tight confidence intervals.

Sometimes there really is a significant correlation between X and Y, but it is so small that it takes a really big sample to find it. If we're working with big samples, we can estimate correlations that are significant statistically (have a high t-statistic) but not significant from a scientific point of view (they are quantitatively very small).

There's a lesson here. Often we see researchers call their findings "significant," but when you stop to look at them, the estimated effects they report are really very small. Calling an effect "significant" does not mean it is important. There is a difference between statistical significance and *real-world* significance. If fertilizer use increases plant growth by a miniscule amount, farmers don't care that the result is statistically significant; they care whether the relationship is big enough to make it worth investing in fertilizer. Don't forget this.

HOW LARGE A SAMPLE IS LARGE ENOUGH?

Large samples have two benefits for our confidence intervals and hypothesis tests. First, a mathematical fact known as the central limit theorem (CLT) ensures that the distribution of b_1 and t are close to normal even if the errors have a non-normal distribution. Second, the more data we have, the more likely it is that the standard error we estimate from our data is close to the correct standard error.

The Central Limit Theorem

The CLT says that if you take a large sample of data and sum it (or average it, which is just the sum divided by N), then you get a statistic with a normal distribution. This is true even if you start with data from a weird distribution that is quite non-normal. The CLT works because when you sum things, the extremes on one side balance out the extremes on the other side, leaving you with a statistic that isn't likely to be too extreme in either direction.

An example will help you understand this. You can find numerous other examples online if you search "central limit theorem demonstration" or something similar.

The US Census, which includes the whole population of the United States, found that the average US household had 2.59 members in 2010. We plot the distribution of household size in figure 6.1. This distribution is certainly not normal. Most households are below the mean—they have either one or two members. Also, the distribution is discrete, meaning that it only takes seven possible values, and it is asymmetric, meaning that it has a different shape on either side of the mean. It does not confirm to the normal bell shape.

(Some households have more than seven members, but the publicly available census data combine all these households into a seven-and-above category. We will assume that all such households have exactly seven members, which means that our computations will produce average household size of 2.52 rather than 2.59. So, from now on, assume no households have more than seven people and that the average household in the population in 2010 had 2.52 members.)

Imagine you want to test whether average household size has changed since 2010. You will sample some number N of households, then compute a

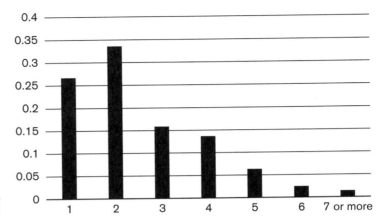

Figure 6.1 Number of people per household (US Census 2010).

t-statistic for the hypothesis H_0: $\beta = 2.52$ versus H_A: $\beta \neq 2.52$. (Here, β is the population average household size.) Your t-statistic is

$$t = \frac{b - 2.52}{s / \sqrt{N}},$$

where b is the average household size in your sample and s is the standard deviation. You will assume a normal distribution for your t-statistic. Then, if your t-statistic is less than -1.96 or greater than 1.96, you will reject the null hypothesis. The CLT says that this procedure will work well in large samples, but not in small samples.

To show this, we did a computer simulation. Our goal in the simulation is to see whether the normal distribution is a good approximation for the t-statistic if H_0 is true. Importantly, if the null hypothesis is true, then the current-year household-size distribution should be the same as the 2010 distribution. We know the 2010 distribution—it's shown in figure 6.1. This means we can pick random samples from the 2010 distribution and, if the null hypothesis is true, they represent potential samples from the current-year distribution.

So, we picked a random sample of size N from the 2010 population and computed our t-statistic. Then we repeated this 10,000 times. If the normal distribution is a good approximation, we should reject the null hypothesis for 500 of these 10,000 cases (5%).

Figure 6.2 shows the results of our simulation for six different sample sizes. When $N = 2$, the normal distribution is a horrible approximation, which is what we expect. Aside from the fact that we should NEVER do statistical analysis based on two data points, there are only 16 possible values that an average of two observations can take on with these data. You won't get a normal distribution out of that. Even worse, we would reject the null hypothesis 36 + 8 = 44% of the time if we used normal critical values.

Things improve a little when $N = 5$. With a sample that size, we would reject the null hypothesis 10.2 + 2.9 = 13.1% of the time. But notice that the histogram is looking a little more normal.

By the time we get to $N = 20$, the magic of the central limit theorem is starting to work. The histogram of t-statistics has a bell shape, apart from some spikes in the middle. The rejection rate is down to 5.5 + 1.5 = 7%, which is close to the correct value of 5%. As N increases beyond 20, the histogram gets closer and closer to normality.

So, your testing procedure will work fine in this example as long as your sample size is at least 20 and preferably over 100.

You may be wondering why we didn't use our California schools example to demonstrate the central limit theorem. The answer is that, unlike the household-size example, the population errors are quite close to a normal distribution, so it wouldn't have made for a very good illustration. Figure 6.3 shows what we get if we plot the 5,765 errors from our regression of API on FLE using the whole population of California schools. The distribution looks like a bell that has been pushed sideways a little. Since the population errors look almost normally distributed, the distribution of the t-statistic from sample regression models will look close to normal even in quite small samples. It is harder to see the CLT at work in a graph for our schools example.

Pictures can be deceiving, though. We simulated the distribution of the t-statistic

$$t = \frac{b_1 - (-1.80)}{est \ s.e.[b_1]}$$

by repeatedly drawing random samples of 20 schools from the population, just like we did in Chapter 5. We tested the null hypothesis $H_0: \beta_1 = -1.80$, because we know the parameter equals −1.80 in the 2013 population of schools. If the population error distribution were truly normal, we'd get a distribution of t-statistics that is bell-shaped, and we'd reject the null hypothesis in 5% of the samples. We do obtain a distribution that looks bell-shaped, but we reject the null hypothesis in 7.3% of the samples. So even though the population distribution *looks* normal, the rejection rate is too high for the standard normal to be the right distribution to use.

HYPOTHESIS TESTING AND CONFIDENCE INTERVALS IN MULTIPLE REGRESSION

For any of the k parameter estimates in our model, to test the null hypothesis that the true parameter $\beta_k = \beta_k^*$, we set up our test statistic exactly as in the

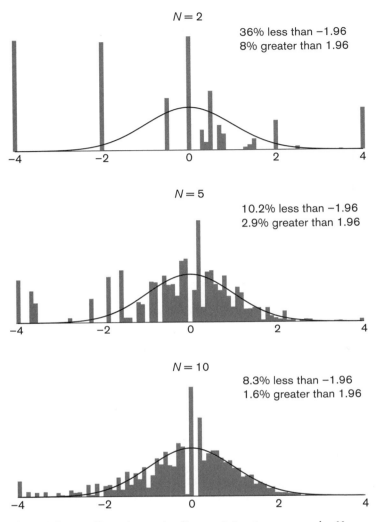

Figure 6.2 Central limit theorem implies t-statistic gets more normal as N increases.

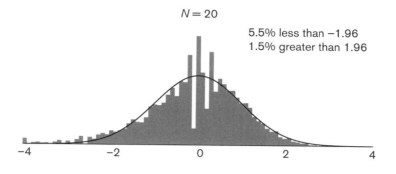

N = 20

5.5% less than −1.96
1.5% greater than 1.96

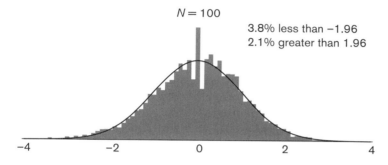

N = 100

3.8% less than −1.96
2.1% greater than 1.96

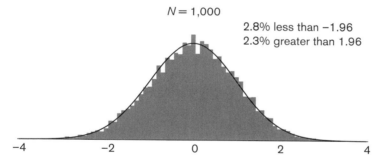

N = 1,000

2.8% less than −1.96
2.3% greater than 1.96

Figure 6.2 *(continued)*

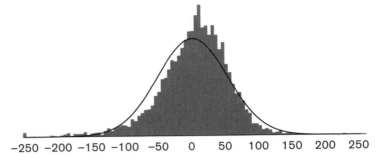

Figure 6.3 Histogram of errors from population regression using all 5,765 California schools.

simple regression model but using our multiple regression formulas for b_k and its standard error:

$$t = \frac{b_k - \beta_k^*}{est\ s.e.[b_k]}.$$

To estimate the standard error, one thing we need is an estimate of σ^2, which we obtain using the regression variance:

$$s^2 = SSE/(N-K-1).$$

This estimate will be different than the one from our simple regression model. The multiple regression model includes new variables that (hopefully) explain more of the variance in Y around its mean. This means that the SSE should be smaller than in the simple regression model, which does not include the new variables. You can verify that, in our schools model, the SSE falls from 43,466 to 17,550 when parental education (PE) is included as well as FLE. On the other hand, K increases with the number of right-hand-side variables in our model. If N is not very large, a larger value of K can have an appreciable positive effect on the regression variance. In our example, the regression variance falls when we include the PE variable, from 2,415 to 1,032.

To obtain the standard errors of our estimators, we must first divide s^2 by $\sum_{i=1}^{N} v_{ki}^2$, then take the square root of the result. The results from our schools-FLE-PE example appear in Table 6.1. You should verify this using the EXCEL spreadsheet in the online appendix for Chapter 6.

The rightmost column reports the t-statistic corresponding to a test of $H_0: \beta_k = 0$ versus $H_a: \beta_k \neq 0$.

We have a small sample, so we have to cross our fingers and hope that CR4 holds along with CR1–CR3. Then, we can use the Student's t critical value. The 5% two-sided critical value for $N - K - 1 = 17$ degrees of freedom is 2.11. We cannot reject the null hypothesis $H_0: \beta_1 = 0$ against a two-sided alternative, but we do reject the null hypothesis $H_0: \beta_2 = 0$ in favor of a two-sided alternative.

Table 6.1 Standard Errors and t-Statistics for Multiple Regression of API

Variable	Parameter	Estimate	Variance	Standard Error	t-Statistic
FLE	b_1	−0.51	0.16	0.40	−1.28
PE	b_2	2.34	0.22	0.47	5.01

Because we fail to reject the null hypothesis $H_0 : \beta_1 = 0$, we can expect the 95% confidence interval around this parameter to contain zero. And we can expect the confidence interval for β_2 not to include zero. You should use the EXCEL spreadsheet to verify that we get the following 95% confidence intervals around our estimates:

For β_1:   −1.35   −0.51   0.33

For β_2:   1.35   2.34   3.

Does this mean that FLE does not correlate with test scores, but PE does? Possibly, but it is far more likely that this results from having too small a sample. With only 20 observations and three parameters to estimate, we have only 17 degrees of freedom. It is no wonder that we do not reject the null hypothesis and that we end up with wide confidence intervals. With a larger sample size N, the summation $\sum_{i=1}^{N} v_{ki}^2$ would be larger, making the standard errors of our estimates smaller. Our estimates would be more precise, and we would be more likely to reject the null hypothesis that the coefficients on FLE and PE are zero.

Do We Have a Model?

Sometimes, you may want to test a null hypothesis about multiple parameters simultaneously. This is known as a joint hypothesis. For example, you may want to test whether both β_1 and β_2 are zero. In this case, the hypothesis is written as

$$H_0 : \beta_1 = 0 \text{ and } \beta_2 = 0 \text{ vs. } H_A : \beta_1 \neq 0 \text{ or } \beta_2 \neq 0 .$$

The alterative hypothesis has an "or" in it because it takes only one nonzero parameter to make the null false. If the null is true, it means that neither of the right-hand-side variables are related to the dependent variable—in other words, that we do not have a model.

Testing a hypothesis involving two parameters might seem difficult, but it is actually fairly simple once we get the intuition behind it. Recall that the R^2 is the part of the variance in Y around its mean that is explained by the regression. So if neither FLE nor PE helps us predict API, then including them in our regression should not increase the R^2 very much. Our test, then, is to compare the R^2 from two regressions, one with the two variables in it and the other without them. The regression without the two right-hand-side variables incorporates the null hypothesis that the parameters are zero. This is a restriction we impose on the more general model, which allows for the effects by allowing the coefficients to take on any value. Thus, we call this the restricted or "null" regression. Let's call the R^2 from this regression "R^2_{null}." The regression with the two right-hand-side variables in it is the unrestricted or "alternative" one. We'll call the R^2 from it "R^2_{alt}."

The statistic for testing a joint null hypothesis is called a Wald statistic and it can be computed as follows:

$$W = \frac{R^2_{alt} - R^2_{null}}{(1 - R^2_{alt})/(N - K_{alt} - 1)}.$$

The term K_{alt} in the denominator is the number of X variables in the main model.

Note that R^2_{alt} will never be smaller than R^2_{null}, because imposing restrictions never makes a model better at explaining something. If the restrictions don't make much difference, the two R^2 values will be similar, and the numerator will be close to zero. The more FLE and PE explain the variation in API, the bigger this test statistic will be.

We need to know how this statistic is distributed if we want to perform a significance test. When we test single parameters, we usually compare the t-statistic to a standard normal critical value, in order to determine whether it is bigger than we would expect it to be under the null hypothesis. We do the same thing with tests involving multiple parameters, but in this case the statistic isn't distributed as a Student's t. The test statistic for a joint hypothesis is a little bit like what you would get if you computed the t-statistics for testing H_0: $\beta_1 = 0$ and $H_0: \beta_2 = 0$, squared them, and then added them together. The formula doesn't look like the sum of squared t-statistics because it also accounts for potential correlations between b_1 and b_2, but the intuition is useful.

What distribution should we use to get critical values for this test? We can use the intuition that W is kind of like a sum of squared t-statistics. We know that if CR1–CR3 hold and you have a large sample (preferably over 100), then you can use critical values from the standard normal distribution for your t-statistic. Squaring the standard normal gets you a Chi-square distribution with one degree of freedom. Adding two squared normals gets you a Chi-square distribution with two degrees of freedom. Adding three squared normals gets you a Chi-square distribution with three degrees of freedom. You get the idea.

So, to test

$$H_0: \beta_1 = 0 \text{ and } \beta_2 = 0 \text{ and } \dots \text{ and } \beta_q = 0 \text{ vs. } H_A: \text{ at least one } \beta_k \neq 0,$$

we get critical values from a Chi-square distribution with q degrees of freedom, where q is the number of equal signs in your null hypothesis, i.e., the number of parameters you are testing. This critical value will work well if CR1–CR3 hold and you have a large sample (preferably over 100). For a test at 5% significance, the critical values are 3.84 if $q = 1$, 5.99 if $q = 2$, 7.81 if $q = 3$, and 9.49 if $q = 4$. (Search online or see the appendix to see critical values for other values of q.)

In Chapter 3, we estimated a regression of school API test scores on FLE and PE for a random sample of 20 schools. Let's test the null hypothesis

$$H_0 : \beta_1 = 0 \text{ and } \beta_2 = 0 \quad \text{vs.} \quad H_A : \beta_1 \neq 0 \text{ or } \beta_2 \neq 0 .$$

This means that our alternative model is

$$Y_i = \beta_0 + \beta_1 FLE_i + \beta_2 PE_i + \varepsilon_i$$

and the null model is

$$Y_i = \beta_0 + \varepsilon_i .$$

In Chapter 3, we saw that the R^2 from the alternative model was 0.84. In the null model, the total sum of squares and the SSE are the same, so the R^2 in the null model is zero. (Have another look at the description of R^2 in Chapter 2 if you are unsure about this, keeping in mind that, in the null model, β_0 is simply the mean of Y, and the R^2 is the share of variation of Y around its mean that is explained by the regression equation.) Thus, the Wald statistic is

$$W = \frac{0.84 - 0}{(1 - 0.84)/(20 - 2 - 1)} = 89.25 .$$

Because 89.25 > 5.99, we reject the null hypothesis at 5% significance.

You've probably noticed a problem here: we have a small sample. What does this imply? As with the t-test, we need to invoke CR4. We need to assume that the errors are normally distributed. With this assumption, we can compute an F-statistic, which is simply equal to W/q. Then, we compare our F-statistic to a critical value from the F distribution with q and $N - K_{alt} - 1$. (That's right, the F-distribution has two degrees of freedom parameters—one for the number of components of the null hypothesis and one to account for the fact that we don't know the standard errors of our estimates.) In our example, the F-statistic is $89.25/2 = 44.63$. The critical value from the F-distribution with 2 and 17 degrees of freedom is 3.59. (Search online or see the appendix tables for critical values.) Because 44.63 > 3.59, we still reject the null hypothesis at 5% significance.

PRESENTING YOUR RESULTS

Now that we have forged ahead to multiple regression, it is important to learn how to present our results. If you peruse some economics journals, you'll come

Table 6.2   API OLS Regression Results

Variable	Estimated Coefficient	Standard Error	t-Statistic
Free-lunch eligibility	−0.51	0.40	−1.28
Parents' education	2.34	0.47	5.01
Constant	777.17	37.92	20.50
Sample size	20		
R^2	0.84		

across two different approaches. Both give readers all the basic information they need to interpret your econometric findings.

The table approach (Table 6.2) presents the estimated parameters, standard errors, and often the t-statistics corresponding to the null hypothesis that the true parameter equals zero. Underneath the table, we provide the sample size and R^2 of the regression.

Actually, the standard error and t-statistic columns are redundant. Knowing one of these (along with the estimated coefficient), we can always derive the other, since for variable k, the t-statistic equals $b_k/est\ s.e.(b_k)$.

The alternative approach is to present the estimated regression equation, along with standard errors and/or t-statistics in parentheses underneath the corresponding estimated coefficient:

$$Y_i = 777.17 - 0.51X_{1i} + 2.34X_{2i} + e_i$$
$$(37.92)\quad(0.40)\quad(0.47)$$

$$\text{Sample size} = 20$$
$$R^2 = 0.84$$

What We Learned

- We reject the null hypothesis of zero relationship between FLE and academic performance in the simple regression model. Our result is the same whether we drop CR4 and invoke the central limit theorem (valid in large samples) or whether we impose CR4 (necessary in small samples).
- The 95% confidence interval for our regression coefficient is −2.11±0.76.
- Confidence intervals are narrow when the sum of squared errors is small, the sample is large, or there's a lot of variation in X.
- How to present results from a regression model.
- The Wald Statistic is useful for hypothesis tests involving multiple parameters as well as to test the overall validity of a model.

Predicting in a Nonlinear World

Gromit was the name of a cat. When I started modeling the cat I just didn't feel it was quite right, so I made it into a dog because he could have a bigger nose and bigger, longer legs.

—Nick Park, creator of Wallace and Gromit

LEARNING OBJECTIVES

Upon completing the work in this chapter, you will be able to:

▶ Articulate what it means to "get the model right"

▶ Learn transformations that can turn a misspecified model into a well-specified model

▶ Test for nonlinearities in an econometric model

Up to now, we have been specifying a linear relationship between right-hand-side and dependent variables. However, economic theory posits that many relationships we might want to study using econometrics are nonlinear. A relationship between X and Y is nonlinear if a given change in X is not always associated with a constant change in Y. Examples include diminishing marginal returns to inputs in production, rising marginal costs of production, and decreasing marginal utility in consumption. There are many other examples, though, because the fact is that we live in a nonlinear world.

Often, a linear model is useful even if the relationship between X and Y is nonlinear. Figure 7.1A shows a nonlinear relationship: Y decreases with X at a diminishing rate, causing the curve to flatten out. The flattening out is gradual enough that this curve could reasonably be approximated by a line (though a logarithmic function almost certainly would give us a better predictor).

As figure 7.1B illustrates, that is not always the case. With the line fitted to the data in figure 7.1B, it looks like X has no relationship at all with Y, when obviously it does—it's just that the relationship is nonlinear (in this case, quadratic). Actually, in figure 7.1B the *average* effect of X on $Y is$ zero, but knowing that is not likely to be very useful.

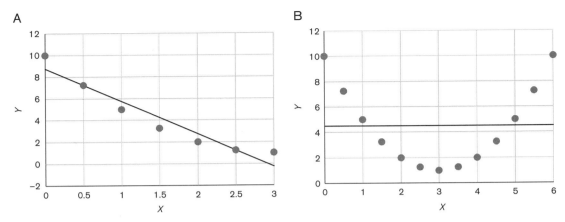

Figures 7.1 A line might approximate a nonlinear relationship between X and Y (A). But it can also fail to capture a nonlinear relationship that clearly is there (B; you might notice that the data used for panel A are simply the first seven data points in panel B).

If we want to use X to predict Y, it is more useful to know that Y first decreases, then increases with X.

GETTING THE MODEL RIGHT

We say we got the model right when the relationship between right-hand-side and dependent variables is represented *reasonably well* by the regression equation we estimate. Often, econometrics books refer to "the true model" or "the true data-generating process," as though we could actually replicate with an econometric model all the complexities of the real world. Often, they leave students with the sense that, if we do not know the "true model," we will estimate the wrong model, and our econometric results are doomed to be useless. That is simply not true. Even if we do not—cannot—estimate the "true model," econometrics can help us make sense of economic data and obtain useful insights into the processes that generate the economic outcomes we see.

We can imagine situations outside of economics in which there really is a "true" model, or something close to it. In physics, we learn that the distance traveled by a falling object (d) is given by the following equation:

$$d = \frac{1}{2} g t^2,$$

where t is the time during which the object has been falling and g is the gravitational acceleration constant. This equation represents a known relationship between t and d. If we performed thousands of experiments dropping objects off of tall buildings and measuring their distance traveled after varying amounts of time, the data would not fit this equation perfectly; other excluded variables, like wind and air resistance, would throw it off a bit from time to time. (Actually, this equation assumes the object is dropped in a vacuum.) Nevertheless, it would come close, provided the object is dense (a rock, not a feather) and it is not dropped from too high up (a building and not an airplane).

If you wanted to predict d as a function of t, this would be the correct model to use. By regressing d on t^2, without an intercept, the estimated coefficient you'd get would be $(1/2)g$. Multiplying this by 2 would give you a good estimate of g, provided that you have measured the $[t, d]$ pairs carefully. It would also make you a good predictor of d.

We could perform a linear approximation of this function by regressing d on t. We would find that d increases with t. A linear model would give us an average effect of changes in t on d, but it would ignore the fact that objects speed up in a nonlinear fashion the longer they have been falling, so it would be a poorer and poorer predictor of d the higher t got.

In economics, of course, we almost never know the true relationship between right-hand-side and dependent variables. When we say "getting the model right," what we really mean is "getting it reasonably right" or "being able to convince our peers and critics that we have it reasonably right." We do our best to imagine what the relationship between right-hand-side and dependent variables might look like, drawing from economic theory, experience, and basic intuition and logic. Then we test our model to see whether it fits the data well. If it doesn't, we fix it.

We follow Albert Einstein's advice: make everything as simple as possible, but not simpler. That means (a) approximating the relationship between right-hand-side and dependent variables with a linear equation when possible, but (b) using simple nonlinear specifications when theory, experience, or logic gives us a compelling reason to make the model nonlinear, and (c) always running models different ways to test whether our assumptions about linearity matter or not (we call this doing *robustness* or *sensitivity tests*).

This general approach reflects a trend in economics research similar to Occam's razor: if you can say something useful with a simpler model, do it. If you need a more complex model to tell the story, fine—do that. But bear in mind that the more complicated your model becomes, the harder it will be to interpret your results. Readers might become confused or, worse, suspicious that the key findings you got were the result of experimenting with ever more complicated model specifications, or throwing in a nonlinearity here and there, instead of reflecting a robust relationship between right-hand-side and dependent variables. In economics, as in science, there is a cost to being more complicated than you need to be.

Getting the functional form reasonably right can improve our ability to predict real-world outcomes. As we shall see in Chapter 11, it is particularly important if we want to make statements concerning causality, because then we need to isolate the effect of one variable from that of another. This means being convinced that we have all the most relevant variables in our model, and it is a reason why establishing causation in econometrics is more difficult than estimating correlations or using econometric models for prediction.

If the relationship between right-hand-side and dependent variables differs from the way it is represented in your econometric equation, problems can result, regardless of whether your main goal is prediction or establishing causation. Because getting the model right is so fundamental for econometric analysis, researchers spend a great deal of time thinking about this. It is not uncommon for econometric findings to be disputed on the grounds that the wrong model was estimated. To make things more challenging (and interesting), there is no surefire way to test whether the model we estimated is the "right" one, because we can never observe the "true" process that generated the data we see.

Often we can formally test one model against another, but sometimes we cannot. The hypothesis tests we consider in this book are what we call "nested tests." The null hypothesis corresponds to a special case of the model we start out with. That is, it is "nested" within that model. The simplest nested test is whether the coefficient we are testing takes on a specified value. For example, the null hypothesis $H_0: \beta_k = 0$ corresponds to a special case in which the variable X_k has no association with the outcome we are modeling. The model without variable X_k is nested within a larger model that has X_k. There are also "non-nested tests," but they are more complicated, few econometric studies use them, and they fall outside the scope of this book.

HOW COULD WE GET THE MODEL WRONG?

There are two main ways that we can get the model wrong. The first is by omitting variables that should be in the model and/or including variables that should not. The second is when we estimate a linear model, but the true relationship between Y and one or more of the right-hand-side variables is not linear. Sometimes, ignoring a nonlinear relationship between X and Y is the same thing as leaving out a relevant right-hand-side variable. For example, if the relationship is quadratic, as in figure 7.1B, but you estimate it as linear, you have omitted a relevant right-hand-side variable: X^2. In many cases, there are easy solutions to either one of these problems. In others, solving the problem is more problematic.

Leaving Out Relevant Right-Hand-Side Variables

We saw in Chapter 3 what happens if we use a single right-hand-side variable, X_i:

$$Y_i = \beta_0 + \beta_1 X_i + \varepsilon_i$$

and apply the simple OLS regression formula:

$$b_1 = \frac{\sum\limits_{i=1}^{N} x_i y_i}{\sum\limits_{i=1}^{N} x_i^2},$$

but there is another relevant variable omitted from the equation. The OLS estimator for the same coefficient, but in a model with two right-hand-side variables, becomes

$$b_1 = \frac{\sum\limits_{i=1}^{N} x_{1i} y_i \sum\limits_{i=1}^{N} x_{2i}^2 - \sum\limits_{i=1}^{N} x_{1i} x_{2i} \sum\limits_{i=1}^{N} x_{2i} y_i}{\sum\limits_{i=1}^{N} x_{1i}^2 \sum\limits_{i=1}^{N} x_{2i}^2 - (\sum\limits_{i=1}^{N} x_{1i} x_{2i})^2}.$$

(Here, we let X_{1i} denote X_i, the variable in the simple regression equation, and X_{2i} is the variable that is omitted from that regression. Remember, also, that the x denotes X minus its mean.)

Only in the extremely rare case where the omitted variable (X_2) is completely uncorrelated with the included variable (X_1), that is,

$$\sum\limits_{i=1}^{N} x_{1i} x_{2i} = 0,$$

will these two formulas give us the same estimated coefficient on X_1. You can safely assume that just isn't going to happen. Omitting a relevant right-hand-side variable will give us a different estimate of the parameter on the included variable. The magnitude of this difference depends on the correlation between the two right-hand-side variables as well as the variance of the omitted variable. (The numerator in the formula for the variance of X_2 is $\sum\limits_{i=1}^{N} x_{2i}^2$, which also appears in both the numerator and the denominator of the formula for b_1.) It also depends on the correlation of the omitted variable with Y, $\sum\limits_{i=1}^{N} x_{2i} y_i$, which appears in the numerator of b_1.

Omitted variables are a major concern when it comes to attributing impacts to specific right-hand-side variables (Chapter 11: Identifying Causation). In Chapter 3, we saw that including parents' education (PE) dramatically altered the estimated association between free-lunch eligibility (FLE) and schools' academic performance (API). If you want to isolate the correlation between FLE and API from the correlation between PE and API, both FLE and API obviously need to be in your model. The coefficient on the PE variable captures influences that are not reflected in the FLE variable, for example, parents' values reflected in their own education, which can affect children's performance.

We have a different problem if we include a variable that should not be in the regression because it does not provide useful information to predict the outcome of interest. If irrelevant right-hand-side variables are included in the equation, it turns out that our OLS estimates are unbiased. You can show this mathematically.

So what's the problem, you might ask? Unbiased doesn't mean best linear unbiased estimator (BLUE). Throwing an irrelevant variable into the model gives us estimators that have higher variance than if we exclude that variable. That means our estimated b could be farther from the population coefficient β. In other words, an irrelevant variable causes us to lose the "B" in BLUE, because even though our estimators are still unbiased, they are not the *best* (lowest variance) unbiased estimators.

In short, there are problems both with omitting relevant variables and with including irrelevant ones. In the first case, our estimators are biased, and in the second case they are unbiased but not efficient (lowest variance). Either way they are not BLUE.

How do we know which variables are relevant and which aren't? Theory is our guide here. Look back at your micro and macro courses. A consumer demand equation better have income and prices in it, along with other key variables that can shift the demand curve (household size, proxies for preferences like age and ethnicity, etc.) A production function should have all of the relevant inputs in it. This is why econometrics requires a good understanding of economic theory as well as math and statistics.

Sometimes you will see people use a trial-and-error approach: put in a variable; see if its estimated coefficient is significantly different from zero (and of the expected sign); leave it in if it is; take it out if it isn't. Then repeat for all variables that could possibly be included in the model. That's definitely not the way to go. We saw in Chapter 4 that, even when we know the model for the whole population, our parameter estimates can take on a whole range of values from one sample of data to another. Sometimes, we're unlucky enough to get a parameter estimate in one of the tails of the distributions. You wouldn't want to take a relevant variable out of your model (or put an irrelevant one in) just because that happens. This approach would also lead you to exclude any variable that gives you a result you weren't expecting, but an unexpected result may actually tell you something important about your model, not to mention the world!

WHAT IF THE TRUE MODEL IS NONLINEAR?

The world is not linear. We see this throughout economics. Decreasing marginal returns to factor inputs. Diminishing marginal utility. Increasing mar-

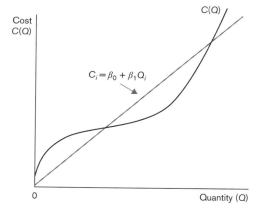

Figure 7.2 Cost functions in microeconomics typically are represented as cubic relationships between quantity (Q) and cost (C). Fitting a line to this relationship provides an estimate of the average relationship between Q and C.

ginal costs. These are not linear functions. Does this mean we cannot use our linear regression methods to model output, demands, or costs?

Not at all. Often, we can use a math trick to make nonlinear models linear. There are two classes of nonlinear models that can be estimated using our linear regression tools: those that are nonlinear in right-hand-side variables and those that are nonlinear in parameters. Fortunately, we have tools to deal with both of these situations.

Linear in Parameters but Not in Right-Hand-Side Variables

It is often the case that a model is linear in parameters but nonlinear in right-hand-side variables.

A Cubic Cost Function

Take, for example, a cubic cost function:

$$C_i = b_0 + b_1 Q_i + b_2 Q_i^2 + b_3 Q_i^3 + e_i,$$

where C_i is total cost and Q_i is output for firm i. (Why cubic? Think back to the cost functions you studied in your intermediate micro theory courses.) Figure 7.2 illustrates a typical cost function in microeconomics.

Functions like this are easy to estimate: just create a new right-hand-side variable that is output-squared and call it whatever you want (say, $Q2_i$):

$$Q2_i = Q_i^2.$$

Then create a second variable that is Q-cubed:

$$Q3_i = Q_i^3.$$

You can do this using the command to generate new variables in any econometrics package, or just do it in EXCEL and add a couple of new columns to your matrix. Then you have a linear model with output, output-squared, and output-cubed as your right-hand-side variables, so you can regress C_i on Q_i, $Q2_i$, and $Q3_i$. Our micro theory would lead us to expect we'd get coefficient estimates that are positive for both b_1 and b_3 and negative for b_2 (why?).

You can see what the problem is if we leave out the quadratic and cubic terms. We omit relevant right-hand-side variables, and therefore our estimated effect of Q on C is inaccurate. Without the higher-order output variables, our model is underspecified—it's missing relevant right-hand-side variables.

In the case of this cost function, micro theory makes it pretty clear that the relationship between dependent and right-hand-side variables is nonlinear. A linear total cost function

$$C_i = b_0 + b_1 Q_i + \varepsilon_i$$

would force the marginal cost to be constant, since $\dfrac{dC_i}{dQ_i} = b_1$. Geometrically, you can imagine trying to draw a straight line through the cubic cost function in figure 7.2. This regression will give you a b_1 coefficient that represents the average relationship between Q and C over the range of the data, but it doesn't really describe what the function looks like. For high values of Q, where the cubic function turns up sharply, the estimated effect of output on cost (the slope of the line) will be too low, and for mid-range values, where the function flattens out, it will be too high.

A Hyperbola

In other applications, theory might be clear on what variables should be in our regression but not necessarily on which functional form the relationship between X and Y should take. A few years ago, Ed wanted to estimate a simple model to illustrate that countries with high per capita income have a small share of their labor force employed in agriculture. He did not use a formal theoretical model to motivate this, only the observation that everywhere, it seems, people move off the farm as nonagricultural opportunities expand. For various reasons, most people prefer nonfarm jobs. Ed wanted to show by how much.

Theory does not offer too much guidance as to what form this regression should take, only that the relationship between the share of workforce in agriculture and per capita income is likely to be negative, and the share in agriculture should never be zero. (How can a country produce crops with no labor?) Ed assembled data from the World Bank and other sources on per capita income (PPP adjusted;[1] he called this variable PCY) and the percentage of the workforce employed in agriculture (AGL) from as many countries as he could. Figure 7.3 shows what he got when he plotted them.

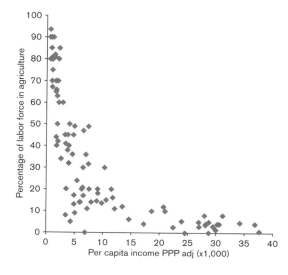

Figure 7.3 Scatterplot of countries' shares of workforce employed in agriculture (vertical axis) against per capita income (PPP adjusted; horizontal axis). The relationship appears to be hyperbolic, asymptoting near zero at high incomes.

Table 7.1   Results from Econometric Estimation of "Moving-Off-the-Farm" Model

Variable	Estimated Coefficient	Standard Error	t-Statistic
$1/PCY$	65.71	4.04	16.25
Constant	11.81	2.05	5.77
Sample size	95		
R^2	0.74		

The relationship between income and farm labor does not look linear—it looks like a hyperbola. Often if you don't have a theoretical model to tell you what the functional form of your econometric model should be, just looking at the raw data can give you a good idea. An equation for a hyperbola looks like this:

$$AGL_i = b_0 + \frac{b_1}{PCY_i} + e_i .$$

That is the equation Ed estimated. Like with the cost function, this model can be estimated using ordinary least squares (OLS), with ($1/PCY$) as the right-hand-side variable. This was not intended to be a causal model: the point is not to argue that per capita income *causes* changes in the labor force employed in agriculture, only to estimate the gross relationship between the two, and to use PCY to predict the share of employment in agriculture. The results appear in Table 7.1.

As you can see, the relationship is very strong: just knowing per capita income allows us to explain 74% of the variation in AGL around its mean. Not a bad predictor. The coefficient on $1/PCY$ is a little hard to interpret, because we don't typically think of the inverse of income as a right-hand-side variable. We can take the derivative of AGL with respect to PCY to see the effect of a $1,000 change in per capita income on the predicted share of workforce in agriculture (using the quotient rule):

$$\frac{dAGL}{dPCY} = \frac{-b_1}{PCY^2}.$$

The derivative is negative, as expected. Since the relationship is nonlinear, its size depends on the PCY at which we evaluate it, which is easy to see from the scatterplot. At the lowest PCY of all the countries in the sample ($590), $1,000 * \frac{-65.71}{PCY^2} = 0.19$. A $1,000 increase in per capita income is associated with a 19-point decrease in the percentage of the workforce in agriculture! At the highest income ($37,610), though, the derivative is virtually zero (0.00005). At the mean per capita income ($10,671), it is also very small (0.00058). In short, at low-income levels, as per capita income increases, the share of workers in agriculture doesn't just decrease—it drops off a cliff. At high-income levels, though, it hardly budges at all, partly because it is already close to zero.

Nonlinear in Parameters

The examples we have looked at so far are nonlinear in the right-hand-side variables but not in the parameters. We were able to solve the problem by defining new right-hand-side variables that are nonlinear functions of the original variables.

In many cases, we encounter models that are nonlinear in parameters. They require new, and sometimes rather creative, transformation strategies.

A Cobb-Douglas Production Function

Consider one of the most famous functions in all economics: the Cobb-Douglas (CD) production function

$$Q_i = F(L_i, K_i) = \beta_0 L_i^{\beta_1} K_i^{\beta_2}$$

or in its constant-returns-to-scale version

$$Q_i = F(L_i, K_i) = \beta_0 L_i^{\beta_1} K_i^{1-\beta_1}.$$

Q_i is firm i's output, L_i is labor, and K_i is capital. With such an important function, it would be a shame if we couldn't estimate it. Fortunately, we can make it linear in parameters simply by taking the natural log of each side. Using the general form of the CD production function, we get

$$\ln(Q_i) = \ln(\beta_0) + \beta_1 \ln(L_i) + \beta_2 \ln(K_i).$$

That's CD in double-log form (meaning that we have natural logs of variables on both sides of the equation). For an econometric regression, we need an error term, too:

$$\ln(Q_i) = \ln(\beta_0) + \beta_1 \ln(L_i) + \beta_2 \ln(K_i) + \varepsilon_i.$$

(Ask yourself: what did the original [untransformed] CD equation have to look like in order to end up with this additive error?[2])

Now we use the trick we learned in the last section to create a linear model. Define three new variables:

$$Q^* = \ln(Q_i)$$
$$L^* = \ln(L_i) \quad .$$
$$K^* = \ln(K_i)$$

Again, these variables are easy to create in Excel or any econometric software program. Then perform an OLS regression of Q^* on L^* and K^*. This will give you estimates of β_1, β_2, and an intercept term, which you can see is not really β_0 but its natural log. To recover β_0, just take the exponential of this intercept.

Economists often like to present their results as elasticities, which we can also calculate using our estimated regression equation. Recall that the elasticity of Y with respect to X is given by

$$\eta = \frac{dY}{dX} \frac{X}{Y}.$$

An advantage of the CD specification is that it gives us direct estimates of output elasticities with respect to each factor input, since (recalling the method to take derivatives of logarithmic functions)

$$\beta_1 = \frac{\partial \ln(Q_i)}{\partial \ln(L_i)} = \frac{\partial Q_i}{\partial L_i} \frac{L_i}{Q_i}.$$

What happens if we estimate a linear production function, when a CD function really created our data? It isn't hard to imagine that major stuff might go wrong, because by trying to fit a straight line to a nonlinear function we are estimating the wrong thing. A regression of Q_i on L_i and K_i is likely to give biased and perhaps misleading estimates of the parameters in a CD production function. The online appendix for this chapter contains a data set on maize production in rural Mexico. You can use it to compare linear and CD estimates of the production function $Q = F(Labor, Land)$. You will find that both *Labor* and *Land* have a significant and positive relationship with output in the CD specification, but not in the linear one.

This CD production function is a special case of the more general constant elasticity of substitution (CES) production function, in which the elasticity of

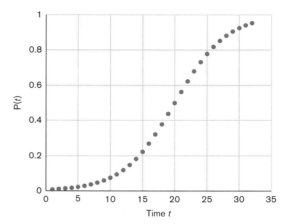

Figure 7.4 Logistic growth function. A logistic growth function generally has an "S" shape.

substitution between the two inputs equals –1. The CES production function looks like this:

$$Q_i = \beta_0(\beta_1 L_i^\rho + (1-\beta_1)K_i^\rho)^{1/\rho}.$$

The parameters to be estimated are β_0, β_1, and ρ. You can play around with this equation all you like, but you will not be able to transform it into something you can estimate using OLS. Unlike the special case of CD, the more general CES production function does not lend itself to estimation using OLS. Instead, a nonlinear estimation approach, like nonlinear least squares, is needed. Although nonlinear least squares is beyond the scope of this book, we include this example to make the point that not all functional relationships can be estimated using OLS.

A Logistic Growth Function

Let's conclude this section by looking at a nonlinear function that seems impossibly hard to transform, but really isn't. Many biological growth processes, as well as the diffusion of new products (like home computers) and technologies (like new seed varieties) can be described by a logistic growth function, like the one illustrated in figure 7.4. It is described by the following equation:

$$Y_t = 1/(1+e^{-(\beta_0 + \beta_1 t)}).$$

How can we estimate this using OLS? You can see that taking the log of both sides does not solve the problem, because we would be left with the log of $(1+e^{-(\beta_0 + \beta_1 t)})$. But suppose we first take the reciprocal of both sides:

$$1/Y_t = (1 + e^{-(\beta_0 + \beta_1 t)}).$$

Subtracting one from both sides and *then* taking the log gives

$$\ln(1/Y_t - 1) = \beta_0^* + \beta_1^* t,$$

where β_0^*, β_1^* are just the negatives of the original coefficients.

Like the CD production function, this logistic growth function has a more general form, given by this equation:

$$Y_t = K/(1 + e^{-(\beta_0 + \beta_1 t)}).$$

This is the function the economist Zvi Griliches used to model the spread of new corn seed varieties in different US states between 1932 and 1956. In his seminal study, Y_t was the share of a state's cropland planted with hybrid seed. In Griliches' equation, you can see that K is the "ceiling" or maximum value that Y_t can attain. (When t is very large, the denominator approaches 1, and the area planted in hybrids approaches K.) In the equation we just transformed, we assumed that K equals 1. Griliches did not want to assume that 100% of all land in a state could be planted in hybrids, though, because some land might not be suitable. Thus, he had to estimate K along with β_0 and β_1. Test your knowledge by trying to figure out whether Griliches was able to estimate his model using OLS.

Other Sources of Nonlinearities

So far, we have seen examples where our model is nonlinear in either parameters or in variables, but these are not the only ways in which a model can deviate from the simple linear model we started out with. The effect of a right-hand-side variable can change depending on the levels of other variables. For example, maybe your work experience has a stronger effect on your earnings if you've also had more education, or maybe the effect of experience on earnings is different for men and women. Knowing whether right-hand-side variables have different effects for different people can be important when thinking about how to translate your econometric models into policy. In these cases, it's important to consider not just which variables should be in your model (education, experience, gender), but also how those variables *interact* with each other.

Interactions

When a model is linear in a variable

$$Y_t = \beta_0 + \beta_1 X_t + \varepsilon_t,$$

the predicted difference in Y values between two observations does not depend on X; the change in Y with respect to X is

$$\frac{dY_t}{dX_t} = \beta_1.$$

When a model is nonlinear in a variable, for example, in the quadratic regression,

$$Y_t = \beta_0 + \beta_1 X_t + \beta_2 X_t^2 + e_t,$$

the predicted difference depends on the level of that variable:

$$\frac{dY_t}{dX_t} = \beta_1 + 2\beta_2 X_t.$$

Sometimes, the impact of a variable depends on the level of *some other* variable. For example, consider the Mincer equation relating people's earnings (E_i) to their years of completed schooling (S_i) and years of work experience (EX_i):

$$\ln(E_i) = \beta_0 + \beta_1 S_i + \beta_2 EX_i + \beta_3 EX_i^2 + \varepsilon_i.$$

This is one of the most famous equations in all of economics. It is a semi-log equation; only the left-hand-side variable is logged. In the double-log CD equation, the slope parameters represented elasticities (percentage changes in output for a 1% change in inputs). In the semi-log Mincer equation, they give the percentage change in earnings associated with a *one-unit* change in the corresponding right-hand-side variable.

The Mincer equation is nonlinear in work experience: at high levels of experience, additional years of experience mean that the worker is getting older, and eventually diminishing returns to experience set in (that is, $\beta_2 > 0$ and $\beta_3 < 0$). The marginal returns to experience depend on how many years of experience the worker has.

Marginal returns to experience might also depend on how much schooling the worker has. Someone with a college education might be able to "move up" more quickly than someone with only a high school education. In this case, the marginal effect of experience on earnings would vary for different levels of schooling.

How do we capture this in our econometric model? Let's include an interaction term $EX_i {}^* S_i$, the product of schooling and experience:

$$\ln(E_i) = \beta_0 + \beta_1 S_i + \beta_2 EX_i + \beta_3 EX_i^2 + \beta_4 EX_i {}^* S_i + \varepsilon_i.$$

The (partial) derivative of the natural log of earnings with respect to experience (the percentage change in earnings associated with a 1-year change in experience) becomes

$$\frac{\partial \ln(E_i)}{\partial EX_i} = \frac{\partial E_i / \partial EX_i}{E_i} = \beta_2 + 2\beta_3 EX_i + \beta_4 S_i.$$

Now the effect of experience on earnings depends on both the level of experience and the level of education. If β_4 is positive, the effect of experience is higher the more schooling person i has.

Interactions are often found in econometric models. Sometimes, including interactions significantly raises a model's predictive power, while omitting them could potentially bias coefficient estimates.

Indicator Variables

Many of the most important variables explaining economic outcomes are not quantitative. Qualitative variables, like where people are, who they are, whether or not an economic policy is enacted, etc., may be important as well.

Consider the Mincer earnings equation again. Human capital theory predicts that workers are paid the marginal value product of their labor (MVPL), as depicted by this well-known picture from microeconomics.

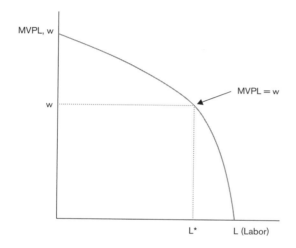

A firm will not hire workers unless the additional value they produce (the MVPL) is at least as large as what the firm will have to pay the workers (that is, the wage).

Characteristics that raise workers' productivity, particularly schooling and work experience, should be associated with higher wages. Econometric evidence, based largely on the Mincer model, confirms that there are significant and high economic returns to these human capital variables.

According to human capital theory, only variables affecting workers' productivity should be in the earnings regression. If women are as productive as men, the earnings of a woman should be similar to those of a man with similar levels of human capital. Do Mincer's human capital variables have the same effect for women as for men? Do women earn the same as men with the same levels of schooling and work experience?

Unless productivity is different for women than men, gender should not be in the earnings equation. If the data show that earnings are lower for women than for otherwise similar men, or if the effect of an additional year of schooling or work experience on earnings is lower for women, there could be something else going on—like gender discrimination in the labor market. How can we use our econometric tools to test whether a person's gender affects his or her earnings?

If we know workers' gender, we can easily test for gender effects by defining an indicator variable (also called a dummy variable), say G_i, equal to 1 if worker i is female and 0 if male. By including this new 0–1 variable in a Mincer regression, we can test whether the intercept of the regression is lower for women than men:

$$\ln(E_i) = \beta_0 + \beta_1 S_i + \beta_2 EX_i + \beta_3 EX_i^2 + \beta_4 G_i + e_i.$$

Because the indicator variable can only take on the values of 0 or 1, it doesn't change the slope of the regression line like the other variables in this equation do. It doesn't make sense to think of the marginal effect of gender on earnings, because gender is a discrete (either-or) variable. Instead, we can think of gender shifting the entire regression line up or down.

The intercept or constant term in our "engendered" Mincer equation is $\beta_0 + \beta_4 G_i$. For men, $G_i = 0$, so the intercept reduces to β_0, while for women, it is $\beta_0 + \beta_4$. If β_4 is negative and significant, our econometric model provides evidence that, controlling for schooling and work experience, predicted earnings are lower for women.

It also is possible that women reap a lower economic return from schooling than men do, or that earnings increase more slowly with work experience for women. For example, many women leave the workforce to have babies. They might be at a disadvantage once they come back into the workforce and try to catch up with the men who never left, even if they are just as productive as their male counterparts. Nothing fair about that.

Mathematically, the (partial) derivatives of earnings with respect to schooling and experience might be lower for women than men. Geometrically, these derivatives are the slopes of the earnings function in the direction of schooling or experience. In other words, now we are considering whether gender might actually *change the slope* of the regression plane.

We can test for differences in the effects of schooling and experience on earnings for men and women by *interacting* our gender indicator variable with these human capital variables. For example, to test for differences in the returns to schooling and experience, we include interactions between gender and both schooling ($G_i \times S_i$) and experience ($G_i \times EX_i$):

$$\ln(E_i) = \beta_0 + \beta_1 S_i + \beta_2 EX_i + \beta_3 EX_i^2 + \beta_4 G_i + \beta_5 G_i S_i + \beta_6 G_i EX_i + e_i.$$

Table 7.2   Results of Mincer Earnings Regression with Gender

Variable	Estimated Coefficient	Standard Error	t-Statistic
G	−0.308	0.142	−2.170
S	0.092	0.006	14.260
$G*S$	0.012	0.010	1.220
EX	0.044	0.004	10.710
EX^2	−0.001	0.000	−7.280
$G*EX$	−0.005	0.002	−2.340
Constant	0.760	0.098	7.790
Sample size	1,289		
R^2	0.36		
$SSE(U)$	284.02		

The (partial) derivative of (log) earnings with respect to schooling then becomes

$$\frac{\partial E_i / \partial S_i}{E_i} = \begin{cases} \beta_1 & \text{for men} \\ \beta_1 + \beta_5 & \text{for women} \end{cases}.$$

The partial with respect to experience is

$$\frac{\partial E_i / \partial EX_i}{E_i} = \begin{cases} \beta_2 + 2\beta_3 EX_i & \text{for men} \\ \beta_2 + 2\beta_3 EX_i + \beta_6 & \text{for women} \end{cases}.$$

A finding that $\beta_5 < 0$ (or $\beta_6 < 0$) reveals that an additional year of schooling (or experience) has a smaller effect on female than male earnings. Geometrically, this would show up as a flatter slope of the regression plane (in the direction of schooling and/or experience) for women than men. Such a finding could be evidence of gender discrimination in the labor market.

The econometrician Paul Ruud assembled a useful data set on the earnings of 1,289 individuals from the March 1995 Current Population Survey of the US Census Bureau. Some of the variables in this data set include E (wage earnings), G (female indicator variable), S (years of schooling), and EX (years of potential experience[3]). These data are available at http://ideas.repec.org/p/boc/bocins/wage.html (though the variable names are a bit different here).

When we use OLS to estimate the regression above, we get the results shown in Table 7.2.

As expected, earnings increase with both schooling and work experience. The negative coefficient on earnings-squared indicates diminishing marginal returns to experience.

The dependent variable is the natural log of earnings, so the estimated coefficients (multiplied by 100) tell us the percentage change in earnings associated with a one-unit change in each of the right-hand-side variables. Other things being equal, an additional year of schooling increases men's earnings by 9.2%.

The effect of an additional year of experience depends on a person's level of experience. For example, for a male worker with 1 year of experience, the effect is $4.4 - 2 \times 0.1 \times 1 = 4.2\%$; for a male worker with 2 years of experience, $4.4 - 2 \times 0.1 \times 2 = 4.0\%$; and so on, since the partial derivative of (log) earnings with respect to experience for males is

$$\frac{\partial E_i / \partial EX_i}{E_i} = \beta_2 + 2\beta_3 EX_i .$$

Here's the bombshell: the coefficient on the gender dummy implies that predicted earnings would be 30.8% lower for females than males with the zero schooling and experience. This effect is equivalent to more than 3 years of schooling! The $G \times S$ interaction implies that the returns to schooling are not significantly different for women than men (the t-statistic, which corresponds to the null hypothesis that the effect of this interaction is zero, is well below the standard critical value of 1.96). However, the experience interaction ($G \times EX$) is negative and significant at the 5% level. This tells us that an additional year of work experience raises predicted earnings by 0.5% less for females than males, which exacerbates the baseline 30.8% gap.

Findings such as these offer evidence that gender is, indeed, correlated with earnings. Econometric studies find similar kinds of negative earnings outcomes for Black and Latino workers. They have spawned a whole literature on the economics of labor market discrimination.

There's an important caveat to be made here. A dummy variable controls for anything and everything about the category it represents (for example, gender) and its correlation with the outcome we are modeling (earnings). We call this "anything and everything" a *fixed effect*. In the earnings example, the gender dummy variable made it possible to document differences in earnings between men and women. It captured an amorphous gender "fixed effect."

Putting gender in our regression did not tell us *why* gender affects predicted earnings; it only let us test *whether* predicted earnings are lower for women, and by *how much*. The evidence for labor market discrimination might seem compelling, but to really answer the "why" question, we need to bring additional information into our analysis. Examples might include employers' attitudes about women, additional controls for differences in productivity across individuals in the same kinds of jobs, and the variables shaping the selection of individuals into different kinds of jobs.

Imagine an experiment in which two people who are truly identical, except for their gender, apply for the same job. One recent study asked scientists to evaluate identical resumes for a candidate named either "Jennifer" or "John." Even female scientists favored "John."[4] This is an example of an experimental approach to test for gender discrimination in the labor market. We will learn more about strategies to test for causation in Chapter 11.

TESTING FUNCTIONAL FORMS

We've emphasized throughout this book that economic theory is our best guide to the art of economic model-building. It often tells us what should be in our model and suggests a reasonable functional form of our model.

In the gender and earnings example, though, human capital theory did not give us much reason to include gender in the earnings regression. According to this theory, it should only be there if somehow women are less (or more) productive than men. We included it in order to test for possible labor market discrimination. Of the three gender variables (gender by itself and gender interacted with education and experience), two were significant and the other was not. Should we conclude from this that gender is, indeed, a significant predictor of earnings? How do we test the null hypothesis that the relationship between *all three* gender variables and earnings is zero? This is different from testing the significance of each variable separately.

We can use the Wald statistic from Chapter 6:

$$W = \frac{R_{alt}^2 - R_{null}^2}{(1 - R_{alt}^2)/(N - K_{alt} - 1)}.$$

The regression with gender in it (Table 7.2) gives us $R^2 = 0.36$. If we run the same model without the three gender terms, we get $R^2 = 0.31$. Our test statistic, then, is

$$\frac{0.36 - 0.31}{(1 - 0.36)/1282} = 100.16.$$

The critical Chi-square value for a 5% significance test, with 3 degrees of freedom, is 7.81. Since 100.16 > 7.81, we reject the null hypothesis that gender is not correlated with (or a predictor of) earnings.

There are many different applications in which we might want to perform hypothesis tests involving more than one parameter. Like single-parameter tests, these are really about trying to use real-world data to get an understanding of the process that generated the data we see.

Usually, the hard part is figuring out what the restricted regression equation looks like. Once we know that, we can easily pop out the R^2 from the restricted and unrestricted regressions and do our Wald test.

Linear Combinations of Parameters

Let's revisit the famous CD production function. Its general form is

$$Q_i = \beta_0 L_i^{\beta_1} K_i^{\beta_2},$$

but often it is written in its restricted, constant-returns-to-scale (CRS) version. (Remember that a CD production function exhibits CRS if its exponents sum to one; CRS means that by multiplying all inputs by the same factor you increase output by the same factor—double all inputs and output doubles.) The CRS form of the CD function is

$$Q_i = F(L_i, K_i) = \beta_0 L_i^{\beta_1} K_i^{1-\beta_1}.$$

(Why is this more restrictive?) Which form of this production function is likely to be the "true" one? That is, which one generated the data we observe on inputs and outputs?

To test this, we transform each equation by taking the natural log of both sides, so we can estimate it using OLS:

$$\ln(Q_i) = \ln(\beta_0) + \beta_1 \ln(L_i) + \beta_2 \ln(K_i) + \varepsilon_i,$$

$$\ln(Q_i) = \ln(\beta_0^R) + \beta_1^R \ln(L_i) + (1 - \beta_1^R)\ln(K_i) + \varepsilon_i^R.$$

(We've given each equation an error to make it econometric, not just mathematical.) Here, the superscript "R" denotes the coefficients in the restricted regression.

Before we can estimate the restricted regression, we need to do a bit of algebra, because β_1 appears in the restricted equation twice:

$$\ln(Q_i) = \ln(\beta_0^R) + \beta_1^R (\ln(L_i) - \ln(K_i)) + \ln(K_i) + \varepsilon_i^R$$

$$\ln(Q_i) - \ln(K_i) = \ln(\beta_0^R) + \beta_1^R (\ln(L_i) - \ln(K_i)) + \varepsilon_i^R.$$

$$\ln(Q_i / K_i) = \ln(\beta_0^R) + \beta_1^R \ln(L_i / K_i) + \varepsilon_i^R$$

Now this is just a simple OLS model, with $\ln(Q_i/K_i)$ as the dependent variable and $\ln(L_i/K_i)$ as the right-hand-side variable. (With CRS, it turns out, the output-capital ratio depends only on the labor-capital ratio.) To estimate the restricted model, then, we regress $\ln(Q_i/K_i)$ on $\ln(L_i/K_i)$. Once we do this, setting up the Wald test is straightforward.

This method generalizes easily to production functions with more than two factors. If there were a third factor in the production function—say, land (T)—the restricted form of the production function would look like this:

$$Q_i = \beta_0 L_i^{\beta_1} T_i^{\beta_2} K_i^{1-\beta_1-\beta_2}.$$

For the restricted regression, we would regress $\ln(Q_i/K_i)$ on $\ln(L_i/K_i)$ and $\ln(T_i/K_i)$.

In this example, we chose capital to be in the denominator of the three terms in the restricted regression, but we could have chosen any factor. For example, we could regress $\ln(Q_i/T_i)$ on $\ln(L_i/T_i)$ and $\ln(K_i/T_i)$. That's because it is just as valid to write the CRS version of the production function as

$$Q_i = \beta_0 L_i^{\beta_1} K_i^{\beta_2} T_i^{1-\beta_1-\beta_2}.$$

Here's another illustration of a test involving more than one parameter. Suppose you work for a firm that sells its product in numerous markets (cities). Your board of directors wants to know which will affect sales more, an increase in TV advertising or an increase in internet advertising. With their blessing, you randomly assign the amount of spending across markets and record the results. You then estimate a model of firm-i sales (Y_i, in millions of dollars) as a function of its spending on television advertising ($tvads_i$) and spending on internet ads ($intads_i$). The unrestricted model is

$$Y_i = \beta_0 + \beta_1 tvads_i + \beta_2 intads_i + \varepsilon_i.$$

The null hypothesis you want to test is that the coefficients on the two advertising variables are equal to each other:

$$H_0 : \beta_1 = \beta_2.$$

The restricted regression is

$$Y_i^R = \beta_0^R + \beta_1^R tvads_i + \beta_1^R intads_i + \varepsilon_i^R$$
$$Y_i^R = \beta_0^R + \beta_1^R (tvads_i + intads_i) + \varepsilon_i^R.$$

Again, a little bit of algebra has reduced the restricted model to a simple OLS model that is easy to estimate by regressing Y on the sum of ad spending. If your Wald test rejects the null hypothesis, you conclude that the two types of advertising have different effects.

$$Y_i = \beta_0 + \varepsilon_i.$$

$$\beta_1 = \beta_2 = \ldots = \beta_K = 0.$$

$$W = \frac{R_{alt}^2}{(1 - R_{alt}^2)/(N - K_{alt} - 1)} \sim \chi^2_{(K_{alt})}$$

What We Learned

- An econometric model will almost never be *literally* right in the sense that it describes precisely how one variable depends on a set of other variables. A good econometric model is as simple as possible and fits the data well.
- Taking logs of the variables, fitting a polynomial, adding interaction terms, and adding right-hand-side variables are easy ways to improve model specification.

Best of BLUE I: Cross-Section Data and Heteroskedasticity (Assumption CR2)

Without deviation from the norm, progress is not possible.

—Frank Zappa

LEARNING OBJECTIVES

Upon completing the work in this chapter, you will be able to:

▶ Demonstrate the problem of heteroskedasticity and its implications

▶ Conduct and interpret tests for heteroskedasticity

▶ Correct for heteroskedasticity using White's heteroskedasticity-robust estimator

▶ Correct for heteroskedasticity by getting the model right

This and the next chapter are about situations in which we are likely to lose the "B" in "BLUE." That is, our estimators are unbiased, but they do not have the lowest variance among linear unbiased estimators; there exists another estimator with lower variance. This is important, because the variance of our estimators is a key ingredient of hypothesis tests and constructing confidence intervals around our parameter estimates. Get that wrong and we may get a very misleading impression of how good our model is.

In general, the "B" in "BLUE" depends on having a constant variance, or homoskedasticity (Assumption CR2) and zero covariance between the errors from one observation to the next (CR3) in the population model. You will recall from Chapter 5 that we did not need either of these two assumptions to show that our OLS estimators are unbiased. However, we *did* need them to show that the OLS estimators are "Best," that is, that they have the smallest variance among all linear and unbiased estimators.

When either of these two assumptions is violated, our parameter estimates are not biased, but the standard errors are. This makes our hypothesis tests and confidence intervals invalid. It also raises an important point about what to do if we find that we have one (or both) of these problems.

When Assumption CR2 or CR3 is violated, our OLS estimators are unbiased even though our standard errors are biased. That means we could opt to keep our OLS estimates. After we get them, though, we'll have to fix the standard errors using a formula that corrects for the problem ex post. This is probably the most common way of dealing with the problems discussed in this and the next chapter.

There is another option, though. If we know something about the statistical characteristics of our problem errors, we might be able to use this information to improve upon our estimator and get a more precise estimate of the model to begin with. In some cases, we *do* know *exactly* what caused the problem, and it's better to attack the problem at its source instead of using ex post corrections that might look more like a Band-Aid than a cure. In fact, we will see that such problem errors often indicate that we got the model wrong, in which case the best response might be to go back to Chapter 7 and use the tips there to fit a better model.

We will take up violations of CR2 in this chapter and violations of CR3 in Chapter 9. In both cases, we will discuss when the assumption is most likely to break down, so that you will know to keep a close eye out for it. We will learn the essentials of testing for the problem and dealing with the problem should it occur.

THE PROBLEM OF HETEROSKEDASTICITY

Assumption CR2 states that the variance of the error in the population model is constant across observations. In real life, this is often not the case. When the error variance is not constant, we call it *heteroskedastic* (from the Greek *hetero* [different] and *skedasis* [dispersion]). When the variance is constant, the error is said to be *homoskedastic*.

Heteroskedasticity means that some observations give you more information about β than others. The data are closer to the regression line for some parts of the sample and farther away for other parts of the sample. The errors still average out to be zero, so you will still get the right β on average.

One example of heteroskedasticity arises when studying climate change. The average temperature on earth has risen by 1.5°F over the past century, and scientists estimate that it will rise another 1–9°F over the next 100 years. These changes might seem small, but they could have large effects on many aspects of human life. The scientific consensus is that the main cause of climate change is emissions of greenhouse gases from burning fossil fuels to produce energy.

Many countries are working on ways to mitigate climate change by reducing fossil fuel consumption. Working against these efforts is the fact that many countries that are currently poor are getting richer, and richer countries tend to use more energy than poorer countries. Even if high-income countries like

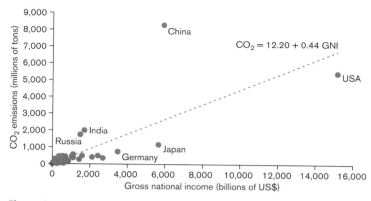

Figure 8.1 2010 CO_2 emissions and gross national income for 183 countries.

the United States cut back on emissions, developing countries such as China and India are likely to increase emissions.

Figure 8.1 plots CO_2 emissions in 2010 against gross national income for 183 countries. Most countries are not visible on the graph because they are so close to zero relative to the United States, China, and other big countries.

High-income countries have higher emissions. You can see this by looking at the graph or by noting the estimated regression equation:

$$CO_{2i} = 12.20 + 0.44 GNI_i + e_i .$$

(In this regression, subscript i denotes countries, CO_{2i} is country i's CO_2 emissions in millions of tons, GNI_i is country i's gross national income in billions of dollars, and e_i is the error.) Every billion dollars of extra income in a country predicts an additional 0.44 million tons of CO_2 emissions. However, you can also see that the error terms are much larger for the high-income countries than the low-income countries. Russia, India, Japan, China, and the United States are all at least 1,000 million tons away from the regression line. In contrast, Lesotho, Kiribati, Vanuatu, Tonga, and 91 other countries are less than 15 million tons from the regression line.

Heteroskedasticity causes OLS to lose its property as the best estimator, and it usually makes OLS less precise. In extreme cases, like in figure 8.1, OLS is really sensitive to the big observations. If we drop China out of the sample and rerun the regression, the slope coefficient goes from 0.44 to 0.34; if we drop the United States from the sample, the slope coefficient jumps from 0.44 to 0.62.

Let's think about this a little more. A country will have high emissions and income if it has a high population. If our goal were to measure the correlation between wealth and emissions, it would be better to do it on a per person basis. Figure 8.2 shows the information in per capita terms. We still have lots of heteroskedasticity, but the extremes are less extreme than in the first figure.

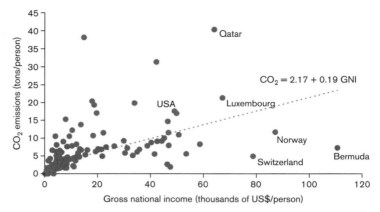

Figure 8.2 2010 CO_2 emissions and gross national income per capita for 183 countries.

Now, the slope coefficient changes by less than 0.03 when we drop any of the most extreme observations.

A great way of illustrating heteroskedasticity is seeing what happens when we work with average data. This is what figure 8.2 does. We do not have data on the CO_2 emissions of each individual. Instead, we have the average CO_2 emissions per individual for whole countries. Instead of estimating a regression of each individual's emissions on individual income, we use the per capita country averages to estimate a model like this one:

$$\overline{CO_{2i}} = \beta_0 + \beta_1 \overline{GNI}_i + \overline{\varepsilon}_i.$$

Here, $\overline{CO_{2i}}$ is average per capita emissions across people in country i and $\overline{GNI}_i$ is the average per capita income. The error, $\overline{\varepsilon}_i$, is the error averaged across country i's population. In a regression like this, it might strike you as odd to give a populous country like China the same weight as a country with a very small population like Bermuda. You're right, and it's because of heteroskedasticity. Think about it: if country i has a population equal to n_i, its average error is

$$\overline{\varepsilon}_i = \frac{\sum_{j=1}^{n_i} \varepsilon_{ij}}{n_i},$$

where ε_{ij} is the error for person j in country i. Even if the individual-level errors ε_{ij} have a constant variance of σ^2, the variance of $\overline{\varepsilon}_i$ is not constant; it depends on country populations:

$$Var(\overline{\varepsilon}_i) = \frac{\sum_{j=1}^{n_i} Var(\varepsilon_{ij})}{n_i^2} = \frac{n_i \sigma^2}{n_i^2} = \frac{\sigma^2}{n_i}.$$

(This derivation assumes independence across individuals.)

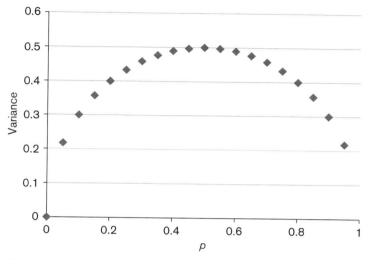

Figure 8.3 Variance of errors in probability model.

In other words, the variance is smaller the bigger the country is, which makes sense. If we use OLS to estimate this model of averages, we know we will have a problem of heteroskedastic errors.

Here's another example: modeling probabilities involves a dependent variable that is limited because it can only take on two possible values—it equals 1 if an outcome occurs and zero if it does not. We can easily show that the variance is not constant. Back in your statistics course, you probably learned that if p is the probability that some outcome occurs, and $(1 - p)$ is the probability that it does not occur, then the variance of the outcome variable is $p(1 - p)$. Figure 8.3 shows this variance for different values of p. It first rises, then falls. At the extremes of $p = 0$ and $p = 1$, it is zero.

Now suppose the probability is a function of some right-hand-side variable. For example, we could test the durability of laptop computers by dropping a large number of $i = 1, \ldots, N$ laptops from different heights. (This could be an expensive experiment, indeed!) Each laptop i either breaks ($B_i = 1$) or not ($B_i = 0$), and the probability of breaking is a function of the height from which you drop it. We estimate a model of this form:

$$B_i = \beta_0 + \beta_1 HEIGHT_i + \varepsilon_i .$$

Because the left-hand-side variable is a 0–1 dummy variable, if we estimate this model and use it to predict the breakage outcome from different heights, the predictions will tend to fall in the 0–1 interval most of the time, the same as a probability. The error, we know, will be heteroskedastic. Logically, if we

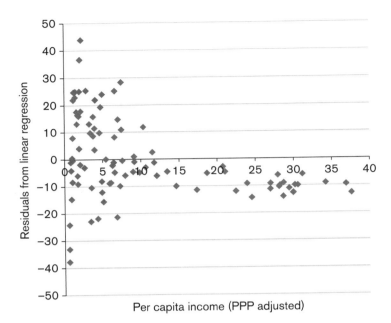

Figure 8.4 Residuals from linear "moving-off-the-farm" regression.

drop laptops from very low heights, say, an inch, they'll never break ($\sigma^2 = 0$). From waist level, sometimes they'll break, and sometimes they'll not ($\sigma^2 > 0$). Drop one from an airplane and it will always break ($\sigma^2 = 0$).

This example illustrates why you definitely need to think carefully about heteroskedasticity if you want to estimate a model involving binary outcomes, like elections or the likelihood of products being defective. We have the same trouble when modeling shares. Take the "moving-off-the-farm" example from Chapter 7.

We modeled the share of country i's workforce in agriculture (AGL_i) as an inverse function of per capita income (PCY_i):

$$AGL_i = \beta_0 + \frac{\beta_1}{PCY_i} + \varepsilon_i.$$

Transforming the right-hand-side variable in this way makes sense theoretically (because, like a probability, shares cannot be less than zero) as well as empirically (shares drop rapidly at low incomes, then level off: remember the scatter plot from Chapter 7). There's heteroskedasticity, though. We should expect this, since we are dealing with shares, which are like probabilities. We can eyeball this by taking the residuals from the linear regression and plotting them against per capita income (see figure 8.4).

You can see that the average of these residuals is zero. However, at low incomes, there is a lot more variability, and the residuals are more likely positive. Above $10,000, there does not seem to be much variability at all, and almost all the residuals are *negative*. If you think about it, there can't be a lot of variation in the error when the share is very low.

TESTING FOR HETEROSKEDASTICITY

The first test for heteroskedasticity is plain old logic. Is heteroskedasticity built into our model? If we're using averages, we don't have to do a test; we just have to fix the problem (see "Fixing the Problem," below.) This basically involves getting the model right.

Once we know we've got the model right, we can test for heteroskedasticity in a number of different ways. We'll cover two of them here: the Goldfeld-Quandt test and White's test. There are other tests out there, but the Goldfeld-Quandt test nicely illustrates the heteroskedasticity problem, and White's test is the basis for most tests and corrections of heteroskedasticity you are likely to encounter.

Goldfeld-Quandt Test

The Goldfeld-Quandt test is very intuitive and straightforward. We can test whether the variance is different for different levels of the right-hand-side variable by splitting the sample into a group of size N_H for which the right-hand-side variable is high and one of size N_L for which it is low. There is no rule about how to divide your data into groups, so common sense and a graph of residuals like the one above can come in handy here. In our moving-off-the-farm example, a natural place to split the sample would be at a per capita income of around $10,000. Or we might divide the sample evenly into thirds and discard the middle third. The subsets we used in our test do not have to be of the same size, and we do not have to use all of the observations.

The test itself is quite simple: we estimate the error variance of each subset and test whether the two subsets' variances are different. The test statistic is the ratio of the two error variances. Whichever is expected to be larger goes in the numerator. The null hypothesis is that these two variances are equal, as they would be if the errors were homoskedastic, so their ratio is one. In the case of the moving-off-the-farm example, we use the following test statistic: $\dfrac{s_L^2}{s_H^2}$.

This is a ratio of two chi-squared variables (the SSEs from the regressions using the two subsets), each divided by its degrees of freedom (the denominators in the two regression variances: $N_L - K - 1$ for the numerator and $N_H - K - 1$ for the denominator). It is distributed as an F with numerator degrees of

Table 8.1   Goldfeld-Quandt Test for Heteroskedasticity in "Moving-Off-the-Farm" Model

Inputs for Goldfeld-Quandt Test	PCY < $10,000	PCY > $10,000
SSE	16,280.48	384.64
df ($N - K - 1$)	62	29
Variance	262.59	13.26
$F(62,29)$	19.80	
Critical F ($\alpha = 0.05$)	1.75	

freedom $N_L - K - 1$ and denominator degrees of freedom $N_H - K - 1$. If we use a cut-off point of $10,000 to split our sample, we get Table 8.1.

The value of our test statistic (19.80) easily exceeds the 5% critical value from an F table (1.75), so we conclude that the two variances are not equal, as we suspected from our scatter plot of the residuals. In other words, we have a heteroskedasticity problem.

There are several drawbacks of the Goldfeld-Quandt test. In a multiple regression model, the sources of heteroskedasticity often involve more than one right-hand-side variable, making it difficult to divide your data into low- and high-variance subsets based on any one right-hand-side variable. Another is that the decision of where to split the sample is somewhat arbitrary. In our case, if we split it 50–50, we would include a lot of countries with large residuals in the H group.

However, the main disadvantage of the Goldfeld-Quandt test is that it requires assumption CR4 (normally distributed errors). If this assumption is false, which it usually is, then the critical value from the F table may not be the right value to determine significance. So, unless you have a strong reason to believe that the errors in your model have a normal distribution, you should not rely only on the Goldfeld-Quandt test.

White's Test

The econometrician Halbert White, building upon work by Herbert Glejser and others, proposed a simple and intuitive way to test for heteroskedasticity involving more than one right-hand-side variable. Simply estimate your regression with the N observations, keep the residuals, square them (then they're all positive), and regress these squared residuals on *all* the right-hand-side variables in the model, their squares, and all their interactions with one another. This approach makes direct use of the fact that, when there's heteroskedasticity, the variance in the population model is potentially different for

Table 8.2   White's Test for Heteroskedasticity in "Moving-Off-the-Farm" Model

Variables in White's Auxiliary Regression	Estimated Coefficient	Standard Error
PCY	−38.27	12.41
$(PCY)^2$	0.91	0.37
Constant	418.11	61.47
R^2	0.14	
N	95.00	
NR^2	13.09	
Critical Chi-square at $\alpha = 0.05$	5.99	

each observation—that is, it equals σ_i^2, not σ^2. The residual-squared, e_i^2, is a noisy but useful proxy for σ_i^2. It even looks like a variance.

The big worry with heteroskedasticity is that the variance is correlated with the regressors, like in the example above where the variance of the share in agriculture is higher for low-income countries. Thus, it makes sense to include all the original right-hand-side variables (regressors) in White's regression. White also pointed out that there might be higher-order heteroskedasticity: even if σ_i^2 is not significantly related to X_i, it might be related to X_i^2, or if there are multiple right-hand-side variables, to their interactions. Thus, White's regression to test for heteroskedasticity in the two-regressor case looks like this:

$$e_i^2 = \alpha_0 + \alpha_1 X_{1i} + \alpha_2 X_{1i}^2 + \alpha_3 X_{2i} + \alpha_4 X_{2i}^2 + \alpha_5 X_{1i} X_{2i} + v_i .$$

(But be careful: to avoid perfect multicollinearity, you will need to exclude some terms if one of the right-hand-side variables is a 0–1 dummy, or if X_{2i} is the square of X_{1i}, as in a quadratic model, for example)

Under the null hypothesis of no heteroskedasticity, the expected value of e_i^2 would be α_0, that is, a constant. (In fact, α_0 would be σ^2.) The right-hand-side variables in this artificial regression would add no explanatory power, so the R^2 would be zero. It can be shown that, if N is large, then NR^2 is approximately distributed as a chi-squared with degrees of freedom equal to the total number of right-hand-side variables in White's regression. (In our two-regressor example, the degrees of freedom equal 5.) If NR^2 exceeds the critical chi-squared value, we reject the null hypothesis that the R^2 of this auxiliary regression is zero and conclude that there's heteroskedasticity.

The moving-off-the-farm example has only one right-hand-side variable, so White's auxiliary regression is

$$e_i^2 = \alpha_0 + \alpha_1 PCY_i + \alpha_2 PCY_i^2 + v_i .$$

The results of White's test are in Table 8.2.

$NR^2 = 13.09$, so White's test easily rejects the null hypothesis of homoskedasticity at the 5% confidence level (the critical chi-squared value with two degrees of freedom is 5.99). Not only that; we can see that the heteroskedasticity bears a quadratic relationship with PCY. You can verify that the estimated coefficients on both the linear and the quadratic terms are significantly different from zero at a high level of significance.

Because of its intuitive appeal and comprehensiveness, White's approach is the basis for most tests of heteroskedasticity you are likely to encounter these days.

FIXING THE PROBLEM

If our data are averages, we know we're likely to run into heteroskedasticity, but fortunately, there is a simple solution. Look again at the regression:

$$\overline{Y}_i = \beta_0 + \beta_1 \overline{X}_i + \overline{\varepsilon}_i .$$

The problem here is that the variance of the error is

$$Var(\overline{\varepsilon}_i) = \frac{\sigma^2}{n_i} .$$

But we can transform the regression equation by multiplying through by $\sqrt{n_i}$, like this:

$$\sqrt{n_i}\,\overline{Y}_i = \sqrt{n_i}\,\beta_0 + \beta_1 \sqrt{n_i}\,\overline{X}_i + \sqrt{n_i}\,\overline{\varepsilon}_i .$$

Then the variance becomes constant; the model now has homoskedastic errors:

$$Var(\sqrt{n_i}\,\overline{\varepsilon}_i) = \frac{n_i^2 \sigma^2}{n_i^2} = \sigma^2 .$$

This transformation is basically a question of getting the model right. Whenever heteroskedasticity results from getting the model wrong, the solution is to use a different specification for the model: different X variables, or perhaps nonlinear transformations of the X variables.

The first step in dealing with heteroskedasticity is making sure we got the model right. This might involve scaling the data, as above, or changing the functional form, as in the "moving-off-the-farm" example. Once we get the model right, our test may conclude that the errors of the transformed model are homoskedastic.

Most of the time, though, the problem isn't so simple. As in our "moving-off-the-farm" example, we think we've got the model right, but the errors turn out to be heteroskedastic.

White's test suggests a solution. Remember that the squared residual, e_i^2, is a rough proxy for σ_i^2, the population variance for observation i, just like s^2 is an estimate of σ^2 in the homoskedastic case. This means that we can replace s^2 with e_i^2 when we estimate the variances of our estimators. For $est\ V[b_1]$ in the simple regression model, instead of

$$est\ V[b_1] = \frac{\sum_{i=1}^{N} x_i^2 s^2}{\left(\sum_{i=1}^{N} x_i^2\right)^2},$$

we can use White's correction:

$$est\ V[b_1] = \frac{\sum_{i=1}^{N} x_i^2 e_i^2}{\left(\sum_{i=1}^{N} x_i^2\right)}.$$

Notice what we've done here: we're letting the regression variance s^2 be different for every observation, as is the case when we have heteroskedasticity. White's procedure, then, is

- Estimate the model and save the residuals
- Square the residuals
- Use them, instead of s^2, when estimating the variance of the parameter estimates

This is also called the heteroskedasticity-robust estimator. Remember that the standard error is the square root of the variance of the parameter estimate.

Econometrics software packages have options to estimate models using the residuals to obtain heteroskedasticity-corrected standard errors (see Appendix). Many analysts forego testing and run their models both with and without the heteroskedasticity correction. If the results of their hypothesis tests are the same with both methods, they conclude heteroskedasticity is not a problem. Otherwise, they conclude it appears to be a problem and use the corrected estimator.

Table 8.3 shows a comparison of estimates of our "moving-off-the-farm" model with and without White's robust correction.

This table illustrates several important points. First, notice that the parameter estimates are exactly the same whether we do White's correction or not. That is, because when we have heteroskedasticity, White's method corrects the standard errors ex post, that is, after the model has been estimated. The fit (R^2) doesn't change either.

The estimated standard errors are different using White's estimator: the standard error of b_1 is higher in the corrected regression, and that of b_0 is lower.

Table 8.3   Comparison of Results for "Moving-Off-the-Farm" Model with and without White's (Robust) Correction for Heteroskedasticity

Variable	Regression A: Uncorrected			Regression B: Robust		
	Estimated Coefficient	Standard Error	t-Statistic	Estimated Coefficient	Standard Error	t-Statistic
1/PCY	65.71	4.04	16.25	65.71	5.86	11.21
Constant	11.81	2.05	5.77	11.81	1.96	6.02
R^2		0.74			0.74	
N		95			95	

This shows that the bias in standard errors when there's heteroskedasticity can go in either direction. Because the standard errors are different, so are the t-statistics. The confidence intervals are also different. Let's construct 95% confidence intervals around b_1 from the uncorrected and corrected regressions:

- *Uncorrected regression:*
  $65.71 \pm 4.04 * 1.98 = 65.71 \pm 8.01$.

- *Robust regression:*
  $65.71 \pm 5.86 * 1.98 = 65.71 \pm 11.61$.

In this particular case, the relationship between PCY and AGL is so strong that heteroskedasticity does not alter the results of our test of the null hypothesis that the relationship is zero. However, when we ignore heteroskedasticity we get a confidence interval that is quite a bit smaller than it should be. Although it does not happen in this case, it is not uncommon for the results of hypothesis tests to change once we correct for heteroskedasticity.

In Chapter 6, we used the Wald statistic to conduct joint hypothesis tests. We computed the statistic based on a formula that uses the R^2 from the null and alternative regressions. That formula is invalid when CR2 or CR3 fails. The correct robust Wald formula is more complicated, so we don't write it here, but most econometrics packages will compute it for you. Just know that, when you're using robust standard errors for your t-tests and confidence intervals, you also need to use a robust Wald statistic for joint hypothesis tests.

BACK TO CLIMATE CHANGE

Look again at figure 8.2, and notice that the errors are much larger when the level of income is higher. In fact, the errors appear to increase proportionately

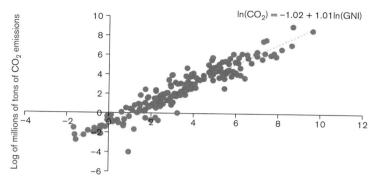

Figure 8.5 Natural log of 2010 CO_2 emissions and natural log of gross national income for 183 countries.

with the level of income. Note also that it looks like a curve may fit the data better than a straight line. With a few notable exceptions, it appears that CO_2 emissions increase, then taper off with per capita income. These facts suggest that taking logs of the data may be helpful. Taking the log compresses the huge differences in income evident in figure 8.2. Whereas country GNIs range from $0.19 billion to $15,170.30 billion, the log ranges from −1.66 to 9.63. As we saw in Chapter 7 with the Cobb-Douglas model, taking logs transforms a multiplicative relationship into a linear function.

Figure 8.5 shows that taking logs appears to remove the heteroskedasticity problem. The data now look to be evenly distributed along a straight line.

Let's look at the regression results for the three model specifications plotted in figures 8.1, 8.2, and 8.5.

First, the regression that uses total CO_2 and total GNI as in figure 8.1 (Table 8.4; standard errors are in parentheses). The only difference between the two regressions in this table is the robust correction to the standard errors. The standard error on the slope coefficient quadruples. It goes from 0.03 in the uncorrected regression to 0.12 in the robust regression. This huge change indicates a big heteroskedasticity problem, which we already know from looking at figure 8.1. White's test agrees. The NR^2 statistic is 50.84, which is much bigger than the 5% critical value of 5.99. We reject the null hypothesis of homoscedasticity.

We should not use the uncorrected regression. We could use the robust regression, but the presence of heteroskedasticity suggests we should first try to fix the model. Let's try the per capita model (see Table 8.5).

This time the standard error doubles when we do the robust correction, from 0.02 to 0.04. It seems we still have some heteroskedasticity. White's test agrees again. The NR^2 statistic is 16.52, which is still bigger than the 5% critical

Table 8.4   Simple and Robust OLS regression of Total CO$_2$ on Total Gross National Income (GNI)

Uncorrected	Robust
$CO_{2i} = 12,282.71 + 0.44 GNI_i + e_i$	$CO_{2i} = 12,282.71 + 0.44 GNI_i + e_i$
(36,713.99) (0.03)	(16,752.29) (0.12)
Sample size = 182	Sample size = 182
$R^2 = 0.61$	$R^2 = 0.61$
White test: $NR^2 = 50.84$	

Table 8.5   Simple and Robust OLS Regression of Per Capita CO$_2$ on Per Capita GNI

Uncorrected	Robust
$\dfrac{CO_{2i}}{POP_i} = 2,155.05 + 0.20 \dfrac{GNI_i}{POP_i} + e_i$	$\dfrac{CO_{2i}}{POP_i} = 2,155.05 + 0.20 \dfrac{GNI_i}{POP_i} + e_i$
(458.28) (0.02)	(407.25) (0.04)
Sample size = 182	Sample size = 182
$R^2 = 0.33$	$R^2 = 0.33$
White test: $NR^2 = 16.52$	

Table 8.6   Simple and Robust OLS regression of Ln(Per Capita CO$_2$) on ln(Per Capita GNI)

Uncorrected	Robust
$\ln(CO_{2i}) = -1.09 + 1.01\ln(GNI_i) + e_i$	$\ln(CO_{2i}) = -1.09 + 1.01\ln(GNI_i) + e_i$
(0.27) (0.026)	(0.25) (0.023)
Sample size = 182	Sample size = 182
$R^2 = 0.90$	$R^2 = 0.90$
White test: $NR^2 = 0.73$	

value of 5.99. We reject the null hypothesis of homoscedasticity, so we have not solved the problem. Let's try the log-log model (Table 8.6).

Success! The robust standard errors are very similar to the uncorrected regression, and White's NR^2 statistic, 0.73, is less than the critical value, 5.99. We cannot reject the null hypothesis of homoscedasticity at the 5% significance level.

We should present results from the log-log model. The slope coefficient of 1.01 in this model means that the elasticity of CO_2 emissions with respect to national income is essentially 1. This means that emissions increase proportionately with income. If one country has twice the national income as another country, we predict that it will have twice the emissions.

The future of climate change turns on whether this relationship holds in the future or whether international treaties can alter the structural relationship between income growth and CO_2 emissions.

What We Learned

- Heteroskedasticity means that the error variance is different for some values of X than for others; it can indicate that the model is misspecified.
- Heteroskedasticity causes OLS to lose its "best" property and it causes the estimated standard errors to be biased.
- The standard error bias can be corrected with White's heteroskedasticity-robust estimator.
- Getting the model right by, for example, taking logs can sometimes eliminate the heteroskedasticity problem.

Best of BLUE II: Correlated Errors (Assumption CR3)

People assume that time is a strict progression of cause to effect, but actually from a non-linear, non-subjective viewpoint—it's more like a big ball of wibbly wobbly . . . time-y wimey . . . stuff.

—Dr. Who

LEARNING OBJECTIVES

Upon completing the work in this chapter, you will be able to:

► Demonstrate the problem of correlated errors and its implications

► Conduct and interpret tests for correlated errors

► Correct for correlated errors using Newey and West's heteroskedasticity and autocorrelation consistent estimator (ex post) or using generalized least squares (ex ante)

► Correct for correlated errors by adding lagged variables to the model

► Show that correlated errors can arise in clustered and spatial data as well as in time-series data

Another situation in which we lose the "B" in "BLUE" is when the errors in our model are correlated from one observation to the next. Here's a picture to drive home the point. It shows the weekly closing values of the Dow Jones Industrial Average stock index between January 7, 2008, and February 27, 2012. Overall, stock prices rose during this period. Let's describe this price increase using a simple trend model:

$$y_i = \beta_0 + \beta_1 week_i + \varepsilon_i.$$

The predicted stock prices from this model are shown by the ordinary least-squares (OLS) trend line overlaid on the graph. The errors in the trend model are anything but random, though. They start out positive until the sharp drop in the second half of 2008 (the start of the subprime crisis). Then they are consistently negative until 2010, when they turn positive for a few weeks, go south again for several months, north, then south, then north again.

If you know the error is positive one week, your best bet is that it will be positive again the next week. And once it turns negative, you can bet it will stay negative for a while.

Figure 9.1 is a stunningly clear picture of correlated errors. The wibbly-wobbly pattern you see happens

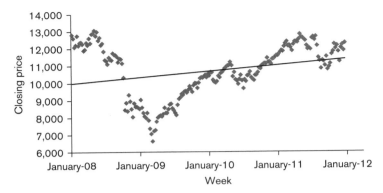

Figure 9.1 Weekly closing values of the Dow Jones Industrial Average stock index between January 7, 2008, and February 27, 2012.

because the errors in the trend model are correlated from one observation to the next. It is a clear violation of CR3, which states that $\mathrm{cov}[\varepsilon_i, \varepsilon_j] = 0$ for $i \neq j$, i.e., zero correlation in the errors from one observation to another.

Time-series data, such as in the figure, present the most common example of correlated errors. Many economic series evolve slowly, so some of the previous period's error remains in the present. This type of correlation between successive observations is known as serial autocorrelation or autocorrelation. However, two other data types also display correlated errors.

Clustered variables contain observations that can be organized into groups, e.g., students in classrooms or employees in firms. Suppose you are predicting test scores of students in a high school. Your sample includes several schools and multiple students from each school. Within each school, you have multiple students who had the same teacher. An excellent teacher may be able to inspire his or her students to perform especially well. These students will have positive errors because their actual scores exceed the model's prediction. A poor teacher may have the opposite effect. Thus, if we look at the errors within each classroom, we will find correlated errors, but we will not find correlations between the errors for students with different teachers.

Spatial variables contain information that is indexed to a particular point in space, e.g., temperature in a set of cities or unemployment in a set of counties. When modeling spatial data, we may expect the errors of neighbors to be correlated with each other because neighboring places tend to have similar demographic and landscape features. Rich counties tend to be located next to rich counties, for example.

We will spend most of this chapter on time-series data and autocorrelation. At the end, we will also address clustered and spatial data.

TIME-SERIES DATA: AUTOCORRELATION

Figure 9.1 illustrates positive autocorrelation: if the error in one time period is positive, the next one is likely to be positive as well. There can also be negative autocorrelation, which means that positive errors tend to be followed by negative errors and vice versa.

Negative autocorrelation is relatively rare. A famous model of fluctuations in agricultural markets, called the cobweb model, is one example. When prices are high, more investments are made, but there is a lag between planting and harvesting (or between breeding pigs and selling them). By the time the crops or pigs are ready to sell, there's a market glut, and prices fall. Investment then decreases. In the next period, prices rise because of the low investment. The economist Nicholas Kaldor observed this see-saw pattern in the prices of corn and rubber, and later studies of cattle prices revealed similar patterns. You've probably worried about the same sort of thing in the labor market. High salaries in one sector (say, information and technology) lure large numbers of students into the subject, but once they all hit the job market several years later, they find themselves competing with all the other students. That, in turn, discourages new students from taking on the major, so a few years down the line there may be a shortage of new workers in the field.

One way of thinking about autocorrelation is that it is a pesky violation of one of our key assumptions. Another way is to think of it as providing information that we can use to make a better model, because knowing that the errors are related from one period to the next is additional information we can use to explain the variation in our data. This means understanding the source of the autocorrelated errors and incorporating it into our modeling.

Start with the simple regression model:

$$Y_t = \beta_0 + \beta_1 X_t + \varepsilon_t.$$

We use a t subscript to remind ourselves that we're working with time-series data. The most common way to express autocorrelation mathematically is a model known as the first-order autoregression. The model is

$$\varepsilon_t = \rho \varepsilon_{t-1} + u_t.$$

The error term in the regression model clearly does not satisfy CR3 because each ε_t is correlated with its value in the previous time period.

You can look at the error as being comprised of two parts: the part that's correlated with the previous period's error ($\rho\varepsilon_{t-1}$) and an additional part that isn't (u_t). To make this thing work, we need to assume that, even though ε_t violates CR3, u_t satisfies the classical assumptions. It is distributed with zero mean and a constant variance, σ^2; that is, $u_t \sim (0, \sigma^2)$.

If $\rho = 0$, ε_t and u_t are the same, and our problem goes away: the model collapses to the classical linear regression model. If $\rho > 0$ we have positive autocorrelation: if last period's value of ε_t was greater than zero, then chances are this period's will be too. If last period's value of ε_t was negative, then chances are this period's will be negative too. If $\rho < 0$, though, we get the opposite: the signs of the error tend to flip-flop from one period to the next, like in a hog cycle. In either case, this is valuable information that we can use to better understand the data.

You can see where we're headed here: we want to test for autocorrelation by testing the null hypothesis that $\rho = 0$. Then, if we reject this null hypothesis, we want to find ways to correct for autocorrelation while estimating our model, just like we did for heteroskedasticity.

The first-order model is surprisingly powerful. It specifies how ε_t relates to ε_{t-1}. The same model in the previous period specifies how ε_{t-1} relates to ε_{t-2}, i.e., $\varepsilon_{t-1} = \rho \varepsilon_{t-2} + u_{t-1}$. So, the model also allows correlation between ε_t and ε_{t-2}. Mathematically, we can write

$$\varepsilon_t = \rho \varepsilon_{t-1} + u_t = \rho(\rho \varepsilon_{t-2} + u_{t-1}) + u_t = \rho^2 \varepsilon_{t-2} + \rho u_{t-1} + u_t.$$

Similarly, we could derive the relationship between ε_t and ε_{t-3}, and so on.

Nonetheless, it is possible that we need more than just a first-order autoregression to capture the autocorrelation. If u_t has autocorrelation, then we may need a bigger model. For example, we might have

$$\varepsilon_t = \rho_1 \varepsilon_{t-1} + \rho_2 \varepsilon_{t-2} + u_t.$$

We want to make our models as simple as possible but not simpler, though, so let's stick to first-order autocorrelation. The techniques we will learn for first-order autocorrelation apply generally to higher-order (that is, with more lags in the error) autocorrelation.

IGNORING AUTOCORRELATION

If we have autocorrelation and we ignore it, what does it do to our OLS estimators? The quick answer is that it does something very similar to what heteroskedasticity does. Our OLS estimators are still unbiased, but, as we'll soon see, they are no longer BLUE. Moreover, the standard error estimate will be biased, so our hypothesis tests and confidence intervals will be invalid.

Positive autocorrelation tricks us by making us think we have more data than we really do. Look at the graph at the beginning of this chapter. The Dow Jones index spent the first 26 weeks of 2008 at about 12,500. We have 26 observations that, in the context of the graph, are all about the same. We would be able to estimate the trend line just about as well if we had only one observation from each six-month period. If the error in this period is comprised partly of last period's error, then only part of the information we get each period is new.

By ignoring autocorrelation, we operate under the false assumption that each observation brings with it completely new information. If much of the information in each observation was already known last period, then we don't have as much information in our data as we thought, and so the variance of our estimator is higher than we thought. Back to the Dow Jones average—the presence of positive autocorrelation does not bias our estimate of the trend line but it makes us think our estimate is more precise than it really is.

Let's dig into the problem more formally, step-by-step. Start with the error equation we looked at above for first-order autocorrelation, which relates the error at times t and $t-1$:

$$\varepsilon_t = \rho \varepsilon_{t-1} + u_t.$$

We saw above that this equation can be rewritten as

$$\varepsilon_t = \rho^2 \varepsilon_{t-2} + u_t + \rho u_{t-1}.$$

We're still not finished, because now we've got ε_{t-2} in our error. We substitute again, and again, and in the end this is what we have:

$$\varepsilon_t = u_t + \rho u_{t-1} + \rho^2 u_{t-2} + \rho^3 u_{t-3} + \ldots.$$

As long as ρ is less than 1 in absolute value, the term involving the lagged ε fades away so that errors from a long time before the current period eventually go to zero. It is a model of exponential decay.

It's easy to see that the expected value of ε_t is zero, since the expectations of u_t and all its lagged values are zero. This, along with Assumption CR1, is sufficient to show that our OLS estimators are unbiased, even when the errors are serially correlated. As in the case of heteroskedasticity, the problem here is with the variance, or what we call efficiency. We lose the "B" in "BLUE." Each ε_t has lots of past u_ts in it, so ignoring autocorrelation means we are counting each u multiple times. When there's autocorrelation, we need to find a new way to estimate that variance, one that counts each piece of information only once. That's what the Newey-West estimator does. We'll look at it below.

In short, ρ is the error correlation. If it's zero, we don't have a problem. If its absolute value is less than 1, then we have what's called a stationary time series, which means that, in the long run, the mean of the data is constant. You're likely to get groups of observations above the mean or below the mean due to autocorrelation, but in general the observations don't wander too far from the mean. Otherwise we have a nonstationary time series, which eventually explodes. Think about it: if $|\rho| > 1$, then each error term is likely to be, on average, larger in magnitude than the one before it, so the observations will deviate further and further away from the mean. Fortunately, this doesn't tend to happen with economic data. If ρ equals 1, we have what is called a "random walk," in which the observations don't return to the mean, but the errors also don't "explode" as when $|\rho| > 1$.

Think of ρ as telling you the direction and strength of the effect of one period's error on future periods' errors: if $|\rho| > 1$, the effect becomes magnified over time; if $|\rho| < 1$, it decays over time; and if $\rho = 1$, it stays constant. If it is zero, we have no problem—Assumption CR3 holds. Otherwise, we lose the "B." This is what we have to test for and, if there turns out to be autocorrelation, we have to fix it. Modern econometrics pays a great deal of attention to understanding the structure of autocorrelation and making it part of our time-series models.

HOW TO TEST FOR AUTOCORRELATION

The Recommended Way

A versatile (and intuitive) way of testing for autocorrelation is with the Breusch-Godfrey or Lagrange multiplier test. Save the residuals from your regression then regress these on all of the right-hand-side variables and all the lags of the residuals that you think should be there. For first-order autocorrelation, regress the residuals on $X_1, X_2, \ldots, X_K$ and on the residual lagged one period. For a simple regression model with first-order autocorrelation,

$$e_t = \rho e_{t-1} + \alpha_0 + \alpha_1 X_t + u_t.$$

(Remember, we use e rather than ε here because this is a regression with our sample data, rather than an expression of a population model.) From this regression, construct the test statistic

$$(T - m) R^2,$$

where m is the number of lags you've included and T is the size of your sample. So in this case, with just one lag, the statistic is $(T - 1)R^2$. The statistic is distributed as χ^2 with m (in this case one) degrees of freedom, provided that the sample size is large. An advantage of this test is that it works for a joint test involving more than one lag, although here we will focus on single-lag models.

The intuition for this test can be seen if we write the regression with first-order autocorrelation as

$$Y_t = \beta_0 + \beta_1 X_t + \rho \varepsilon_{t-1} + u_t.$$

If we ignore autocorrelation, then ε_{t-1} is an omitted variable in this regression. To test whether we have such an omitted variable, we first run the regression without ε_{t-1}. Then we see whether the residuals in that model are related to their lag. We include X_t in the regression to take proper account of how we got the residuals (from a regression of Y on X) and guarantee that the χ^2 table is the right place to look for a critical value. (You can actually use a test like this whenever you want to see whether an omitted variable should have been included in your regression. It's known as a Lagrange Multiplier, or LM, test.)

The Old Way

The classic test for autocorrelation is the Durbin-Watson test. It is gradually fading out of the econometrics textbooks, but it's still out there, so you should know about it. James Durbin and Geoffrey Watson came up with the following statistic:

$$DW = \frac{\sum_{t=2}^{T}(e_t - e_{t-1})^2}{\sum_{t=1}^{T}e_t^2}.$$

You don't have to derive this to know what it's about. With some algebra, you can prove that DW is almost identical to $2*(1 - r)$, where r is the correlation between e_t and e_{t-1}. If r is close to 1, then DW will be close to 0. If r is close to -1, then DW will be close to 4. In short, DW ranges from 0 to 4, with 2 being the case of no autocorrelation. The degrees of freedom in a DW test equal the number of parameters in your model (including the intercept).

Unfortunately, the bounds of this test are not entirely clear-cut, unlike in a t, χ^2, or F-test. There is a "gray area" that depends on the values of the regressors. Durban and Watson derived lower (d_L) and upper (d_U) bounds such that, if DW falls outside these bounds, we reject the null hypothesis of no positive autocorrelation (if $DW < d_L$) or no negative autocorrelation (if $DW > d_H$). There is a zone around 2 in which one fails to reject the null hypothesis of *either* type of autocorrelation. On either side of this middle zone, though, there is an *indeterminate* zone, in which we can neither reject nor fail to reject the null hypothesis of autocorrelation.

The spectrum and zones of the DW test are shown below. Usually, the concern is that we have positive autocorrelation, so we look to see whether our DW statistic is close to zero, that is, whether it has a value less than d_L at the left end of this spectrum.

Reject H_0: no positive serial correlation	Indeterminate zone	Fail to reject H_0: no positive or negative serial correlation	Indeterminate zone	Reject H_0: no negative serial correlation
0	d_L	d_U ... 4-d_U	4-d_L	4

Econometrics packages have options to calculate the DW statistic: see the website for examples.

If whichever test we choose concludes that there is no autocorrelation, we can just use OLS to estimate our model. Otherwise, we have to fix the problem.

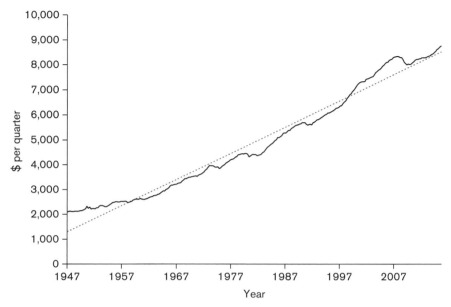

Figure 9.2 Total real personal consumption expenditure per capita, 1947–2015 (quarterly frequency, seasonally adjusted, 2009 dollars).

An Example: National Consumption and Income

The US government regularly compiles data on national income and consumption expenditures. Dividing these numbers by the US population, we get the average per capita income and consumption spending. Figure 9.2 shows average quarterly consumption expenditures per capita from 1947 to 2015. The figure shows that per capita consumption quadrupled in this 69-year period, from $2,094 to $8,749 per quarter. That is quite amazing growth. What makes it even more amazing is that the data adjust for inflation—they are in constant, seasonally adjusted, 2009 dollars.

The figure includes a trend line. Notice that the series has an exponential growth pattern, which causes it to hardly ever cross the trend line. Consumption is above the trend line until 1958, then below the trend line until 1998, and then above the trend line for the remainder of the sample. This pattern arises because consumption tends to increase by a certain percentage each year rather than a certain dollar amount.

To straighten out this exponential shape, we can take logs. Figure 9.3 shows the natural logarithm of consumption. This series is much more linear.

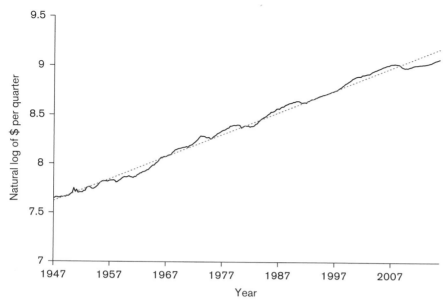

Figure 9.3 Log of total real personal consumption expenditure per capita, 1947–2015 (quarterly frequency, seasonally adjusted, 2009 dollars).

We want to explain consumption as a function of income. Let's use C to denote the log of consumption and X to denote log income. (We'll continue using the logs of our consumption and income data throughout the rest of this chapter, which will let us interpret estimates as elasticities.) This relationship comes straight out of consumer theory:

$$C_t = \beta_0 + \beta_1 X_t + \varepsilon_t.$$

The parameter β_1 is the elasticity of consumption with respect to income.

We first estimate an OLS regression, which gives us the results in Table 9.1. We estimate the income elasticity to be 1.03, which implies that consumption increases (approximately) proportionally with income.

Our DW coefficient is close to zero, indicating positive autocorrelation, and it is far below the lower critical value, so we easily reject the null hypothesis of no positive autocorrelation. (We use a 2.5% critical value from the Durbin-Watson tables to create a 5% two-sided test.)

For the Lagrange multiplier test, we regress the residual on its own one-period lagged value and on income (Table 9.2).

The value of our test statistic, 217.80, vastly exceeds the critical χ^2 value for a 5% test, and the estimated coefficient on the lagged residual, 0.89, is positive.

Table 9.1   A Simple OLS Regression of Consumption on Income

Variable	Estimated Coefficient	Standard Error	t-Statistic
Ln(income)	1.030	0.003	317.93
Constant	−0.379	0.028	−13.70
Sample size	275		
R^2	0.997		
Durbin-Watson	0.21		
Lower critical value (d_L), 2.5% test, 2 df	1.76		
Upper critical value (d_U), 2.5% test, 2 df	1.77		

Table 9.2   Lagrange Multiplier Test for Autocorrelation in the Simple OLS Regression of Consumption on Income

Variable	Estimated Coefficient	Standard Error	t-Statistic
e(t − 1)	0.885	0.027	32.70
Ln(Income)	0.001	0.001	0.56
Constant	−0.007	0.012	−0.58
Sample size	274		
R^2	0.80		
(T − 1)*R^2	217.80		
Critical χ^2, 1 df, 5%	3.84		

These results confirm that we have positive autocorrelation. The next question we have to address is what to do about it.

FIXING AUTOCORRELATION

Sometimes autocorrelation results from getting the model wrong. Recall the logistic model from Chapter 7, which gives us an S-shaped curve describing the diffusion of new products and technologies (figure 9.4).

All of the points on the S curve in figure 9.4 were generated from a logistic function. Because the "true" function is logistic, it appears that the errors are negative in the first part of the sample and positive in the second part. That is,

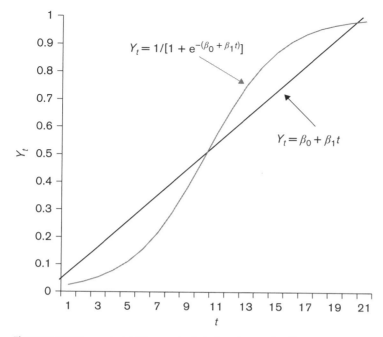

Figure 9.4 Fitting a straight line to a logistic function artificially creates autocorrelated errors.

there seems to be autocorrelation, but really it's because we tried to fit a line to a cubic function.

You'll notice the similarity of this example to the one we saw in Chapter 8, in which we modeled a cost function wrong and ended up with heteroskedasticity. Both illustrate how getting the model wrong can create what appears to be a violation of our classical error assumptions. The first step in dealing with autocorrelation is making sure we got the model right.

If we still have autocorrelation once we have the model right, the next step is to find a solution. The problem of autocorrelation, like the problem of heteroskedasticity, is really twofold. First, OLS is inefficient, even though it remains unbiased. Second, the standard errors that come out of the OLS estimation are biased.

AN EX POST ERROR CORRECTION METHOD: NEWEY-WEST

One option is to keep the OLS estimates but calculate the standard errors using a formula that corrects for the bias. This approach may be reasonable, because our parameter estimates, though imprecise, are unbiased. It is analogous to what we did in Chapter 8 to correct for heteroskedasticity using White's method. You'll recall that in White's method, for the simple regression model the corrected variance used the observation-specific e_i^2 instead of the constant regression variance, s^2, when calculating the variance of b_1. In that case, we got

$$s_{b_1}^2 = \frac{\sum_{i=1}^{N} x_i^2 e_i^2}{\left(\sum_{i=1}^{N} x_i^2\right)^2} = \sum_{i=1}^{N} w_i^2 e_i^2,$$

where, as always,

$$w_i = \frac{x_i}{\sum_{i=1}^{N} x_i^2}.$$

The analog for autocorrelation is the Newey-West correction. Variants of this method are the most common way to correct standard errors for autocorrelation ex post. For the simple regression model, it is

$$s_{b_1}^2 = \sum_{t=1}^{T} w_t^2 e_t^2 \left(1 + 2\sum_{j=1}^{L}\left(1 - \frac{j}{L}\right) r_j\right),$$

where r_j is the autocorrelation between $w_t \varepsilon_t$ and $w_{t-j} \varepsilon_{t-j}$, which we can write mathematically as

$$r_j = \frac{\sum_{t=j+1}^{T} w_t e_t w_{t-j} e_{t-j}}{\sum_{t=1}^{T} w_t^2 e_t^2}.$$

The formula looks intimidating, but look at it closely. The r_j term has the covariance of errors across pairs of observations in the numerator and White's variance in the denominator—it is an autocorrelation. If there is no autocorrelation, the covariance in the numerator is zero, and the whole term inside the parentheses in the $s_{b_1}^2$ formula equals 1. Then we are left with what's outside of the parentheses, which you should recognize as White's estimator. On the other hand, if the covariance is not zero, the formula will use it to adjust the standard errors for autocorrelation.

As you can see, the Newey-West correction is a "twofer": it includes White's correction for heteroskedasticity, but it also corrects for autocorrelation. Because of this, it gives us what are called "heteroskedasticity and auto-correlation consistent (HAC) standard errors."

Table 9.3   Newey-West Estimates of the Consumption-Income Regression

Variable	Estimated Coefficient	Standard Error ($L = 0$)	Standard Error ($L = 1$)	Standard Error ($L = 4$)	Standard Error ($L = 20$)	Standard Error ($L = 40$)
Ln(income)	1.030	0.004	0.005	0.008	0.013	0.015
Constant	−0.379	0.033	0.044	0.065	0.111	0.132
Sample size	275					
R^2	0.997					

The term in the interior parentheses is a weight that helps ensure that we get a positive value. (Variances by definition cannot be negative, but, without this weight, you might randomly get a negative value.) The weight de-emphasizes correlations between more distant pairs.

The Newey-West estimator requires choosing L large enough to capture the autocorrelation. There is no agreed-upon way to choose L, so a good rule of thumb is to choose a value large enough that increasing it further has little effect on the estimated standard errors. If you cannot find such a value, then it is an indication that the autocorrelation may be too large for the Newey-West estimator to correct effectively. In that case, it is best to explore the fixes we discuss in the next section.

You should also be wary of setting L too large, as it makes the standard error estimates imprecise. Again, there is no agreed-upon definition of "too large." In our opinion, L is probably too large if it reaches one quarter of the sample size. Ten percent of the sample size might be a better maximum.

Table 9.3 shows Newey-West estimates for our consumption-income regression. The $L = 0$ case corresponds to the White correction for heteroskedasticity, but it makes no correction for autocorrelation. The standard errors double when we set $L = 4$, which corresponds to a year with these quarterly data. They increase by more than 50% when we go to a 5-year lag ($L = 20$). The rate of increase slows as L increases, but the standard errors still increase by more than 15% when we go from $L = 20$ to $L = 40$. Because the standard errors still have not stabilized, and we are past 10% of the sample size, we would not recommend the Newey-West standard errors for this application.

EX ANTE: USING WHAT WE KNOW TO IMPROVE ON OLS

An alternative is to use what we know about the nature of the autocorrelation to improve upon the OLS estimator (that is, use this additional information about the structure of the errors to get a more precise estimate). There are many different types of autocorrelation processes and whole courses and texts that deal with them. In the spirit of keeping things simple, let's continue with the case of first-order autoregression.

Look again at our simple regression model with errors that follow a first-order autoregression:

$$Y_t = \beta_0 + \beta_1 X_t + \varepsilon_t$$
$$= \beta_0 + \beta_1 X_t + \rho \varepsilon_{t-1} + u_t.$$

The relationship holds for all time periods. Let's lag our original equation by one period and consider the observation for time period $(t-1)$:

$$Y_{t-1} = \beta_0 + \beta_1 X_{t-1} + \varepsilon_{t-1}.$$

Solve for ε_{t-1}:

$$\varepsilon_{t-1} = Y_{t-1} - \beta_0 - \beta_1 X_{t-1}.$$

In a stroke of mathematical wizardry, substitute this last expression for ε_{t-1} in the equation for Y_t, and you'll get

$$Y_t = \beta_0 + \beta_1 X_t + \rho \left(Y_{t-1} - \beta_0 - \beta_1 X_{t-1} \right) + u_t.$$

Now rearrange terms:

$$Y_t - \rho Y_{t-1} = \beta_0 \left(1 - \rho \right) + \beta_1 \left(X_t - \rho X_{t-1} \right) + u,$$

$$Y_t^* = \beta_0^* + \beta_1 X_t^* + u.$$

See what we've done? We've made the problem error vanish! Dr. Who would be proud of us for this sleight of hand. If we knew ρ, we could do this transformation and just use OLS regression of Y^* on X^*. This process is called GLS, and it is BLUE.

Unfortunately, we do not know ρ, so we have to estimate it. You already know how to do that: just estimate a regression of e_t on e_{t-1} to get

$$r = \frac{\sum_{t=2}^{T} e_{t-1} e_t}{\sum_{t=2}^{T} e_{t-1}^2}.$$

Once we have r, we use it in place of ρ to transform the variables in our regression.

This is called feasible generalized least squares (FGLS). Like GLS, it involves transforming the data to eliminate the autocorrelation problem. But unlike GLS, it does not assume that we know the population ρ; it estimates it using sample data, thus the word "feasible." Sometimes people iterate the FGLS esti-

Table 9.4 FGLS and Prais-Winsten Estimates of the Consumption-Income Regression

Variable	FGLS		Prais-Winsten	
	Estimated Coefficient	Standard Error	Estimated Coefficient	Standard Error
Income	1.012	0.013	0.438	0.045
Constant	−0.026	0.012	4.660	0.452
Sample size	274		274	
R^2	0.88		0.999	
Durbin-Watson	2.47		2.11	
Lower critical value ($4-d_U$), 2.5% test, 2 df	2.23		2.23	
Upper critical value ($4-d_L$), 2.5% test, 2 df	2.24		2.24	

mator. After getting the FGLS estimates, they compute a new value for r and redo GLS. They continue this process until their estimates stop changing. This iterative process is known as the Cochrane-Orcutt procedure (named after Cambridge University statisticians Donald Cochrane and Guy Orcutt) or the Prais-Winsten procedure (named after Sigbert Prais and Christopher Winsten, who developed their procedure while at the University of Chicago).

If we do this with our consumption-income data, we get results in Table 9.4.

According to the Durbin-Watson statistic, we did not quite correct the autocorrelation problem with FGLS (2.47 > 2.24). There is now some negative autocorrelation in that model. The Prais-Winsten procedure (i.e., iterative FGLS) converges to a higher value of r and a Durbin-Watson statistic that shows no significant autocorrelation (2.11 > 2.23).

At this point you might say, wait a minute, the coefficient estimates changed. I thought our OLS estimators were still unbiased when there is serial correlation. FGLS is unbiased in large samples, as well, so you would expect the parameter estimates from the two methods to be close. But in this example, clearly they are not: 1.03 (OLS) and 1.01 (FGLS) versus 0.44 (Prais-Winsten). OLS can be very imprecise when there is severe autocorrelation. Because of this, the two methods can give quite different results, even though both are unbiased. However, this large difference is a warning sign that the model is not right. Next, we try to understand this better.

Table 9.5   Autoregressive Distributed Lag Model of the Consumption-Income Regression

Variable	Estimated Coefficient	Standard Error	t-Statistic
Consumption($t-1$)	0.927	0.020	47.20
Income	0.297	0.046	6.44
Income($t-1$)	−0.222	0.048	−4.66
Constant	−0.021	0.012	−1.75
Sample size	274		
R^2	0.9997		

Yet a Better Way (Most Likely): An Autoregressive Distributed Lag Model

We can rearrange terms in our transformed regression a slightly different way, keeping the lagged dependent variable on the *right-hand* side of the equation:

$$Y_t = \beta_0 \left(1 - \rho\right) + \rho Y_{t-1} + \beta_1 X_t - \beta_1 \rho X_{t-1} + u_t.$$

If we do this, we end up with a model in which we regress Y_t on its lagged value, Y_{t-1}, and on X_t and its lagged value, X_{t-1}. Notice that the coefficient on X_{t-1} equals the product of the coefficients on the other two variables. This is what we call an autoregressive distributed lag model. "Autoregressive" means it includes the lagged dependent variable on the right-hand side. "Distributed lag" means it also includes the lagged right-hand-side variable.

To estimate this model, first generate the lagged dependent and independent variables. In a spreadsheet, this is tantamount to cutting the top cell in a data column, then moving the whole column up. Then run the regression with the lagged variables along with your X variable on the right-hand side.

To this point in the chapter, we have specified a model in which the only autoregressive component is in the error. We just saw that, when we transform this model and write it in autoregressive form, the coefficient on X_{t-1} equals the product of the coefficients on the other two variables. In practice, there usually isn't a good reason to impose this restriction, so we will not do so when we estimate the model. Here's what our consumption-income model looks like without out the restriction:

$$C_t = \beta_0^* + \beta_1^* C_{t-1} + \beta_2^* X_t + \beta_3^* X_{t-1} + u_t.$$

We put * superscripts on the coefficients so as not to confuse them with the β coefficients in the restricted model.

Table 9.5 shows what we get when we estimate the autoregressive distributed lag model without the restriction.

Table 9.6   Breusch-Godfrey (Lagrange Multiplier) Test for Heteroskedasticity in the Autoregressive Distributed Lag Model

Variable	Estimated Coefficient	Standard Error	t-Statistic
$e(t-1)$	−0.072	0.066	−1.09
$Ln(Cons(t-1))$	−0.001	0.021	−0.04
$Ln(Income)$	0.031	0.048	0.64
$Ln(Income(t-1))$	−0.029	0.051	−0.58
Constant	−0.003	0.012	−0.28
Sample size	274		
R^2	0.0056		
$(T-1)^*R^2$	1.53		
Critical value, 5% test, 1 df	3.84		

Including the lagged dependent variable on the right-hand side of our regression eliminates the autocorrelation problem. We cannot show this using the Durbin-Watson test, because it is not valid when there is a lagged dependent variable in the regression. But we can use the Breusch-Godfrey (Lagrange multiplier) test. It gives us the results in Table 9.6.

The test statistic, $(T-1)R^2 = 1.53$, is below the critical value, 3.84. Thus, with this model, we fail to reject the null hypothesis of no autocorrelation. Including the lagged variables in our regression eliminated the problem.

Fortunately, it is rare for autocorrelation to persist once the lagged dependent variable is included as a regressor. If it does persist, it might be worth experimenting with putting additional lags of the dependent and/or X variables on the right-hand side of your regression. If the errors from one period are a function not only of the errors from last period but also of the errors from two periods ago, including Y_{t-2} or X_{t-2} might clean up the autocorrelation problem.

Interpreting Results from an Autoregressive Model

How do we interpret the results of our autoregressive model? The model is

$$C_t = -0.021 + 0.927C_{t-1} + 0.297X_t - 0.222X_{t-1} + e_t.$$

It looks like these numbers are quite different from those in our OLS and FGLS models, but they are not. There are two tricks for understanding what the coefficients in autoregressive distributed lag models mean.

The first trick is to drop all the time subscripts and the error term. This gives the equilibrium or long-run relationship implied by the model. Our model is

$$C = -0.021 + 0.927C + 0.297X - 0.222X,$$

which we can rewrite as[1]

$$C = -0.29 + 1.03X.$$

So, the estimated long-run consumption elasticity is 1.03, i.e., aggregate consumption tends to increase about one for one with income. Notice how similar the 1.03 coefficient is to the OLS and FGLS estimates obtained earlier.

The second trick is to subtract the lagged dependent variable from both sides of the original equation, then add and subtract $b_3^* X_t$ from the right-hand side. Our model becomes

$$C_t - C_{t-1} = -0.021 + (0.927 - 1)C_{t-1} + 0.297X_t + 0.222X_t - 0.222X_t - 0.222X_{t-1} + e_t$$
$$C_t - C_{t-1} = -0.021 - 0.073C_{t-1} + 0.075X_t + 0.222(X_t - X_{t-1}) + e_t$$

Now group the first three right-hand-side terms into a single term (this might seem a bit tricky, but if you check you'll see that it works out):

$$C_t - C_{t-1} = -0.073(C_{t-1} + 0.29 - 1.03X_t) + 0.222(X_t - X_{t-1}) + e_t.$$

This model is known as an *error correction model*.[2] It says that the change in consumption each quarter, $C_t - C_{t-1}$, has two components. The term in the first set of parentheses you should recognize as the long-run relationship we just derived. The error correction model says that, if consumption in $t - 1$ is high relative to its long-run value, then $C_{t-1} - 1.03X_t + 0.29 > 0$, and we expect consumption to decrease by 0.073 times the excess. In addition, if income increases this month, then we expect consumption to increase by 0.22 times the increase in log income.

So, changes in consumption are a function of how large consumption is relative to income and whether income is increasing or decreasing at the moment. These two insights could not have been gleaned from the OLS or FGLS estimates, so we recommend using autoregressive distributed lag models in time-series modeling rather than leaving the autocorrelation in the error.

Getting a Time-Series Model Right

The best way to approach time-series analysis is to try and get the dynamics right, starting out with the simplest model to describe the trend in question. An autoregressive model with a time trend often is a useful way to begin:

$$Y_t = \beta_0 + \beta_1 Y_{t-1} + \beta_2 t + u_t.$$

Such a model can be used to describe the underlying dynamics, and though simple, it can give us some important insights. Including a time trend can help capture much of what's going on, as it's often the case that a dependent variable is increasing or decreasing linearly with time. The parameter β_2 denotes the trend in the dependent variable over time.

The parameter β_1 gives us information about the stability of the model as well as about what happens if our dependent variable is knocked off its linear time trend. Remember that with autocorrelation, if the error in one period is positive it's likely that the error in the next period will be positive too, so the observations will linger above the trend line. β_1 tells us how long it will linger above the trend line.

Provided β_1 is less than 1 (the model is stable) and greater than zero, the half-life of return to the trend from an unexpected change in Y_t is given by the formula $h = -\ln(2)/\ln(\beta_1)$, where ln is the natural logarithm. For example, if t denotes years ($t = 1, 2, \ldots, T$) and $\beta_1 = 0.70$, it will take $-\ln(2)/\ln(0.7) = 1.94$ years to get half way back to the trend after an unexpected shock to the dependent variable.

A way to think about β_1 is that it tells you how persistent a shock is, or how long its effect is likely to linger. A large value for this parameter tells you that if there is a large positive shock that moves the variable above its trend line, then observations are likely to stay above trend for a fairly long time. In contrast, a small value tells you that observations will return more quickly to the time trend after a shock.

It is important to realize that a positive trend could result from a steady increase in the dependent variable over time, but it could instead be an artifact of some omitted variable. For example, policy changes or other exogenous shocks could have caused the dependent variable to increase suddenly. If we do not include variables that measure these shocks in our regression, there may appear to be an upward trend when really there was a one-time jolt; the increase in Y_t might be a sharp step-up (a "stepwise function") instead of a continuous upward trend.

By including additional right-hand-side variables in the simple dynamic model, we may be able to test for shifts or breaks in the trend due to those shocks. In fact, testing whether particular policies or other exogenous changes cause breaks in a trend often is the focus of many time-series econometric studies. This is essentially what we do by including X variables in the autoregressive distributed lag model.

The univariate autoregressive model insulates us from the perils of autocorrelation because we are *starting* by modeling the autocorrelation. Other variables matter in addition to the autocorrelation, and we can add them to the model to see their effect, just like we did in the autoregressive distributed lag model for consumption and income. We do so knowing that, if we find them to be significant, our result will not be an illusion generated by ignored autocorrelation.

CLUSTERED AND SPATIAL DATA

In 1990, an economist at the Bureau of Labor Statistics named Brent Moulton conducted an influential study.[3] He ran a regression to predict the wages of 18,946 workers in the United States. He included in his regression variables such as education and work experience. Then, he added 14 variables that he thought should not have any relationship with wages. These 14 variables included land area of the state in which the person lives, the divorce rate in the state in which the person lives, and random normal digits. He found that 6 of the 14 were statistically significant. Even the random number variable was significant.

Moulton's result was worrying for econometricians. If our models say that garbage variables are important, then can we really trust our models?

Thankfully, Moulton had the solution. He noticed two things. First, the error terms in his model were correlated within states. That means workers in some states tended to earn more than the model predicted and workers in other states tended to earn less than predicted. This is clear violation of CR3, which states that $\text{cov}[\varepsilon_i, \varepsilon_j] = 0$ for $i \neq j$, i.e., zero correlation in the errors from one observation to another. Autocorrelation can be spatial as well as temporal!

The second thing Moulton noticed was that his 14 garbage variables were measured at the state level—they were the same for all individual-worker observations within a state. These variables, obviously, have a very high correlation across observations within a state because they are the same for all observations in the state. Putting these two things together caused the standard errors to be 3–5 times smaller than they should have been. To pick one example, the t-statistic on the random numbers variable should have been 1.09 and insignificant, but it was instead reported to be 4.13 and highly significant.

This is known as the clustering problem. It causes us to think we have more data than we really do. Even though Moulton had 18,946 data points, many of these observations were from the same state and therefore contained the same information. Thus, when dealing with clustered data, we need to adjust the standard errors in the same way that we did for heteroskedasticity with White's estimator and for autocorrelation with the Newey-West estimator.

The formula for the cluster-robust estimator in a simple regression is

$$s_{b_1}^2 = \sum_{i=1}^{N} \sum_{j=1}^{N} 1\left(i, j \text{ in same cluster}\right) w_i e_i w_j e_j.$$

The expression $1(i, j$ in same cluster) equals 1 if i and j are in the same cluster and zero otherwise. This means that we add up $w_i e_i w_j e_j$ for all combinations of observations i and j that are in the same cluster. We exclude all pairs of observations in different clusters. In Moulton's case, each state is a cluster. This means that he allows errors from the same state to be correlated with each other, but assumes zero correlation between errors in different states.

Compare this to White's heteroskedasticity-robust formula

$$s_{b_1}^2 = \sum_{i=1}^{N} w_i^2 e_i^2.$$

The two formulas are the same if each observation is its own group of one. But they are different if we have more than one observation from the same group.

To work well, the cluster-robust estimator needs the number of clusters to be large enough. In settings with fewer than 20 clusters, it becomes unreliable (just like the Newey-West correction is unreliable when L is large).

How should you define a cluster? Each of Moulton's 18,946 wage earners worked in a firm that was located in a county, which is located in a state, which is located in a region (West, Mountain, Midwest, South, or Northeast). You need to define your clusters large enough to soak up the error correlation, but not so large that you end up with fewer than 20. You could try clustering by county, then by state. If the two produce similar results, then you can be confident that you have addressed the error correlation problem. On the other hand, if you see evidence that there is error correlation between states, then you may need to find some more variables to control for macro effects or collect more data.

Spatial econometrics aims not to group the data into discrete clusters, but rather to model the relationship between each pair of observations based on how far apart they are. It's like time series, except instead of the observations being separated in one dimension by time, they are separated by the two dimensions of latitude and longitude. Spatial analysis is beyond the scope of this course. Many practitioners choose to treat spatial data like clustered data, which works well in many settings.

What We Learned

- Correlated errors cause OLS to lose its "best" property and the estimated standard errors to be biased.
- As long as the autocorrelation is not too strong, the standard error bias can be corrected with Newey and West's heteroskedasticity and autocorrelation consistent estimator.
- Getting the model right by adding lagged variables to the model is usually the best approach to deal with autocorrelation in time-series data.

Sample Selection Bias (Assumption CR1)

10

Three econometricians go hunting, and spot a large deer. The first econometrician fires, but his shot goes three feet wide to the left. The second econometrician fires, but also misses, by three feet to the right. The third econometrician starts jumping up and down, shouting "We got it! We got it!"

—Econometrician Joke

LEARNING OBJECTIVES

Upon completing the work in this chapter, you will be able to:

► Articulate in words the implications of a nonrepresentative sample
► Explain using mathematics the implications of a nonrepresentative sample
► Apply a model of sample selection to correct sample selection bias
► Describe the experiment you would like to run if you could

In the 2012 US presidential election, many polls predicted that Mitt Romney would beat Barack Obama. As it turned out, Obama won easily. How could so many polls have been so wrong? The famous polling organization, Gallup, discovered that its polls were skewed toward people who did not vote, whites, and people with listed phone numbers. All of these groups tended to support Romney. Gallup avoided the biggest pitfall in modern polling (omitting people who do not have a landline telephone), but it still made a large error. It did not have a representative sample of the population of voters.

Our first classical assumption is that the sample is representative of the population we want to say something about. If we were to select a random sample from the population, it would have the same distribution as our sample. Without this assumption, we cannot expect our sample to be informative about the population.

Of course, we almost never see the whole population. All we see are the sample data on the right-hand-side and dependent variables. This makes violations of CR1 very tricky to deal with.

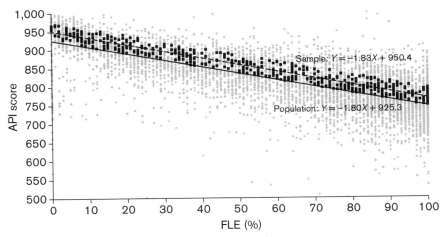

Figure 10.1 API score and free lunch eligibility (FLE). A nonrepresentative sample of California schools that produces a parallel shift in the regression line.

WHAT IF WE HAVE A NONREPRESENTATIVE SAMPLE?

The answer to the question "what if this assumption is violated?" depends on *how* it is violated. To illustrate some possibilities, let's go back to the schools example we used beginning in Chapter 2, for which we do happen to have data on the whole population of California schools.

Figure 10.1 shows a scatter plot of free-lunch eligibility (FLE) and the academic performance index (API) for the population of California schools (gray diamonds) and the population regression line (solid line).

Because this regression line was estimated from data on the whole population, it is the target we are aiming for when we run a regression with a sample. You can see that, as always, there's a scatter of errors above and below the regression line. A scatter plot of these errors against FLE would show a flat relationship.

Suppose we obtain a sample of 500 observations by randomly choosing only from observations with positive errors. (Perhaps, we want to focus our analysis on good schools.) The new sample is shown by the black squares in figure 10.1. We fit a regression line to those data points (the dashed line in the figure) and get a slope of −1.83. You can see that this line has a similar slope to the line we want to estimate.

The sample in the figure is not representative. It includes only schools that outperform their predicted API scores. So, why is the sample slope so similar to the population? The answer is that we picked our sample in a way that kept the errors uncorrelated with FLE. Our sampling process did not distort the relationship between API and FLE.

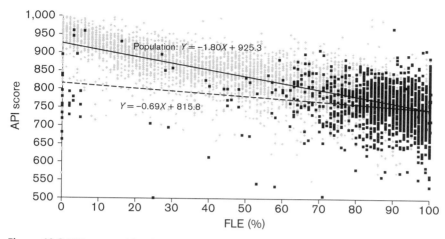

Figure 10.2 API score and free lunch eligibility (FLE). A nonrepresentative sample of California schools that produces a change in the slope of the regression line.

To generate this sample, we restricted ourselves to the 2,346 schools with a population error that was positive but no greater than 50. We then randomly selected 500 schools from this set. With this setup, we were just as likely to select a large error from a high-FLE school as a low-FLE school. This means that our sample regression line looks just like the population regression line, except shifted up.

A parallel shift in the error distribution doesn't affect our slope estimate. The intercept clearly takes a hit, though: it is higher in the sample than in the population. If all we care about is getting a good estimate of β_1, we're okay in this case, even though CR1 is violated. If we care about β_0, though, we're in trouble.

Now let's look at a different (and much more common) situation: CR1 is violated in such a way that the errors *are* correlated with the X variable.

We took the 1,901 schools with no more than 10% of parents who are college graduates. This subpopulation is shown in figure 10.2 (black squares) along with the subpopulation regression line (dashed). The slope is −0.44, much smaller than the population value of −1.80. This subpopulation is clearly not representative of the population of CA schools, so any sample from this subpopulation will not be representative. If we only look at less-well-educated areas, then there is only a small relationship between FLE and API.

We have a big problem: our estimates of β_0 and β_1 are biased.

HOW DOES IT HAPPEN?

Political pollsters understand sampling bias well. Before the 2012 election, if you wanted to know whether Obama would be reelected, you wouldn't limit your polls to college campuses or coastal cities, which are likely to vote

Democrat. You also wouldn't limit your polling to conservative rural counties in the heartland (or to Wall Street, or Occupy Wall Street). You'd do your best to poll a random sample of all likely voters in the United States.

That's easier said than done. Finding a truly random sample is typically harder than you might imagine. Many firms use phone surveys. Traditional polls randomly draw phone numbers from a master list—of what? Landline phones. If you do not have one of those, there's no risk you'll be called. Ed polled his econometrics class last winter, and no one had a fixed-line phone (though many of their parents did).

Are people with landline phones similar to people without them in terms of whatever it is you want to model? Think of how many of your friends have land-line phones, compared with how many of your parents' friends do. If you think those groups are similar, then a landline-only sample would be representative. If not, then we've got a problem.

Landline phone surveys have always been a pretty bad idea in poor countries, where only relatively high-income people tend to have phones. They used to be a fairly good strategy in the United States, when landline phones were almost universal. Today, many people have only cell phones, and people with landline phones may differ from those without them. Modern pollsters use a mix of cell and landline phone numbers to get around this problem, but they face another problem: who answers a call from a number they don't recognize?

Political polls typically aim to predict the proportion of votes a candidate will receive. Econometric models often aim not just to predict the dependent variable, but also to estimate how the dependent variable correlates with some right-hand-side variables. In our schools example, we were interested not just in predicting API score, but also in how API scores differ across districts with different FLE rates.

HOW SAMPLE SELECTION BIAS AFFECTS REGRESSION MODELS

Let's look more at potential sample selection bias in our California schools example. Suppose you are trying to predict how API score correlates with FLE in California schools. Your population of interest is the 2013 population of schools in California.

The population model is

$$API_i = \beta_0 + \beta_1 FLE_i + \varepsilon_i \qquad \text{cov}\left[FLE_i, \varepsilon_i\right] = 0.$$

The parameters β_0 and β_1 are constants, as usual. Because we have the population in this example, we know that $\beta_0 = 925.3$ and $\beta_1 = -1.80$.

Recall from Chapter 4 that in our population model FLE has zero covariance with the error term. This means that our population model is the best linear predictor of API using FLE.

Suppose you know school i's *FLE*. Then, this school's expected *API* is

$$E\left[API_i\right] = 925.3 - 1.80FLE_i + E\left[\varepsilon_i\right].$$

In the population, the error has a mean of zero. So, using the population model, the predicted *API* for school i would be

$$E\left[API_i\right] = 925.3 - 1.80FLE_i.$$

If you had a sample of data rather than the population, you would not know β_0 and β_1. You could use your sample to compute the OLS estimates b_0 and b_1, and you could use these in place of β_0 and β_1 to predict *API*.

How will you draw your sample? You could select a random sample of schools like we did in Chapter 5. Or take a random sample of urban schools, or schools in Northern California, or large schools, or schools in districts with low parental education. Would such samples be representative of the whole state? It turns out that selecting the 500 largest schools produces $b_0 = 937.9$ and $b_1 = -1.93$, so large schools represent the population pretty well.

As we saw in figure 5.2, sampling only from districts with low parental education produces a nonrepresentative sample. There are 1,901 schools with no more than 10% of parents who are college graduates. Let's define a population model for this population of 1,901 schools:

$$API_i = \beta_0^{low} + \beta_1^{low} FLE_i + \varepsilon_i^{low}.$$

We use the superscript low to distinguish this model from the whole-state model. The parameters β_0^{low} and β_1^{low} are different from the parameters β_0 and β_1. Using the 1,901 schools, we computed that $\beta_0^{low} = 815.8$ and $\beta_1^{low} = -0.69$, compared to $\beta_0 = 925.3$ and $\beta_1 = -1.80$ for the whole-state population.

To create figure 5.2, we randomly selected 500 schools from within this low-parental-education population. Our sample model is

$$API_i = b_0^{low} + b_1^{low} FLE_i + e_i^{low}.$$

Notice we now use Roman, not Greek, letters, because the equation no longer refers to the whole population of low-parental-education schools. When we estimated this regression, we got $b_0^{low} = 792.8$ and $b_1^{low} = -0.44$.

Let's focus on the slope. If we kept randomly drawing samples, like in Chapter 5, we would get different values for b_1^{low}, some smaller than -0.69 and some larger. But on average we would estimate the value of the slope for the low-education population, which is $\beta_1^{low} = -0.69$.

Putting the two population models together helps us understand what this nonrepresentative sampling process does to the model. We have

$$\beta_0^{low} + \beta_1^{low} FLE_i + \varepsilon_i^{low} = \beta_0 + \beta_1 FLE_i + \varepsilon_i.$$

Rearranging, we get

$$\varepsilon_i = \left(\beta_0^{low} - \beta_0\right) + \left(\beta_1^{low} - \beta_1\right) FLE_i + \varepsilon_i^{low},$$

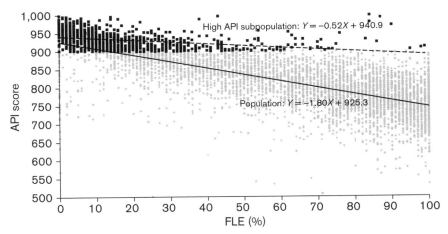

Figure 10.3 Subpopulation with API > 900. Selection on the *Y* variable (high-API schools) results in a regression line that is flatter than that for the whole population.

or, if we plug in the numbers we got from the two population models,

$$\varepsilon_i = 815.8 - 925.3 + \left(-0.69 - (-1.8)\right) FLE_i + \varepsilon_i^{low},$$

$$\varepsilon_i = -109.5 + 1.11 FLE_i + \varepsilon_i^{low}.$$

Here, we can see how sample selection bias affects the error term. We are interested in the whole-state population, but we are sampling from the low-education subpopulation. If our two populations have different slope parameters (which they do in this case), then the error term we are interested in is correlated with FLE.

So, selecting your sample in a way that makes the error correlated with the right-hand-side variable will cause bias in your slope parameter. Even if there is no such correlation (i.e., if $\beta_1^{low} = \beta_1$) you may still have a biased intercept if you sample from a subpopulation that does not have an error with mean zero.

This can get confusing. Here's what to do if you get confused about the various populations. Think of a scatter plot of the whole population, the population you are interested in. Then, imagine the population regression line running through those points. Next, overlay a set of points that define the subpopulation that you are actually sampling from. Does your subpopulation have the same regression line?

We finish this section with three more examples, shown in figures 10.3–10.5.

To get the plot in figure 10.3, we select only from the subpopulation of schools with high API. Selection on the dependent variable eliminates many

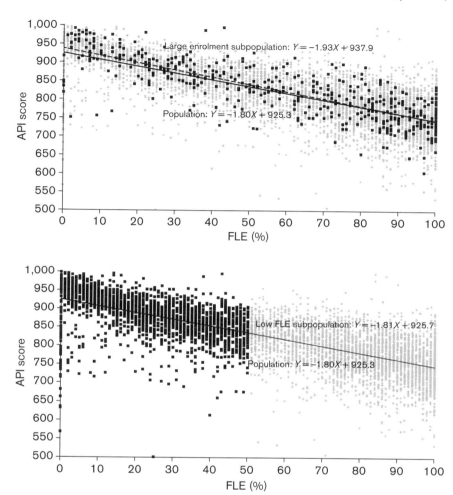

Figure 10.4 (Top) Subpopulation with enrolment > 600. Selection on X variables (school size and FLE) does not bias the slope estimate in a well-specified model.

Figure 10.5 (Bottom) Subpopulation with FLE < 50%. Selection on X variables (school size and FLE) does not bias the slope estimate in a well-specified model.

observations with negative errors and causes bias. The subpopulation has a much flatter regression line than the full population.

Figures 10.4 and 10.5 show subpopulations that introduce little to no bias. Selecting on enrollment (figure 10.4) avoids any serious bias, as we mentioned earlier. Selecting on the X variable (FLE) does not introduce bias as long as the population model is well specified (see figure 10.5).

WHAT TO DO ABOUT IT

Obviously, the best thing you can do is get a random sample of the whole population. Good survey firms (and political pollsters) put a lot of thought into strategies to get representative random samples of the relevant population. What the relevant population is depends on the nature of your research question. For politics, it is likely to be the population of voters. For a study of workers' wages, it is probably the entire working-age population. If it's a study of voting or wages in California, it's the population of voters or the working-age population in California. If it's about marketing a new gadget to the 20-something generation, it's the population of 20-somethings. It probably isn't the population of 20-somethings at UC Davis, though, because that's not anything like a random sample of all 20-somethings. It is a self-selected sample. Whatever made students come to Davis put them in the Davis sample. Variables that explain *why* someone is a UC Davis student might also be correlated with the outcome we want to measure. This is the big worry when CR1 breaks down.

In many cases, the only credible solution is to get more or better data. In fact, you may not know whether your sample is representative without collecting more data. For example, if you have a sample of API and FLE for large schools, you could look up census data on socioeconomic and economic characteristics of the regions that contain the large schools and compare them to the state as a whole. Is there any sign that your selected sample differs from the rest of the population?

In some cases, you can account for selection bias with the data you have. We turn to that next.

SELF-SELECTION

A few years back Ed and a colleague (Antonio Yúnez-Naude) asked a simple question: does education make farmers more productive? They compared productivity in basic grains production between Mexican farmers with lower and higher levels of education. (Basically, they included years of schooling in the farmers' production functions, then tested whether it significantly affected yields.)

Like a number of prior studies, they found little evidence that farmers with more schooling were more productive. They dug deeper and found that once farmers got more schooling, they tended to move out of agriculture. This makes perfect sense, because the economic returns to schooling are generally higher in nonfarm jobs.

Of course, *some* farmers with relatively high schooling did keep on farming. Were they like the farmers with schooling who left farming? Maybe the educated farmers with the most drive—the ones who would have had high yields—left the farm, and the less enterprising ones stayed behind. Ed and Antonio could imagine all kinds of stories here, but the nagging question was this one: is the process that sorts people with schooling into the farmer and nonfarmer samples random? If not, they aren't answering the question of whether schooling makes *farmers* more productive.

As farmers increase their education, they essentially select themselves out of the sample, leaving the farm for better-paying jobs. This finding raises an interesting prospect: that rural education programs could negatively affect agricultural productivity by encouraging the most productive farmers to quit farming. (That isn't necessarily a bad thing, provided that it grows the nonfarm economy.)

Ed and Antonio's study produced some reassuring findings. Among farmers who continued farming, those with higher schooling were, indeed, more productive. Schooling also induced farmers to shift from low-valued basic grains to high-valued cash crops. But to show these things, they had to solve the CR1 problem.[1]

There's a whole class of outcomes on which it is not possible to get information: the things people could have done but did not do. In their case, the big question was: "What would a farmer's production have been if he had kept on farming?"

Here's another one, which you'll likely come across if you take a labor economics class: many people join unions. What effect does this have on their wages? To really answer this question, we would have to compare the same people's wages at a given point in time with and without joining a union. Unfortunately, we can only see one of the two: workers are either "in" or "out."

There are many other examples. How does adopting a new production technology affect profits? We only see profits under the new technology for producers who choose to adopt it. How does migration affect wages? We only see migrants' wages for the people who actually migrate. How much are people willing to spend on new cars? We only see this for the people who choose to buy a new car. In cases like these, getting the sample right isn't really the answer, because you can't sample hypothetical outcomes. We need to solve the problem econometrically.

How do we control for hypothetical stuff we can't even see? The Nobel Laureate James Heckman, an economist at the University of Chicago, studied this problem, which has become known as "self-selection." He posed the question: how do people respond to higher wages? Do they work more? Many economists had regressed hours worked on wages in an effort to estimate the relationship between the two. The trouble is that a lot of people are not in the workforce. Those who drop out, you could imagine, might be people who would earn low wages if they were in the workforce. (If you expect to earn low wages, why bother working?) Or maybe they won the lottery, but that's not very likely.

This problem is called "self-selection" because people select themselves into and out of the workforce. Those who select out cannot be in the sample of wage earners. Yet we want to know how they, too, might respond to higher wages. If wages go up, there are really two effects. The people already in the workforce might work more (or maybe less: what if you could pay your bills working fewer hours and have more free time?). In addition, people who weren't in the workforce might come in, and those "workers at the margin" are likely to differ in fundamental ways from the people who were in the workforce all along. If we ignore the selection problem and forget about those who aren't in the workforce, our estimates of how wages affect hours worked are likely to be biased.

To write this formally, define I_i to be a dummy variable that equals one if person i is in the workforce and zero otherwise. Taking wages as given, the expectation of hours worked (HW_i), the dependent variable, is given by

$$E\left[HW_i \mid I_i = 1\right] = \beta_0 + \beta_1 W_i + E\left[\varepsilon_i \mid I_i = 1\right].$$

The last term in this equation is the conditional expectation of the error—that is, the error conditional upon person i being in the workforce and getting a wage. If the conditional expectation of the error is not zero, we get biased estimates. The problem here is that variables (call them Z_{1i}, Z_{2i}, . . ., Z_{ki},—these might include education, gender, whether you have children, etc.) that affect people's decision of whether or not to be in the workforce are also likely to affect their hours worked once they are in.

We can solve this problem. First, we get data on people who are in the workforce earning wages and on people not in the workforce, for whom no wages are observed. We use these data to estimate a model of labor-force participation, in which the dependent variable is the dummy variable I_i.

You could imagine an OLS regression of I_i on Z_i, the variables affecting labor-force participation:

$$I_i = \alpha_0 + \alpha_1 Z_{1i} + \alpha_2 Z_{2i} + \ldots + \alpha_k Z_{ki} + u_i.$$

The predicted value of I_i from this regression, $\hat{I}_i$, can be thought of as person i's ex ante probability of being in the workforce. Since the dependent variable in this side regression only takes on the value of 0 or 1, the predicted $\hat{I}_i$ usually will fall into the (0,1) interval, like a probability.

Now include $\hat{I}_i$ as a new right-hand-side variable in the hours worked regression:

$$HW_i = \beta_0 + \beta_1 W_i + \beta_2 \hat{I}_i + \varepsilon_i.$$

That is a way of controlling for self-selection. It is not exactly what Professor Heckman did. He used a different method to estimate participation, called a probit regression, which among other things insures that the predicted $\hat{I}_i$ are always in the (0,1) interval.

There are some other issues with this regression, not the least of which is that the right-hand-side wage variable (W_i) is not randomly assigned to individuals but rather is determined by productivity of the worker. (Remember our Mincer wage regression back in Chapter 7? It had the wage on the left hand side) This violates CR5. (We will address this problem in Chapter 11.) Just the same, our new regression captures the spirit of what has become known as the Heckman procedure, so we will set these problems aside for now.

Looking at these two regression equations, it's easy to see that variables affecting whether or not someone is in the workforce (Z_i) also affect hours worked, through $\hat{I}_i$. Heckman used his model to explain why the wage gap between black and white men in the United States narrowed between 1940 and 1980. It was almost entirely the result of low-wage black men dropping out of the workforce! What seemed like a good outcome, we learned thanks to Heckman, actually was the sign of a very bad outcome, because the sample of working men changed over time.

In all of these cases, if people were randomly sorted into the different groups, there wouldn't be a problem. But the kinds of people who self-select into our samples (e.g., those who choose to get more education or choose to enter the workforce or pick up the phone when a pollster calls) are likely to be different, perhaps in unseen ways, than the people who do not. If those we can see are different than those we can't, CR1 is likely to be violated.

An Application to Migration and Remittances

About 1 in 10 Mexicans live in the United States, and these international migrants send more than $25 billion a year back to their families and friends in Mexico. This makes people Mexico's second most valuable "export" (after oil) in terms of the revenue they generate. Much of this remittance income goes to relatively poor households and regions in Mexico. Mexico's Central Bank reported that remittances fell sharply during the subprime crisis and recession of 2008. Understanding what determines remittances is vital from both an economic and welfare point of view.

There's a double self-selection problem when it comes to modeling migrant remittances. In order to observe remittances by person i, two things have to happen: the person has to migrate, and then she has to decide to send money home.

Why does this matter? Say we want to know how some variable (say, employment in the United States) affects remittances. As employment increases, migrants who already were remitting might remit more. But migrants who weren't remitting before might begin to remit. And new people might decide to migrate. We don't have remittance information for the last two groups, even though they could *become* remitters. In other words, they could become part of our sample if certain conditions, like employment, changed, so we can't ignore these potential remitters when modeling the effect of some right-hand-side variable of interest on remittances.

Fortunately, the Mexico National Rural Household Survey collects data on both migrants and nonmigrants. We can use the data from the 2003 and 2007 rounds of this survey to estimate a remittance model of the following form:

$$R_i = \begin{cases} \beta_0 + \beta_1 X_{1i} + ... + \beta_K X_{Ki} + \varepsilon_i & \text{if } I_i = 1 \\ 0 & \text{if } I_i = 0 \end{cases}$$

where

$$I_i = \alpha_0 + \alpha_1 Z_{1i} + \alpha_2 Z_{2i} + ... + \alpha_K Z_{Ki} + u_i.$$

Similar to Heckman's method described above, we first model people's (joint) decision of whether to migrate to the United States and remit ($I_i = 1$) or not ($I_i = 0$), using data on both migrants and nonmigrants. I_i is similar to the dummy variables we introduced in the last chapter; only in this case, individuals *choose* whether I_i is equal to 1 or 0. Here's what we get from the (0, 1) migration regression:

Variable	Estimated Coefficient	t-Statistic
Migrant from the household 5 years ago	0.135	26.96
Number of family members	0.000	0.35
Gender (1 = male, 0 = female)	0.118	17.55
Years of education	0.000	0.04
Potential work experience	0.001	1.42
Potential work experience-squared	0.000	−4.03

Clearly, migrating and remitting are selective. Human capital variables matter when it comes to predicting who migrates and remits and who does not. Rural Mexicans with more schooling are not more likely to migrate and remit, because the economic returns to schooling for (mostly undocumented) immigrants in the United States are minimal. However, there is evidence of a quadratic relationship between potential work experience and migration. The first year of experience raises the probability of migrating and remitting by about one-tenth of a percentage point (not significant at the 10% level, however), and additional years a little less. Males are 11.8% more likely to migrate and remit than females. People are nearly 14% more likely to migrate and remit if someone else in their family migrated previously.

We use this dichotomous (0–1) regression to estimate the probability that each person in our sample migrates and remits:

$$\hat{I}_i = a_0 + a_1 Z_{1i} + \ldots + a_k Z_{ki}.$$

Then we include the predicted probabilities as right-hand-side variables in our model of the level of remittances, which we estimate using only the people who remitted (since they are the only ones for whom we can observe remittances).

Notice we have an important identification problem here. We need to have at least one variable in the selection equation, above, that is not in the outcome equation (remittances). Otherwise, our predicted probability will be a perfect linear combination of other variables in the remittance equation! This would result in perfect multicollinearity. Again, this is where you might have to draw on your microeconomic theory to think about which variables might affect whether people migrate and remit and which variables affect how much people remit, given that they are remitting.

The results of correcting for self-selection using the linear probability model are presented in the table below. The first two columns (Model A) give the estimated coefficients of the remittance regression if we ignore self-selection and simply run an OLS regression of the level of remittances on our right-hand-side variables. (All standard errors estimated using White's heteroskedasticity robust estimator.) The results show that males remit about $968 more than females each year. There is some evidence that people remit more to larger families: as the number of children in person j's household increases by one, remittances increase by $176, although this effect is not significant at the 10% level. Human capital variables don't seem to affect remittances significantly at all. None of the three Mincer variables, years of education, potential work experience, and experience-squared, has an effect that is significantly different from zero.

Variable	Model A: without Selection		Model B: with Selection	
	Estimated Coefficient	t-Statistic	Estimated Coefficient	t-Statistic
Number of children in the household	175.88	1.37	115.75	0.89
Gender (= 1 if male, 0 if female)	967.62	2.32	1,416.67	3.17
Years of education	39.87	0.57	34.58	0.50
Potential work experience	48.17	0.79	69.53	1.13
Potential work experience-squared	−0.76	−0.64	−1.27	−1.06
Constant	−2,408.17	−0.50	−2,336.85	−0.49
Linear probability ($\hat{I}_i$)		NA	−3,516.743	−2.77

Mincer would point out that these results are likely to be biased, because the sample of remitters is self-selected. The second pair of data columns (Model B) show the results if we include the predicted probabilities in the model for remitters, in the spirit of Heckman's approach. In the selection-corrected remittance regression, the effect of children in the household is still insignificant. Gender is still highly significant, but now its effect is much larger: $1,417 instead of $968. The human capital variables remain insignificant. Evidently, any effect they have on remittances is indirect, through the selection equation: human capital variables affect *whether* people choose to migrate and send remittances home, but they do not affect *how much* they send home.

The predicted migration probability has a very significant and negative effect on remittances. People with a high ex ante probability of migrating and remitting, those whom we predict would migrate based on our selection equation, remit less. This result is interesting. Remember that people are much more likely to migrate and remit once others in the family have done so. The new regression tells us that the more likely people are to migrate and remit, the less money they send home once they migrate. As more and more people migrate, migration becomes less selective: there are more below-average remitters in the mix. The fact that the predicted probability of migration has a significant effect on remittances tells us that self-selection is an important concern here.

Although the procedure we just used captures the spirit of the Heckman procedure, Heckman does it differently, for a couple of reasons. A linear probability model, which estimates the probability of migrating (I_i) using OLS, is easy to estimate but has some problems. It has heteroskedastic errors. (We saw in Chapter 8 that the variance when we have a binomial distribution is $p(1 - p)$, which at the extremes of $p = 0$ and $p = 1$ is zero and reaches a maximum in between.) There is no guarantee that predicted probabilities from a linear model will fall into the (0,1) range.

The Heckman procedure is beyond the scope of an undergraduate econometrics course, but the idea behind it is fundamental. When endogenous variables, like the choices people make, determine whether or not individuals are in our sample, we need to control for those choices as we model the outcome. If we do not, there is a missing variable in our outcome model. Our estimates are likely to be biased if the same variables, observed or unobserved, determine both whether or not someone is in the sample and the outcome *given* that they are in. It is like we really have two models here: one for whether or not the outcome is observed for given individuals and the other for the outcome itself.

EXPERIMENTS

An increasingly common application of self-selection is in regard to experiments. Experiments are all the rage in economics these days. Experimental methods, in their purest form, are not really econometric at all. A perfectly designed and executed experiment should control for everything we could put into an econometric regression.

That is what drug trials try to do. Start with what we hope is a random sample from the population for which the drug is being tested (say, heart patients). Randomly split this group into those who will get the real treatment (the treatment group, TG) and those who will get the placebo (the control group, CG). Then administer the treatment and compare the outcome of interest (say, the incidence of heart attacks over the following five years).

Randomization avoids the self-selection problem. It ensures that, on average, the TG and CG are identical except for the treatment. Even if other factors (age, weight, etc.) affect the outcome, these variables don't affect which group an individual ends up in, and they should have the same distribution in each of the two groups, so you don't have to worry about them. If the process determining whether or not someone is in the treatment sample is truly random, you don't need econometrics to test whether or not the treatment worked. A simple comparison will do (say, of shares of people in the TG and CG who later suffer a heart attack).

Unfortunately, it is very hard to design clean economic experiments. That's because it's usually hard to argue that the TG and CG really are identical. Take a cash transfer program aimed at improving the nutritional and educational status of poor children. We give the cash to randomly selected households in some villages but not in others. Yet villages are different. Some are close to roads, others more remote; some are hilly, others flat; some have access to irrigation, others water-scarce. They may have different ethnic or religious mixes. The list of possible differences goes on and on.

We could choose both the TG and CG from within the same villages, but then we run a high risk that the treatment will affect the control group, too. For example, the households that get the income transfer use it to buy stuff from the control households, so the control households are not the same as households in villages where nobody receives cash transfers. We call this "control group contamination." On top of that, if you're in the control group and aren't getting, say, the government subsidy or training program, you probably know it—there's no such thing as an economic placebo. This is why we need econometrics: we have to control for the ways in which people in the TG and CG might be different, using methods that are related to the ones we've looked at in this chapter.

Even when an economic treatment is given out randomly, the treatment's impacts will be different for different kinds of people. Here's an example: millions of Africans, mostly in their prime working years, suffer from AIDS. A key to controlling the spread of AIDS is getting people tested. You hypothesize that, for poor people, cost discourages getting tested. You design a program that gives randomly selected poor Africans coupons to get free AIDS tests. But some people live closer to AIDS clinics than others. Transportation costs are likely more of an obstacle for those living farther away from clinics, so distance to the nearest clinic may determine how effective the coupon is at encouraging people to get tested.

We can control for distance to clinics ($DIST_i$) while evaluating the program's impact on the likelihood of being tested for AIDS. Let $T_i = 1$ if person i is randomly chosen to get a coupon, 0 otherwise. Let $Y_i = 1$ if person i gets tested for AIDS, 0 otherwise. Instead of just comparing shares of people in the TG and CG who get tested, we can estimate a regression model like this one:

$$Y_i = \beta_0 + \beta_1 T_i + \beta_2 DIST_i + \beta_3 T_i DIST_i + \varepsilon_i.$$

As long as the coupons are given out randomly, we do not have a self-selection problem: T_i is given. We can estimate this model using OLS. The estimated effect of the treatment will be

$$\beta_1 + \beta_3 DIST_i.$$

In other words, it will depend on how far a person lives from an AIDS clinic, and ex ante, we'd expect β_3 to be negative. If we reject the null hypothesis $H_0: \beta_1 = 0$, we conclude the treatment was effective at getting people tested. This is one of many examples in which experiments and econometrics come together.

Even if you randomly assign the TG and account for heterogeneous impacts, you may still face the issue that your sample is nonrepresentative. It may be easier to conduct an experiment on a population that is more receptive to the treatment than a different population.

Here's an example: Opower is an energy conservation program that mails "Home Energy Reports" to a random selection of consumers. These reports include energy conservation tips and compare energy use to that of neighboring households. This looks like an ideal experiment. A random set of households receives some information. Comparing actual energy use in these households to those that did not receive the information enables us to estimate the effect of the information on energy use.

Opower was rolled out gradually. The economist Hunt Alcott[2] studied how the estimated treatment effects differed between early and later trials. He found that estimates in the first 10 experiments substantially exceeded the estimates in the subsequent 101 experiments. This occurred because utilities in more environmentally inclined areas tended to adopt the program first and they tended to apply it to subpopulations of high energy users. The experiments gave great estimates of the effects of the program in each subpopulation, but the subpopulations that adopted the program first were not representative of the population of US residential energy consumers.

Experiments have changed the way we think about and teach econometrics. Any econometric analysis can be recast as a "thought experiment." Whatever it is you are estimating or testing, ask yourself what the ideal experiment would look like. It would undoubtedly involve randomization. Then compare this ideal to what you actually have, figure out what biases you are dealing with, and devise an econometric strategy to deal with them.

For example, you want to test the effect of income on the demand for smartphones. If you were all-powerful (and didn't have to worry about ethical details), how would you design the perfect experiment to do this? Here's an idea: randomly give money to some people (these people would be in the TG), while leaving everyone else alone (the CG). Then measure each group's difference in demand for smartphones before and after the exogenous income change. Since other things (like recessions) could also affect demand, you'll probably want to compare the TG's change in demand to the CG's. (This is called the "difference-in-difference" estimator.)

Or take our remittance example. You could randomly pluck people out of some Mexican households and make them migrate. If you could somehow make migration random, you wouldn't have to worry about self-selection anymore! Or unionism and wages: randomly force some workers into unions and keep others out.

Obviously, these experiments are impossible, but thinking about the perfect (though typically not feasible) experiment can help you design the econometric strategy you need to get as close as possible to the conditions of your idealized thought experiment.

What We Learned

- Nonrepresentative samples cause estimates of population coefficients to be biased if you sample from a subpopulation that has nonzero correlation between the X variable and errors. Examples include sampling on outcomes of the Y variable and (sometimes) selection on X variables not in the model.
- If you can build a model of selection into the sample, you may be able to correct for selection bias.
- Experiments can solve the sample selection problem in theory, although they are limited by the practical difficulties of generating a truly random sample and ethical restrictions on social experiments. Regardless, imagining the perfect experiment can help you design a defensible econometric modeling strategy.

Identifying Causation

Ice cream sales and forest fires are correlated because both occur more often in the summer heat. But there is no causation; you don't light a patch of the Montana brush on fire when you buy a pint of Haagan-Dazs.

—Nate Silver

LEARNING OBJECTIVES
Upon completing the work in this chapter, you will be able to:

► Explain how correlation differs from causation in regression models
► Learn the three sources of the endogeneity problem and how they cause assumption CR5 to fail
► Learn about some solutions to the endogeneity problem

U p to now, we have focused largely on the mechanics of estimating correlations between right-hand-side and dependent or outcome variables. We used sample data to predict outcomes and gain an understanding of a population. In Chapters 2 and 3, we derived the formulas for estimating model parameters using ordinary least squares (OLS). Chapters 4–7 were about using sample data to make statements about the population that the sample data represent. In Chapter 10, we focused on the process that generated the sample data from that population.

Often, economists seek more than correlations and an ability to predict. For many, the chief goal of econometric research is to determine whether *X causes Y*. If that is your goal, then it is not enough to show that *X* and *Y* are significantly correlated with each other, or that having information about *X* makes you a good predictor of *Y*. Thomas Sowell, an American economist, wrote: "One of the first things taught in introductory statistics textbooks is that correlation is not causation. It is also one of the first things forgotten."

Here's how to think about the difference between correlation and causation: correlation means that if you tell me what the value of *X* was, I can make a prediction of what *Y* was. Causation means that if you *change X* to a different value, then I expect *Y* to change by some amount.

Our study of schools' academic performance indexes (API) and free or reduced-price lunch eligibility (FLE) in Chapters 2–5 provides a good example of the difference between correlation and causation. We found a high and statistically significant negative correlation between FLE and API. This enabled us to make good predictions about a school's academic performance based on the share of its students receiving free or reduced-price lunches. Schools where most students qualify for free lunches perform significantly worse than schools where few students do.

Does this mean that free school lunches *explain* academic performance? Would expanding free-school-lunch programs reduce the API? The notion that FLE *causes* API seems preposterous. Why would kids' academic performance decrease if a free-lunch program made them better fed?

In short, FLE is correlated with API. It is a good predictor of API. But there is no reason to think that it *causes* API, because it is not clear why changing the school lunch program would change API. This illustrates the difference between correlation and causation.

We might reasonably hypothesize that *poverty causes* low academic performance. That would be in line with the theory in Chapter 1, because poverty induces stress in students from poor families, poor households generally are able to invest less money in their children, and schools in poor neighborhoods lack many of the facilities that schools in rich neighborhoods have. In Chapter 2, we first proposed FLE as an indicator or "proxy" for poverty. Only poor children qualify for free school lunches under most circumstances. Viewed this way, an economist might say that our findings are consistent with poverty causing poor school performance. However, they do not prove it, and they do not tell us how, say, a change in the local poverty rate would affect school performance.

WHY CARE ABOUT CAUSATION?

Suppose you want to design a policy to improve school performance at the lowest cost possible. What should that policy look like? Give schools more money to hire teachers and reduce classroom size? Give teachers raises and other incentives to teach better? Provide poor parents with cash welfare payments, so that they can invest more in their kids? Launch a campaign to educate parents on the importance of making sure their kids go to school and study hard?

Economists often use econometrics to try and provide answers to questions like these. They are questions of causation, not simply correlation. Determining whether an explanatory variable *causes* an outcome is often called "the identification problem" in econometrics. If your goal is to design policies and projects to achieve specific outcomes, you need to think hard about causation.

Here are a few examples of questions of causation that economists have asked and found strategies to answer using econometrics:

- Does joining a union or getting more education raise workers' earnings?
- Do immigrants reduce wages and employment for native workers?
- Do good roads make economies grow faster?
- Does economic growth make civil wars less likely?
- Do smaller class sizes make kids learn more?
- Do welfare payments to poor women make their kids better educated and well-fed?
- What makes some nations rich and others poor?

A NEW CLASSICAL REGRESSION ASSUMPTION

If we want to make statements about causation, we have to add a new assumption to the list of classical regression assumptions presented in Chapter 4:

- *CR5: The values of the right-hand-side variables are exogenous, or given (there are no errors in the X-direction).*

Most econometrics textbooks lump this together with the four assumptions listed in Chapter 4, giving the false impression that econometrics is not useful—or at worst, is misleading—if this assumption does not hold.

We saved assumption CR5 for this chapter in order to make the point that econometrics can be extremely useful even if right-hand-side variables have errors associated with them. We can still use our econometric tools to learn about correlations between explanatory and outcome variables, as well as to predict. However, when it comes to making statements about causation, we need CR5 along with the other classical regression assumptions.

The challenge in establishing causation between X and Y largely boils down to demonstrating that X does not have an error attached to it, or, if it does, that this error is not correlated with the error in the equation we're estimating. Otherwise, we have to find a convincing way to deal with the problem. When X has an error in it, we say that X is endogenous, and we are likely to have *endogeneity bias* when estimating the causal impact of X on Y.

THE ENDOGENEITY PROBLEM

The *endogeneity problem* is a general way of saying that a right-hand-side variable in the econometric equation has an error attached to it. There are three main reasons why an explanatory variable might be endogenous.

First, it might simply be *measured with error*. Ed carried out surveys in rural Mexico that ask people to recall their family members' migration histories, with questions like "Did your son work as a migrant in the United States in 1990? In 1991? Etc." Households' past migration experience is found to be an important determinant of their income, but some people recall family members' migration experience better than others. This creates an error-in-variable problem: our information on migration depends on people's memory as well as on what really happened.

Second, the explanatory variable might be determined as part of the same process that determines the outcome we are modeling. They are both outcomes in the same model, *determined jointly*. By "jointly" we do not necessarily mean "at the same time." It could be that X is determined before Y, but both are determined as part of the same larger process.

Third, we may have *omitted an explanatory variable* from the model that we want to hold constant in our causal experiment. Causal analysis involves changing the explanatory variable and estimating the effect of this change on a Y variable. But we usually want to hold other variables constant when changing the variable of interest. If we are estimating the effect of changing schooling on earnings, we want to hold constant cognitive ability. If we change schooling and cognitive ability, then we don't know whether it is ability or schooling that caused the change in earnings. However, ability is typically not observed; it is omitted from the model.

Often, an endogeneity problem can be explained as arising for any combination of the three reasons. This can be confusing. Is ability an omitted variable in an earnings model? Or are schooling and earnings jointly determined by ability? The answers are: yes and yes. These two questions are different ways of framing the same econometric problem. (Some econometricians reserve the term "endogeneity" for the "jointly determined" problem and do not use the word endogeneity to describe measurement error or omitted variables problems. We follow the modern trend of using endogeneity as a catch-all to describe failure of CR5.)

If you can imagine there being an equation that determines X as well as Y, you've probably got an endogeneity problem. On the other hand, if X is given, determined outside the model, then we say it is *exogenous*, and assumption CR5 is satisfied.

Here's an example of a likely endogeneity problem: our decision to go to college and the earnings we get once we join the workforce are likely to be part of the same process or "life plan" to maximize utility or earnings over time. People who are more likely to get high earnings from going to school are also more likely to go to school. In this case, schooling affects earnings, but prospective earnings also affect schooling, and cognitive ability affects both.

Let's consider the three reasons for endogenous variables in more detail, one at a time.

MEASUREMENT ERROR

We'll begin by looking at the simplest case, in which X is measured with error. In the simple regression model,

$$Y_i = \beta_0 + \beta_1 X_i + \varepsilon_i,$$

we have an error-in-variable problem if X_i has an error (call it u_i) attached to it. In this case, we observe $\tilde{X}_i$, but we want to estimate the effect of X_i on Y_i. The measurement error equation is

$$\tilde{X}_i = X_i + u_i,$$

where X_i is the part of $\tilde{X}_i$ that is deterministic, or measured without error. When Ed asks people about their migration histories, X_i is the true history and $\tilde{X}_i$ is the answer he gets. The recall error is in the difference between the two, u_i. If there is no error, $\tilde{X}_i$ is the same as X_i, and there isn't a problem.

What happens if we ignore the measurement error? Regressing Y_i on $\tilde{X}_i$ while ignoring u_i will result in a biased estimate of β_1, the population parameter—unless u_i is independent of the error ε_i. The regression equation you estimate is

$$Y_i = \beta_0 + \beta_1 \tilde{X}_i + \tilde{\varepsilon}_i.$$

The error term is $\tilde{\varepsilon}_i = \beta_1 \left(X_i - \tilde{X}_i \right) + \varepsilon_i = -\beta_1 u_i + \varepsilon_i.$ (You can see this by substituting in $\tilde{X}_i - u_i$ for X_i in the regression equation we want to estimate.) Notice that the measurement error u_i is in the regression error term. This means that the right-hand-side variable, which includes u_i, is correlated with the regression error. This correlation causes a bias in the OLS estimator.

Here's the math. Let's revisit the proof that b_1 is an unbiased estimator of β_1 (Chapter 5):

$$E\left[b_1 \right] = E\left[\frac{\sum_{i=1}^{N} \tilde{x}_i Y_i}{\sum_{i=1}^{N} \tilde{x}_i \tilde{X}_i} \right] = \beta_1 + E\left[\frac{\sum_{i=1}^{N} \tilde{x}_i \tilde{\varepsilon}_i}{\sum_{i=1}^{N} \tilde{x}_i \tilde{X}_i} \right].$$

If the observed value of the right-hand-side variable $\tilde{x}_i$ is uncorrelated with the error, the last term is zero, and our estimator is unbiased. But, look closely at the last term:

$$E\left[\frac{\sum_{i=1}^{N} \tilde{x}_i \tilde{\varepsilon}_i}{\sum_{i=1}^{N} \tilde{x}_i \tilde{X}_i} \right] = E\left[\frac{\sum_{i=1}^{N} \tilde{x}_i \left(-\beta_1 u_i + \varepsilon_i \right)}{\sum_{i=1}^{N} \tilde{x}_i \tilde{X}_i} \right] = -\beta_1 E\left[\frac{\sum_{i=1}^{N} \tilde{x}_i u_i}{\sum_{i=1}^{N} \tilde{x}_i \tilde{X}_i} \right].$$

The last term is nonzero because the measurement error is in both the observed variable $\tilde{x}_i$ and the error. Even if our model is a good predictor of Y, b_1

will not be an unbiased estimate of the effect of X on Y. We will not be able to say that a change in X *causes* a change in Y by an amount equal to b_1.

We can say something about the direction of this bias. As the sample size increases, this is what the parameter estimate in the uncorrected model gets closer to:

$$\beta_1 \left(\frac{1}{1 + \sigma_u^2 / \sigma_{\tilde{X}}^2} \right).$$

You can see that this collapses to β_1, the true population parameter, if $\sigma_u^2 = 0$ (no measurement error). Otherwise, the term in parentheses is less than one (since variances are always positive), and the OLS estimate is biased toward zero. In other words, it is harder to show that X causes Y if X has an error in it. Econometricians call this *attenuation bias*. The attenuation bias is larger the bigger the error u_i is compared to X_i.

The bias toward zero makes good intuitive sense. Imagine a science experiment in which you test the effect of fertilizer on the growth of bean plants. You arrange identical boxes of bean plants and randomly give each one a different amount of fertilizer. (We'll come back to the usefulness of random treatments at the end of this chapter.) Your plan is to check a month later to see whether the plants with more fertilizer grew larger than the plants with less fertilizer.

But in the meantime, a clueless janitor comes into your lab in the night and rearranges the boxes or accidentally spills fertilizer on some of the boxes. The janitor just created an error-in-variables problem. Your records show some boxes having less fertilizer than they really do have, and others more. You'll be surprised to find that some plants you thought got a low-fertilizer treatment grew large, while others you thought got a lot of fertilizer didn't grow much at all. It will be harder to show that fertilizer promotes plant growth. The error in fertilizer measurement biases the estimated effect of fertilizer on plant growth toward zero.

Measurement error happens all the time in the social sciences (and even in the laboratory sciences). Most econometric studies use data gathered in surveys of individuals, firms, and other entities. We ask people questions like how old they are, how many years of schooling they have, how many days they worked or how much fertilizer they applied to their corn fields last year. Some of these things (age, schooling) seem easier to remember than others (days worked, fertilizer applications). Sometimes people have an incentive to not tell the truth. Systematic underreporting or overreporting is a common problem when surveys ask people sensitive questions, like how sexually active they are, how much money they have saved, or whether they have engaged in illegal or questionably legal activities (Do you smoke weed? Speed on the highway? Cheat on your taxes?).

Attenuation bias toward zero applies to the simple measurement error problem. In multivariate regression (that is, when there are multiple explanatory variables), it turns out the direction of the attenuation bias is indeterminate. The nature of the bias is also more complicated in models that are nonlinear in parameters, which are outside the scope of this book.

Dealing with the Measurement Error Problem

Naturally, when we measure explanatory and outcome variables, we want to be as careful and precise as possible. Tremendous thought goes into designing surveys to minimize errors and make sure that we get the information we *think* we are getting. A major recent innovation in field surveys has been the use of electronic tablets to record people's answers. The tablets can be pre-programmed to spot likely data-recording errors, for example, by putting logical bounds around responses (years of schooling from 0 to 22 and not exceeding age; 1 = male, 2 = female; nonnegative prices, fertilizer use, etc.). Data can be checked instantly in the field. Strict quality control is critical in order to minimize measurement errors in primary data collection.

Most of the time, economists work with data gathered by other researchers, governments, and agencies. They do not have much control over data quality. Almost everything is measured with error.

If there is a strong reason to believe that an explanatory variable was measured with a lot of error, it is sometimes possible to find another variable that is highly correlated with the problem variable but measured with less error. It might be used instead of the problem variable in the regression we are estimating. When one variable "stands in" for another in a regression equation, we call it a *proxy variable*. In our school performance example, we used free-school-lunch eligibility as a proxy variable for poverty, which we did not observe.

Sometimes, knowing the direction of the bias can be useful. If, despite the error in X, you still find that X has a significant and positive effect on Y, you can conclude that the true effect is likely to be greater than what you estimated. If you find that X has a negative effect on Y, you can conclude that the true effect is negative and likely to be even larger in magnitude than what you estimated. In other words, you have a lower-bound estimate of the impact of X on Y, in absolute value.

Jerry Hausman, one of the best-known econometricians, insisted that because almost everything is measured with error, when we do econometrics, "The magnitude of the estimate usually is smaller than expected."[1]

Even though in a simple regression model the parameter estimate is biased toward zero, that might not be a problem if your goal is to use X to *predict Y*. In large samples, simple OLS gives us the best linear predictor of Y given X. Thus, we say it is a *consistent* estimator of the parameter needed to predict Y given X.

X AND *Y* JOINTLY DETERMINED

Let's return to the schooling-and-earnings example. It is similar to the fertilizer-and-growth example, in that both involve a treatment (schooling, fertilizer) that is expected to affect an outcome (earnings, plant growth). That's where the similarity ends, though. A huge difference between the two is that, in a laboratory situation, fertilizer application is exogenous, whereas people's decision about whether or not to go to school is endogenous.

Fertilizer application is exogenous because it is determined outside the model of plant growth. The conscientious scientist randomly determines how much fertilizer to apply to each box. The plants have no choice about how much fertilizer they get, and the scientist makes sure that the fertilizer application is independent of the error in the plant-growth equation. For example, he doesn't apply more or less fertilizer depending on how much a plant has grown each day.

That isn't the case for schooling. People decide how many years to go to school, and they make this choice in part to increase their future earnings. We can easily imagine there being a separate equation to determine people's schooling. It might look something like this:

$$X_i = \gamma_0 + \gamma_1 Z_{Xi} + u_i.$$

In this model of schooling, X_i is person i's years of completed schooling, and Z_{Xi} is a variable (or set of variables) that determines how much schooling person i gets. In theory, Z_{Xi} might include people's access to schools (in poor countries, many people do not have schools in their village), school quality, parents' schooling, or people's ability to pay schooling costs.

This equation has an error, u_i, which contains the effects of everything besides Z_{Xi} that explains schooling. If we do not have information on relevant right-hand-side variables, we cannot include them in Z_{Xi}, and they fall into the error term.

Earnings depend on the schooling people have accumulated as well as on other things, which we could call Z_{Yi}. In a Mincer model, those other things include people's years of work experience, but they also might include other characteristics that affect people's productivity, how they are treated in the labor market (e.g., gender and ethnic discrimination), and access to well-paying jobs (people in rural areas are less likely to have access to well-paying jobs than people in urban areas, for example). This is what the earnings equation might look like:

$$Y_i = \beta_0 + \beta_1 X_i + \beta_2 Z_{Yi} + \varepsilon_i.$$

In this earnings equation, the error term, ε_i, contains everything besides X_i and Z_{Yi} that determines earnings. These things include variables that we do not observe.

One variable that we are not likely to observe is ability. High-ability people might be more likely to attend school because learning is easier for them, so in terms of effort the cost of getting an education is lower for them. If we do not have a measure of people's ability, ability becomes part of the error in the schooling equation. But high-ability people also earn more, so ability is part of the error in the earnings equation, too.

It is clear that we have an endogeneity problem here. The schooling variable, X_i, has an error that is likely to be correlated with the error in the earnings equation: $\text{cov}(u_i, \varepsilon_i) \neq 0$. A simple OLS regression of earnings on schooling will give a biased estimate of the true returns to schooling, β_1. The sign and size of this bias will be

$$E\left[\frac{\sum_{i=1}^{N} u_i \varepsilon_i}{\sum_{i=1}^{N} x_i X_i}\right].$$

If unobserved ability affects both schooling and earnings, there is a good chance that the estimated coefficient on schooling in the earnings equation will be too high. The returns to ability will "load onto" the returns to schooling. We might have a good equation to *predict* earnings using people's schooling, but we will not have an unbiased estimate of the economic returns to schooling. We will not be able to distinguish between the effects of schooling and the effects of other variables that influence both schooling and earnings.

Notice that this is not a case of measurement error. We can have perfectly accurate information on people's schooling. The problem here is that schooling is determined inside the schooling-and-earnings model, instead of by some exogenous force outside the model. Anything that unexpectedly shocks schooling (through u_i) is also likely to affect earnings (through ε_i). If a child gets a chronic illness, it might affect his ability to work as well as go to school. Health shocks are a vivid illustration of how schooling and earnings are both endogenous.

To really drive home the point, imagine a thought experiment in which we randomly gave different people different amounts of schooling, then observed their earnings. People's schooling would then be exogenous, determined by the experiment instead of by the choices people make. If schooling were given out randomly, it would not be correlated with the error in the earnings equation, and we could estimate the returns to schooling simply by regressing Y on X.

Such an experiment, of course, would be unrealistic, not to mention completely unethical, because it would deny schooling to people who want it and force schooling onto people who otherwise would not choose to have it. In other situations, it might be possible to design randomized experiments to establish causation. As we shall see later in this chapter, some economists design experiments involving randomized treatments to overcome the endogeneity problem.

Simultaneity Bias

In the example we just looked at, the relationship between schooling and earnings was sequential, but schooling was endogenous. In other situations, the relationship between a dependent and right-hand-side variable may be *simultaneous*. Simultaneity is a particular case of endogeneity, in which each variable directly determines the other.

The most famous example of simultaneity in economics is the market supply-and-demand model. Both the quantity supplied and the quantity demanded depend on price, but the price is endogenous. It is determined by the market-equilibrium condition that the quantities supplied and demanded are equal. In this model, quantity and price are determined simultaneously.

The market demand for a good at time i depends on the price of the good at time i (P_i) and other stuff (XD_i):

$$D_i = \beta_0 + \beta_1 P_i + \beta_2 XD_i + \varepsilon_{Di}.$$

(Typically, XD_i would include things like income and population in the market we are modeling, because they shift around the market demand curve, raising or decreasing the quantity demanded at each price.)

We can't just do an OLS regression of D_i on P_i and XD_i. There's another side to this market: supply.

The market supply equation is

$$S_i = \alpha_0 + \alpha_1 P_i + \alpha_2 XS_i + \varepsilon_{Si},$$

where XS_i is other things that shift around the (upward-sloping) market supply curve (technology, input prices, weather, etc.). It, like XD_i, is exogenous to our market supply-and-demand model.

Considering that the quantities of market supply and demand are equal to each other when the market is in equilibrium, should the quantities we see increase or decrease with the observed market price? We would expect a price increase to *reduce* the quantity demanded but *increase* the quantity supplied.

The problem here is that the market price is not exogenous. It is determined by the intersection of supply and demand—the point where the quantities demanded and supplied are equal to each other:

$$D_i = \beta_0 + \beta_1 P_i + \beta_2 XD_i + \varepsilon_{Di} = S_i = \alpha_0 + \alpha_1 P_i + \alpha_2 XS_i + \varepsilon_{Si}.$$

We can solve this for P_i to get an equation for price as a function only of the exogenous shifter variables:

$$P_i = \frac{\alpha_0 - \beta_0 + \alpha_2 XS_i - \beta_2 XD_i + \varepsilon_{Si} - \varepsilon_{Di}}{(\beta_1 - \alpha_1)}.$$

We can rewrite this equation more compactly as

$$P_i = \gamma_0 + \gamma_1 XS_i + \gamma_2 XD_i + \varepsilon_i.$$

where

$$\gamma_0 = \frac{\alpha_0 - \beta_0}{(\beta_1 - \alpha_1)}, \quad \gamma_1 = \frac{\alpha_2}{(\beta_1 - \alpha_1)}, \quad \gamma_2 = \frac{-\beta_2}{(\beta_1 - \alpha_1)}, \quad \text{and} \quad \varepsilon_i = \frac{\varepsilon_{Si} - \varepsilon_{Di}}{(\beta_1 - \alpha_1)}.$$

You probably have performed an exercise similar to this one in a microeconomic class, but in an econometric course the equations you end up with have errors in them. You can see that the market price has an error in it, and this error is a composite of the errors from the supply and demand functions.

If our goal is to predict the equilibrium market price (or quantity) using information on XS_i and XD_i, there is no problem—we can simply regress P (or Q) on the demand and supply shifters. If we want to estimate the impact of P on supply or demand, though, we've got a problem, because there is a blatant violation of CR5. There are errors in the P_i direction as well as in the quantity $(D_i = S_i)$ direction. Any stochastic shock on supply (say, a drought) or demand (say, a recession) hits our model through the errors in the supply and demand equations, but this gets transmitted to the error in our price equation, ε_i. The relationship between quantity and price is simultaneous.

OMITTED VARIABLES

A common concern is that omitted variables that influence Y (and thus fall into the error term) also are correlated with X. If so, then a regression of Y on X will give a biased estimate of the causal effect of X on Y. It will reflect the effects of the other, omitted variables as well as the effect of X, confounding one with the other. We have seen an example of omitted variable bias in the Mincer model, where unobserved ability can affect people's schooling as well as their earnings.

Wouldn't it be nice to make the problem of omitted variables, well, just disappear? Here's one example where you can do that.

Extreme Dummy: Fixed-Effects Model with Panel Data

Panel, or longitudinal, data make it possible to control for omitted variables that do not change over time. Here's how it works.

Consider a model of household consumption $(C_{i,t})$ as a function of income $(Y_{i,t})$:

$$C_{i,t} = \beta_{0,i} + \beta_1 Y_{i,t} + \varepsilon_{i,t}.$$

In this equation, the subscript "i,t" refers to "household i at time t." There are many intangibles that might explain why consumption behavior is different for different households, even with the same income levels. They include household tastes, which we cannot observe. The "$0,i$" subscript on the intercept in this regression equation indicates that the consumption function shifts up or down on the vertical (consumption) axis for different households, in ways reflecting these unobserved household characteristics. In effect, each household has its own consumption function, anchored on the consumption axis by the household-specific intercept.

In Chapter 7, we learned how to use indicator or "dummy" variables to permit the intercept to shift for qualitatively different groups of observations in the data—men and women, for example. The coefficient on the dummy variable captures the effects of any unobserved characteristics that are correlated with the outcome of interest. For example, the coefficient on a gender dummy variable in an earnings equation captures the correlation of earnings with anything having to do with gender.

With panel data, we can do something similar in order to control for the effects of unobserved variables *that do not change over time* on the outcome of interest—that is, differences in the intercept from one observation to another. In effect, we can have a different intercept for each individual in the sample. These intercepts capture the effects of characteristics that vary across individuals but remain constant over time for each individual (like natural ability in an earnings model, or household taste in a consumption model).

We may not be able to measure intangibles, but if we have panel data we can control for them just the same by creating a dummy variable for *each individual in our sample.* That's a lot of dummy variables, but by including them all (minus one—to avoid the dummy trap) in the earnings regression, we could control for *all* of the unobserved time-invariant characteristics of people that might influence their earnings. No one will be able to tell you that you did not take into account hard-to-measure variables like ability, taste for work, or whatever.

How can we generate so many dummy variables, you might ask? With cross-section data we clearly could not: there would be just as many dummy variables as observations, so once we added in other variables, we would end up with $K > N$, that is, more parameters to estimate than data. That clearly is a problem.

Not so with matched panel data. If we have observed earnings, education, and experience in at least two different periods for each person in the sample, there will be enough data to make dummies for everyone! By including all these dummies ($N - 1$ of them) in our regression, we will end up with a different intercept for each person in the sample. These person-specific intercepts are called "fixed effects." They capture the effects of all of the (time-invariant) characteristics of individuals on the outcome being modeled, even though we can't directly observe these intangible characteristics.

You can accomplish pretty much the same thing by regressing the *change* in the dependent variable on the *change* in each right-hand-side variable. For example, consider the Mincer earnings model:

$$E_{i,t} = \beta_{0,i} + \beta_1 S_{i,t} + \beta_2 EX_{i,t} + \beta_3 EX_{i,t}^2 + \beta_4 G_i + \varepsilon_{i,t}.$$

The outcome variable is earnings of person i at time t, and the right-hand-side variables are schooling, experience, experience-squared, and a dummy variable for person i's gender. Earnings in the previous period, then, are

$$E_{i,t-1} = \beta_{0,i} + \beta_1 S_{i,t-1} + \beta_2 EX_{i,t-1} + \beta_3 EX_{i,t-1}^2 + \beta_4 G_i + \varepsilon_{i,t-1}.$$

We get the change in consumption by taking the difference between the two:

$$E_{i,t} - E_{i,t-1} = \beta_1 \left(S_{i,t} - S_{i,t-1} \right) + \beta_2 \left(EX_{i,t} - EX_{i,t-1} \right) + \beta_3 \left(EX_{i,t}^2 - EX_{i,t-1}^2 \right) + \varepsilon_{i,t} - \varepsilon_{i,t-1},$$

$$\Delta E_{i,t} = \beta_1 \Delta S_{i,t} + \beta_2 \Delta EX_{i,t} + \beta_3 \Delta EX_{i,t}^2 + \varepsilon_{i,t}^*.$$

You can see that the individual fixed effects (intercepts) vanish, because for a given individual they are the same in both periods. In effect, our model now compares individuals with themselves over time, by regressing the difference in their outcome on the difference in the right-hand-side variables.

The great thing about fixed-effects models is that they let us control for time-invariant unobservables that are likely to be correlated with included right-hand-side variables. If we ignore them, they become part of the error term, and the included variables are then correlated with the error, violating CR5. By controlling for the time-invariant unobservables, we can take an important step toward identifying the causal effect of X on Y, not simply the correlation between the two. In a fixed-effects earnings model, we might be able to control for ability and other time-invariant unobservables while estimating the causal effect of schooling on earnings.

There are a couple of catches, though. First, notice that gender disappeared in the FE model. That's because "dummying out" everyone in the sample controls for *all* characteristics, observed as well as unobserved, that do not change over time. Work experience is a time-varying variable, so it stays in our model. Gender for most people is time-invariant, so it would be captured in the individual dummies; we probably would not be able to test for gender differences in earnings in a fixed-effects model (that is, unless we had enough people in the sample who changed their genders during the time period covered by the data).

Schooling could be a problem, too, if individuals' education does not change over the time period covered by the data. Since schooling attainment can only stay the same or go up, we could only estimate an effect of education on earnings for people who went back to school and subsequently reentered the workforce. As you can see, given the same set of data, your approach might be quite different depending on whether you are interested in the effect of gender, schooling, experience, or something else on earnings.

The second big catch is that the fixed-effects model only controls for the effects of time-invariant unobservables. It does not control for the effects of things we cannot see that change over time. The results of FE models often are questioned on the grounds that there is likely to be something that we cannot see that did change. If omitted time-varying variables are correlated with the included variables, their presence can still bias estimates of causal impacts.

Someone might look at your gender-and-earnings model and say, "Hey, the economy is changing in complex ways that affect men's and women's earnings over time." Not only that, peoples' attitudes about gender might evolve over time in ways that make educated women more mobile in the workforce. Changes in economies, attitudes, and the world are notoriously hard to measure, so they are not in our regression equation. Is it schooling, or is it that the economy and attitudes are changing, that explains changes in people's earnings over time?

All is not lost, because a clever econometrician can control for changes in unobserved variables over time by including time in the original earnings model:

$$E_{i,t} = \beta_{0,i} + \beta_1 S_{i,t} + \beta_2 EX_{i,t} + \beta_3 EX_{i,t}^2 + \beta_4 G_i + \beta_5 t + \varepsilon_{i,t}.$$

In this equation, β_5 literally measures the effect of time on earnings—the effect of anything that is changing out there, including things you cannot measure or put a finger on, that otherwise would be missing from the equation. The catch here is that t only controls for changing unobservables that affect *everyone's* income in the same way—that is, by β_5.

What about changes in attitudes toward gender over time? We could include a time-gender interaction term, like this:

$$E_{i,t} = \beta_{0,i} + \beta_1 S_{i,t} + \beta_2 EX_{i,t} + \beta_3 EX_{i,t}^2 + \beta_4 G_i + \beta_5 t + \beta_6 t G_i + \varepsilon_{i,t}.$$

The new parameter, β_6, measures changes in the effect of gender on earnings over time.

Once we do our differencing trick with these modifications to the model, this is what we end up with:

$$\Delta E_{i,t} = b_1 \Delta S_{i,t} + b_2 \Delta EX_{i,t} + b_3 \Delta EX_{i,t}^2 + b_5 + b_6 G_i + e_{i,t}^*.$$

Some curious things happen. The differenced model now has an intercept, β_5, which is the coefficient on the new time-trend variable. Gender makes a reappearance in the model, with a coefficient of β_6. The interpretation of these two coefficients stays the same: the impact of time and the *change* in gender effect *over time*, respectively, in the augmented earnings model.

By controlling for individual and time fixed effects, we have made substantial progress toward identifying the impact of schooling on earnings. Nevertheless, some worries persist. A big one is that we can only identify the effect of schooling on earnings with information on people whose schooling changed during the time period covered by the data. Who are these people? People who returned to school as adults. Are these people representative of the population of all adults? How are they different from people who, like Ed and Aaron, ripped through college to grad school and then into the workforce? Can we use the results of our FE model to make statements about the population of all working adults, or only those who went back to school as adults?

We're back to the problem of defining our population, discussed in Chapter 4. If we want to say something about the population of all working adults, not only those who went back to school, we might have to abandon the FE approach and estimate an earnings equation like this one:

$$E_{i,t} = \beta_0 + \beta_1 S_{i,t} + \beta_2 EX_{i,t} + \beta_3 EX_{i,t}^2 + \beta_4 G_i + \beta_5 t + \beta_6 t G_i + \varepsilon_{i,t}.$$

Estimating this regression lets us use data on all individuals and all years. But it does not let us control for unobservables, like ability, that might confound our estimates of the causal effects of schooling on earnings. If we have access to IQ scores or some other ability measure, we can include them in this regression equation, but someone will always be able to come up with a reason why the endogeneity of schooling biases the estimate of the economic returns to schooling, versus the economic returns to other, omitted variables. We face a cruel trade-off between controlling for these unobservable variables, on the one hand, and being able to generalize findings to the population of all working adults, on the other.

We have seen that fixed effects provide a potentially powerful way to deal with a certain type of endogeneity problem. We have not yet offered any solutions that could work outside the panel data context. In the next chapter, we study an estimation method that can solve the endogeneity problem.

What We Learned

- Correlation means that if you tell me what the value of X was, I can make a prediction of what Y was. Causation means that if you *change* X to a different value, then I expect Y to change.
- The three sources of "endogeneity" are (i) measurement error, (ii) simultaneity, and (iii) omitted variables.
- Measurement error in X variables usually (but not always) leads to coefficient estimates that are smaller than they should be (biased toward zero). Proxy variables can help reduce measurement error bias.
- Simultaneity means that X and Y cause each other. A standard regression of one on the other cannot disentangle the directions of causation.
- Variables that affect Y and are correlated with X may be omitted from the model, causing the coefficients on X to represent the effects of the omitted variables as well as the effect of X, confounding one with the other. Fixed-effects estimation can mitigate this problem in panel data.

Instrumental Variables: A Solution to the Endogeneity Problem

What we call Man's power over Nature turns out to be a power exercised by some men over other men with Nature as its instrument.

—C. S. Lewis

LEARNING OBJECTIVES

Upon completing the work in this chapter, you will be able to:

▶ State the two necessary properties of a good instrumental variable

▶ In real-world settings, articulate the two properties of a good instrument and critique the instruments used by researchers.

▶ Apply the instrumental variables, or two-stage least squares, estimator to solve the endogeneity problem

If the right-hand-side variable in a regression is endogenous, then we need an equation to determine X as well as our equation for Y. We need to find a new variable with certain special characteristics to include in the X equation. We call this variable an *instrument* for X. If you are lucky enough to find more than one instrument, so much the better. But finding good instruments is not easy; applied econometricians spend more time in the pursuit of good instruments than perhaps any other endeavor! Instruments are the Holy Grail that econometricians seek in an effort to solve the endogeneity problem.

WHAT ARE INSTRUMENTAL VARIABLES?

An instrument is like a proxy variable, but instead of "standing in" for the endogenous variable, it is used to purge the endogenous variable of the error that caused the endogeneity problem. Doing this can be extremely useful if our goal is to establish a causal effect of X on Y. We don't want to know how *the instrument* affects the outcome. We want to know how X affects the outcome.

Let's get concrete right off the bat with an example of instruments in econometrics. Suppose we want to estimate households' marginal propensity to consume out of their income (X_i). The equation we want to estimate is

$$C_i = \beta_0 + \beta_1 X_i + \beta_2 SIZE_i + \varepsilon_i.$$

where C_i is the logarithm of household i's total expenditure on consumption, X_i is the logarithm of its income, and $SIZE_i$ is the family's size (number of mouths to feed). The parameter of most interest here, the marginal propensity to consume, is β_1. We want to get a consistent estimate of that.

A problem with this model is that people don't make consumptions decisions based only on current income. Income may go up and down over time, influenced by the work choices people make and stochastic shocks, like illnesses, bonuses, injury, or unemployment. Financial advisors urge people to save in good years and spend down their savings in bad years—that is, let their permanent income, not their current income, determine consumption. If people follow that advice, the income variable we really want in this regression equation is permanent income, not observed income. The observed income variable is a "noisy" version of the permanent income variable that really drives consumption. Current income is endogenous and measured with error.

It should come as no surprise that there is an error in this income variable. For most people, income is mostly earnings, and we just finished modeling earnings as a function of other variables (ability and schooling). Income should have its own equation.

How do we measure permanent income? Mincer would say that permanent income is determined by people's schooling and experience (we could include ability, too, if we knew it—but usually we do not):

$$X_i = \alpha_0 + \alpha_1 S_i + \alpha_2 EX_i + \alpha_3 EX_i^2 + \varepsilon_{Xi}.$$

Panel A of Table 12.1 shows what we get when we model income using a data set on 3,254 households in the Dominican Republic. (Note that we are using heteroskedasticity robust standard errors.)

The Mincer variables are highly significant in explaining household income. Remember that, with log variables, we can interpret the coefficients as percentage effects. So, an additional year of household-head schooling raises predicted log income by 21%. The first year of experience is associated with a 3.9% income gain, and additional years add somewhat less. The high F-statistic (50.18) tells us that we can easily reject the null hypothesis that schooling, experience, and experience-squared do not explain income.

We could use this regression to predict income for each household and then use predicted income in place of actual income in the consumption regression. The idea is that predicted income captures permanent income and excludes the noisy income fluctuations that don't affect consumption.

To make this work, we need to make one modification. The $SIZE$ variable appears in the consumption model, but we excluded it from the Mincer equation.

Table 12.1   Mincer Model of Household Income in the Dominican Republic

Variable	Panel A: without Family Size			Panel B: with Family Size		
	Estimated Coefficient	Robust Standard Error	t-Statistic	Estimated Coefficient	Robust Standard Error	t-Statistic
Schooling	0.21	0.02	9.49	0.20	0.02	9.23
Experience	0.039	0.005	7.16	0.028	0.005	5.31
Experience-squared	−0.00050	0.00067	−7.43	−0.00036	0.00064	−5.69
Family size				0.11	0.01	12.00
Constant	10.18	0.12	85.87	9.96	0.12	84.02
Sample size		3,252			3,252	
R^2		0.057			0.098	
F-statistic for H_0: $\alpha_1 = \alpha_2 = \alpha_3 = 0$		50.18			43.24	

This could be a problem. Large households tend to generate more income and more consumption—they need more income to feed more mouths. If we exclude *SIZE* from the Mincer regression, then we impose that permanent income is unaffected by family size. That means the relationship between consumption and family size has to be picked up by the coefficient β_2, even if the way family size affects consumption is through income.

Panel B of Table 12.1 shows results from the Mincer equation including *SIZE*. The regression equation is

$$X_i = \alpha_0 + \alpha_1 S_i + \alpha_2 EX_i + \alpha_3 EX_i^2 + \alpha_4 SIZE_i + \varepsilon_{Xi}.$$

The coefficient on *SIZE* implies that families with one more member have income that is 11% higher.

We generate predicted income from this regression as

$$\hat{X}_i = a_0 + a_1 S_i + a_2 EX_i + a_3 EX_i^2 + a_4 SIZE_i$$

and then we substitute predicted income for X_i in the consumption regression:

$$C_i = \beta_0 + \beta_1 \hat{X}_i + \beta_2 SIZE_i + \hat{\varepsilon}_i.$$

Using the predicted explanatory variable, $\hat{X}_i$, instead of the observed variable, X_i, in the equation of interest is called the instrumental variable (IV) method. The variables used to predict X_i are called instruments. In our example, we used the Mincer variables S_i, EX_i, and EX_i^2 as instruments for income.

Sometimes this method is called two-stage least squares (2SLS). In our example, the first stage is the income regression and the second stage is the consumption regression.

Good instruments must satisfy two conditions in order to convincingly solve the endogeneity problem.

- *IV1*: an instrument must be strongly correlated with the endogenous right-hand-side variable.
- *IV2*: an instrument must not be correlated with the error term in the main equation of interest.

We can definitively test whether IV1 holds by testing the null hypothesis that the coefficient(s) on the instrument(s) equal zero in the first-stage regression. It is standard practice to compute an F-statistic for the null hypothesis that the coefficients on the instruments all equal zero. (Remember that the F-statistic equals the Wald statistic divided by the number of restrictions being tested.)

Unlike a regular hypothesis test, we do not compare the F-statistic to a value from the F-tables. That is because we don't just need the coefficients to be nonzero; we also need them to be large enough to make the instrument(s) strongly correlated with the endogenous right-hand-side variable. A good rule of thumb is to only use a set of instruments if the F-statistic exceeds 10. Econometricians continue to debate the right criterion for determining whether IV1 holds, but we believe this rule of thumb is a good start.

In our example, schooling and experience clearly are correlated with current income, and the F-statistic for testing the null hypothesis that the coefficient(s) on the instrument(s) equal zero is 43.24. This is greater than 10, so our instruments clearly pass the first test to be good instruments for permanent income.

In our example, the Mincer variables are used to predict income for the second-stage (consumption) estimation. For predicted income to satisfy IV2, the Mincer variables must be independent of the error in the consumption equation. This is another way of saying that they do not belong in the original equation: S_i, EX_i, and EX_i^2 influence C_i only through their effect on X_i. Otherwise, the new income variable we constructed from them, $\hat{X}_i$, will suffer from the same problem as the original income variable.

Do the Mincer variables pass the IV2 condition? Unfortunately, there is no definitive way to test whether the IV are correlated with the error in the primary equation. Normally, economists rely on theory and logic to argue why an instrument is not likely to be correlated with the outcome of interest except through its effect on the endogenous right-hand-side variable. We need to ask whether, *at the same permanent income level* (that is, holding permanent income constant), people with more schooling consume differently than people with less schooling, or people's work experience somehow influences

Table 12.2   OLS and IV Estimates of Consumption Function for Dominican Republic Households

Variable	Panel A: OLS			Panel B: IV Method		
	Estimated Coefficient	Standard Error	t-Statistic	Estimated Coefficient	Standard Error	t-Statistic
Income	0.35	0.01	24.44	0.75	0.06	12.14
Family size	0.14	0.01	20.02	0.09	0.01	9.06
Constant	7.27	0.16	46.11	2.93	0.67	4.38
Sample size		3,252			3,252	
R^2		0.34				

their consumption choices. If they do not, then our instrument passes the second test.

If the two conditions are satisfied, an OLS regression of C_i on $\hat{X}_i$ and $SIZE_i$ will give us a *consistent* estimate of the effect of income on consumption.

Table 12.2 presents estimates of the consumption model ignoring the errors in variables problem (Panel A), and using the IV method (Panel B).

The marginal propensity to consume in the uncorrected, OLS model is very low (0.27) compared to the one we get using the IV method (0.75). This illustrates the problems we may encounter if we do not address the endogeneity problem.

Remember that, in the first stage of 2SLS, we should always regress the problem variable on *all* the exogenous variables in the model, including those in the main equation. (Here, X is regressed on S, EX, EX_i^2, and $SIZE$.) If we had excluded $SIZE$ from our first-stage regression, we would have gotten a similar estimate of the income coefficient (0.64), but a much larger coefficient on $SIZE$ (0.17). (We didn't put these numbers in a table, but you can verify them for yourselves using the data and instructions on the website.) That model overstates the effect of family size on consumption because it doesn't account for the fact that family size also affects income.

In the second stage of 2SLS, we will get the wrong standard errors if we just use a standard OLS regression command. The problem is that we are interested in one regression (consumption on family size and income), but we are estimating the coefficients using a different regression (consumption on family size and predicted income). This problem is solved through a technical correction as part of 2SLS or IV routines in econometrics packages. These corrections adjust the standard errors and t-statistics to account for the error in $\hat{X}_i$.

Solving the Simultaneity Problem

Endogeneity arises naturally in a simultaneous equation system, like a model of market supply and demand. In the market supply-and-demand model, we can use OLS to estimate a price regression.

In Chapter 11, we solved for the equilibrium price in a market model. We got

$$P_i = \gamma_0 + \gamma_1 XS_i + \gamma_2 XD_i + \varepsilon_i.$$

where XS_i and XD_i denote variables that shift the supply and demand functions, and the error term includes the errors in both the supply and demand equations. Provided these errors satisfy CR1–CR3, an OLS regression of P_i on XS_i and XD_i gives us BLUE estimators of γ_0, γ_1, and γ_2. The estimated regression

$$\hat{P}_i = c_0 + c_1 XS_i + c_2 XD_i$$

is a model of how supply and demand "shifters" explain the equilibrium market price. This can be interesting in and of itself, but it does not tell us how prices affect demand and supply.

The problem in our original supply and demand equations is that the price is correlated with the error—it is endogenous. If only we could replace it with a variable that is highly correlated with price, but not correlated with the error, we'd be set.

We have just such a variable: the predicted price from our regression of P_i on XS_i and XD_i, which we can denote $\hat{P}_i$. We'll need good instruments (exogenous shifters XS_i and XD_i), which will be a challenge. (We'll see how one team of economists dealt with this at the end of this chapter.) If we can find such instruments, we can use them to get predicted prices that should be highly correlated with the observed prices, P_i, but uncorrelated with the errors in the supply or demand equations. These are the conditions IV1 and IV2.

This discussion suggests a way to deal with endogeneity bias when estimating our supply and demand equations.

First, estimate the price regression, above, and use it to get predicted prices, $\hat{P}_i$.

Second, substitute $\hat{P}_i$ for P_i in the supply and demand regressions. That is, estimate the following:

demand: $Q_i = \beta_0 + \beta_1 \hat{P}_i + \beta_2 XD_i + \hat{\varepsilon}_{Di}$

and

supply: $Q_i = \alpha_0 + \alpha_1 \hat{P}_i + \alpha_2 XS_i + \hat{\varepsilon}_{Si}$,

where Q denotes quantity. This is an IV estimation, because it uses exogenous shifter variables as instruments for the endogenous price variable. In this estimation, we are using the part of the variability in price that is explained by the variables XD and XS, while eliminating the problematic part that's correlated with the error.

As in our consumption example, this method gives estimates of the parameters that are consistent. That is, as the sample size increases, the estimates of β_1 and α_1 converge in probability to the true parameter values, and given the central limit theorem, our usual hypothesis tests and confidence intervals will be (approximately) valid.

Drawbacks to IV Methods

You may have noticed in Table 12.2 that the standard errors in the IV and 2SLS regression are higher than in the OLS regression. By using the predicted values of income, we are removing quite a bit of the variation in our income variable. For example, in the consumption example, observed incomes are bound to vary more than the part of income predicted using education and experience (which is our estimate of permanent income).

Of course, removing the part of the variation correlated with the error was our objective, but we learned back in Chapter 5 that the precision of our estimates decreases when there is less variation in the explanatory variable. That's why we look for a high F-statistic in the first-stage regression. If it does not exceed 10, there's good reason to worry that your predicted values will not capture enough of the variation in the problem variable (income, price) to give reliable results in the second stage.

If you're sensing that there's a trade-off here, you are right. In trying to deal with the endogeneity bias, the IV method sacrifices precision. The weaker your instruments are, the greater the trade-off. If you have good instruments, though, there's likely to be a strong case for using IV methods—especially if you want to say something about causation. Often you will see economists report the results of their OLS and IV (or 2SLS) estimation, so that readers can compare for themselves.

You can learn how to do IV or 2SLS regression with Stata and Shazam in the Econometrics Rosetta Stone in the online appendix to this book.

THE QUEST FOR GOOD INSTRUMENTS

When it comes to establishing causation, endogenous explanatory variables are the single greatest challenge confronting econometricians, and finding good instruments is the challenge to solving the endogeneity problem. Because IV estimation uses only the variation in the endogenous variable that is explained by the instruments, you need instruments that are good predictors of the endogenous variable. Otherwise, you will not have enough variation in the predicted values to predict the outcome in your second-stage regression.

And you have to be able to convince your critics that the instruments you use are not correlated with the error in the primary equation of interest.

A great deal of effort and creativity goes into finding good instruments. We conclude this section on endogeneity by giving a few examples of instruments that econometricians have used to address the endogeneity problem. They are taken from a very rich literature involving identification strategies. You will see that some of these instruments are quite imaginative, and not all of them are without controversy. Most of the controversy surrounds assumption IV2—that the instrument is not correlated with the error in the primary equation of interest.

The Supply and Demand of Food

The prices of the world's most important food crops—corn, wheat, rice, and soybeans—nearly quadrupled between 2005 and 2008. This had major ramifications for human welfare and political stability in countries across the globe. What drives the supply and demand for food? Could US ethanol policy, which subsidized the use of food for fuel, be a culprit in the food price spikes? Economists Michael J. Roberts and Wolfram Schlenker wanted to find out.[1] However, they faced a classic endogeneity problem: prices determine supply and demand, but supply and demand also determine prices. They needed to find a convincing instrument that is correlated with prices but not directly with shifts in supply and demand.

They found an instrument in past yield shocks due to random weather. (Yield is the amount of production per acre of land.) Here's their argument: farmers decide how much land to plant to a crop based on futures prices. The actual amount they produce depends on the weather, which is unpredictable and out of their control. If bad weather hits, then there is less production and consumers pay a higher price. This means that current yield shocks can be used as an instrument for the price to consumers.

In addition, food crops can be stored from one year to the next. When bad weather hits, production goes down and so does the amount of inventory saved for the next period. This low supply of inventory causes futures prices to rise, which induces farmers to plant more of the crop next year. This means that past yield shocks can be used as and instrument for the futures price, which is the price that producers use when making their planting decisions.

The authors found that the yield-shock instrument passes IV1: current and past yield shocks do indeed significantly explain prices. To pass IV2, the yield shocks cannot directly affect current demand or future supply. A large part of world food output is traded. Thus, typically the weather shocks happen far away from where the food is demanded. This, the authors argue, makes it unlikely that yield shocks directly affect food demand. On the supply side, weather and therefore yield shocks are almost uncorrelated from year to year. The authors argue that this fact means that last year's yield shock doesn't directly affect this year's supply.

Using the supply-shock instrument to control for futures prices, this study found that US ethanol use increased world food commodity prices by about 30% and the total area planted in food crops by 2%. Higher prices shift surplus from consumers to producers and hurt most developing countries, which are net importers of basic food crops.

How Much Does Schooling Increase Wages?

Human capital theory posits that schooling increases people's earnings by making workers more productive. However, we have seen that estimating the effect of schooling on earnings is challenging, because people decide whether or not to go to school. This is a classic endogeneity problem.

Development economist Esther Duflo came up with a novel solution.[2] In poor areas of rural Indonesia, often there is not a school nearby. This makes it costly and difficult for children to attend school, even if they want to. Between 1973 and 1979, the Indonesian government launched a massive school-building campaign. Could new school construction be a good instrument for school attainment? If so, then we might use it to predict people's schooling levels, then use an IV method to estimate the impact of schooling on earnings.

There's a catch, though. While school-building intensity was higher in some parts of the country than others, we do not know why. The government decided where to build the schools; thus, school construction might be endogenous. Moreover, Duflo noted that timing is everything. If a new secondary school gets built in your community when you are the right age to take advantage of it, it will have the potential to increase your schooling and, later on, your earnings. Otherwise, it probably will not.

How old you are when the new school gets built depends largely on when you were born, which is pretty random. That sounds like a good instrument! Duflo defined a dummy variable equal to 1 if a person was young enough to take advantage of the new school (aged 13 or younger) and zero otherwise. She multiplied this by the number of new schools constructed in the region where the person lived. In the first stage, she regressed individuals' schooling attainment on this instrument. New school construction was found to significantly increase educational attainment—but only for the people who were young enough at the time the schools were built to benefit from them. Each new primary school constructed per 1,000 children raised average educational attainment by 0.12 to 0.19 years.

Using 2SLS, Duflo regressed people's 1995 wages (logged, as in the Mincer model) on their predicted schooling from the first-stage regression. She found that a 1-year increase in predicted schooling caused a highly significant increase in wages ranging from 6.8% to 10.6%, depending on how she specified her model.

Do Migrant Remittances Increase Income Inequality?

More than 1 in 10 people born in Mexico live in the United States. In the first half of 2015, the money Mexican migrants sent home, or "remitted," was $14.3 billion. That was more than Mexico earned from oil exports during that period. David Mckenzie and Hillel Rapoport wanted to know how migration affects income inequality in Mexico.[3] They proposed the following model:

$$Ineq_i = \alpha_0 + \alpha_1 mig_i + \alpha_2 mig_i^2 + \varepsilon_i.$$

The left-hand-side variable is income inequality of community i, measured by a widely used index of inequality, the Gini coefficient.[4] Migration prevalence (mig_i) is measured as the share of people 15 or older who have ever migrated to the United States. The migration-squared term is included to test for a possible nonlinearity in the impact of migration on inequality.

The problem with this regression is that migration is endogenous. People decide whether or not to migrate. Inequality could affect migration, as well as the reverse, and both migration and inequality might be affected by other variables excluded from this regression. To estimate the effect of remittances on inequality, the authors needed to find an instrument, correlated with migration but not directly with inequality.

They used state-level migration flows in 1924 as instruments for current migration. Labor contractors followed railroads built in the early 1900s to recruit men to work in the United States. The layout of the railroads, then, largely determined which places in Mexico had high migration rates and which did not. The authors also used migration rates over the 1955–1959 period. This was the peak period of the bracero program, a temporary worker program under which large numbers of Mexicans were able to work legally in the United States.

Both of these instruments were significant in explaining contemporary Mexico-to-United States migration. Thus, they passed IV1, the first test for a good instrument. When there is an endogenous right-hand-side variable, econometricians sometimes try to use the same variable observed in an earlier period as an instrument. The historical migration rates used here are in this spirit, though past migration is measured at a different level (state) than the inequality outcome (community). Since migration that happened many years ago cannot be affected by inequality today, that might seem like a good strategy.

However, there is a danger here. Even though the migration instrument is predetermined, there might be other, omitted variables that affect both inequality and migration over time. The migration instruments could be correlated with inequality in some way besides through current migration.

Historical data on inequality at the community level are hard to come by. The authors managed to find one data set on inequality in Mexico, in 1960. They tested whether their migration instruments were correlated with this historic inequality measure, and they failed to reject the null hypothesis of zero correlation. They interpret this as evidence that the migration instruments are likely to pass IV2 as well.

Using predicted migration from this regression, the authors found a nonlinear relationship between migration and inequality. At first, as migration increases, so does inequality. International migration is costly and risky; thus, the first migrants tend to come from wealthier households in Mexico. As migration prevalence increases, though, so do networks of contacts with family and friends, who can assist new migrants. This makes migration more accessible to poorer households. The two-stage least-squares model found that inequality first rises and then falls as a result of migration.

What's a Year of College Worth?

How can we measure the effect of college education on earnings if people's decision to attend college obviously is endogenous? Wouldn't it be ideal to have an experiment in which a lottery determined who went to college and who didn't? Then college educational attainment would be exogenous, determined by the lottery instead of by whatever it is that makes some of us go to college and others not to. But a lottery determining who goes to college? Preposterous.

Not so, said Joshua Angrist and Alan Krueger.[5] There was such a lottery—more or less—thanks to the Vietnam War. A lottery determined who got drafted to fight in the war and who did not. If you happened to get a low lottery number, too bad. Until 1971, there was one way out, though: you could get a deferment by going to college. That's how a lot of men at risk of being drafted avoided military service. Between 1965 and 1975, the college enrollment rate rose, then fell sharply.

Could it be that men with low draft lottery numbers got more college education than men with high numbers? Angrist and Krueger argued that men's draft numbers passed IV1 because lottery numbers were significantly related to educational attainment. However, later researchers found that their F-statistic was less than 10, so the instrument was not a strong enough predictor of college education. In modern econometrics, this is considered a case of *weak instruments* and a failure of IV1.

Does this instrument pass IV2? Might drawing a low draft number affect people's earnings directly? On the one hand, being random, draft numbers might seem like a good instrument. On the other hand, it isn't hard to imagine how getting drafted might affect one's earnings in ways other than through schooling. Ed knew people growing up who took drastic measures—including fleeing to Canada—to avoid the draft after drawing a low number. Those who got drafted could have been affected in ways that influenced their future earnings, from time lost at war to the legacy war left on their minds, hearts, and bodies.

The lottery instrument was clever but controversial, which probably is why this paper did not make it into a top economics journal.

The lottery IV strategy did produce an interesting outcome. Angrist and Krueger found that an additional year of schooling, as predicted from the lottery instrument, was associated with a 6.6% increase in earnings later in life. A simple OLS regression of earnings on schooling gave a smaller estimate, 5.9%.

Economic Growth and Civil Wars

Civil conflict is an enormous source of human suffering in many countries around the world. Since World War II, it has caused three times more deaths than wars between nations. Most of these deaths have been in poor countries. Does poverty *cause* civil wars? If so, then economic policy might be a tool to help prevent them.

How do we test the hypothesis that countries' (poor) economic performance causes civil conflict? You might imagine a model in which we regress a measure of deaths due to civil conflict ($conflict_{it}$) on income growth ($growth_{it}$) in a sample of countries over time:

$$conflict_{it} = \alpha_1 + \gamma_1 growth_{it} + \gamma_2 growth_{it-1} + \beta X_{it} + \delta t + \varepsilon_{it}.$$

In this equation, we include a measure of both current and last-period economic growth, because economic problems could affect civil conflict with a lag. X_{it} is a variable (we could include a set of variables) that controls for country-i characteristics at time t that might be correlated with conflict and growth. The time trend, t, controls for unobserved variables that might be associated with civil conflict across countries over time (like the Arab Spring).

Even with these extra controls, there is an obvious endogeneity problem. It may well be that economic growth explains civil conflict, but there is no doubt that civil wars also affect economic growth. Not only that; there might be other omitted variables that affect both civil conflict and economic growth.

We need an IV that is correlated with economic growth but not with civil conflict except through economic growth. What might that variable be?

Economists Edward Miguel, Shanker Satyanath, and Ernest Sergenti came up with one: the weather.[6] They found that higher rainfall (in the present and previous year) is significantly and positively correlated with economic growth in a sample of African countries. Thus, it passes IV1. When the rains come, economies do better.

Does the rainfall instrument pass the second test? Could rainfall affect civil conflict directly? Maybe people are less likely to engage in civil conflict during rainy periods. On the other hand, inclement weather might affect *when* civil conflict occurs during the year, rather than *whether* it occurs. These are the sorts of things you might think about in deciding whether or not the weather instrument passes IV2. The reviewers of this article were sufficiently convinced to approve it for publication in a top economics journal.

Miguel et al. used the rainfall instrument to predict income growth in the present and past year. Using 2SLS, they estimated an equation like the one above to test whether (low) income growth causes deaths from civil conflicts. They found that a 5-percentage-point drop in national income increases the likelihood of civil conflict involving 25 deaths or more the following year by more than 12 percentage points. This represents more than a 50% increase in the chance of civil war—a big causal impact.

Incidentally, if we do not care how weather affects civil conflict, only whether or not it does, we could regress civil conflict directly on current and lagged rainfall growth. This is called a *reduced-form* estimate. When Miguel and coauthors did that, they found that a 1-percentage-point increase in lagged rainfall growth causes a 12% decline in the likelihood of civil conflicts involving 25 deaths or more, and a 6.9% decrease in conflicts involving 1,000 deaths or more. Those findings, while interesting, do not give us much policy guidance. After all, there isn't much we can do about the weather.

Because it is random, the weather would seem like an ideal instrument to use to correct for endogeneity in a right-hand-side variable. Indeed, it has been used in so many studies that it is almost a trope. However, if we use the weather, we have to be convinced that it does not affect the outcome we are modeling directly, in addition to affecting it through the instrumented right-hand-side variable.

Malaria, Institutions, and Economic Growth[7]

As we have seen, economists sometimes rely on strange connections between events in their quest to establish causation. An influential study on why nations are poor created huge controversy over the key findings as well as the use of a novel instrument: malaria.

In economics, institutions are the operating system or "rules of the game" that underpin people's economic interactions. They include legal systems, markets, and conventions, and they can be extremely important in promoting or retarding countries' economic development. (Witness the high cost to society of government corruption.)

It is relatively easy to show that weak institutions *correlate* with (lower) economic growth. It is much harder to show that they *cause* it. To show causation, we need an instrument that is highly correlated with the development of institutions but not directly correlated with income growth—that is, an instrument that affects countries' economic growth *only through its effect on institutions.*

Daron Acemoglu, Simon Johnson, and James Robinson thought they came up with such an instrument.[8] Here's the story they tell: As European powers were colonizing much of the world in the seventeenth, eighteenth, and nineteenth centuries, the kinds of institutions they imported to a given place depended on how pleasant they found the place to be. If Europeans could live in a place without a constant threat of tropical diseases, like malaria, or other hazards, they tended to import institutions that were pluralistic, protected individual rights, and created the conditions that reward innovation and entrepreneurship, including secure private property and competitive markets. If, instead, mortality risks kept Europeans from settling en masse in a location, they became more interested in extracting value from the resources they controlled there (land, minerals, monopoly rights, public coffers, people, foreign aid, etc.)—a sort of "take the money and run" mindset. They put a few colonial masters in place to maintain (heavy-handed) order.

Could "settler mortality risk" be a good instrument for extractive institutions? Acemoglu et al. argued that it could be. They found that higher settler mortality caused Europeans to put extractive colonial institutions in place. Places that had extractive colonial institutions, in turn, had lower income per capita in 1995. Based on this finding, the authors claim that institutions *cause* economic growth.

This novel instrument, which comes to us mostly thanks to malaria-carrying mosquitos, passes IV1: it is significantly correlated with extractive institutions. But does it pass IV2? Is settler mortality in colonial times correlated directly with income today?

Since this paper was published in 2001, several critics have claimed that mortality risk is not a valid instrument, because it can directly affect current income levels. Many places that had high malaria risk 200 years ago continue to have high malaria risk today, and current disease pressure in a society directly affects current income through lost productivity. Thus, it is not clear whether extractive institutions or malaria caused the lower incomes. The analysis shows conclusively that nineteenth-century mortality is correlated with income levels in 1995. It is less clear whether this is because of the institutions European powers left behind or the current disease ecology.

This study provides a good example of a particularly original IV strategy, and also of the kinds of controversy that can arise when researchers try to make statements about causality as well as correlation.

Technology and Income Growth

Technological innovation is the single most important driver of economic growth, yet endogeneity issues make it difficult to estimate the impacts of new technologies on income. These impacts depend not only on new inventions, but also on how innovations spread, which is a complex process. We cannot simply regress income growth on the adoption of new technologies, because technological adoption is endogenous. We need an instrument that is correlated with the adoption of new technological innovations, but not correlated with income growth except through these innovations.

Jeremiah Dittmar came up with an IV approach to estimate impacts of the printing press on income growth in European cities.[9] The printing press was the great innovation in early information technology. Dittmar noticed that cities' adoption of the printing press in the 1400s was correlated with their distance from Mainz, Germany, the birthplace of this new technology. Thus, distance from Mainz passes IV1. The second test requires that cities' income growth did not depend on their distance from Mainz. Dittmar showed that incomes were not significantly different between the cities that adopted the printing press and those that did not at the time the adoption took place. This suggests that the distance instrument passes IV2.

Using an IV approach with distance as an instrument, this study found that cities that adopted the printing press in the 1400s grew 60% faster between 1500 and 1600 than cities that did not adopt. This study is unique in its use of a clever IV method to document the economic importance of technological innovation.

Class Size and Children's Economic Performance

Do smaller class sizes improve students' academic success? This turns out to be a tough question to answer, because class size is the result of decisions taken by school boards and potentially shaped by an array of variables, from funding availability to parent pressure. These variables are also likely to affect children's school performance in other ways, as discussed in the first few chapters of this book. Thus, we cannot hope to get an unbiased answer by regressing children's scholastic achievement on their class size. We need an instrument that is correlated with class size but not with children's school performance *except through class size.*

Joshua Angrist and Victor Levy spotted a fascinating instrument in Israel.[10] A twelfth-century rabbinic scholar named Maimonides argued that classes should have no more than 40 students. Israel follows this rule in its public schools today. That means that if there are, say, 38 students in a school's third grade class, they will all be put into a single classroom. However, if a school has

41 third graders, they will be split into two classrooms, one with 20 and the other with 21 students. It seems pretty random whether there are 38 or 41 third graders at a given school, but the result is a large variation in class sizes from one school to another, and from one grade to another within the same school, over time. Maimonides' "Rule of 40" results in an apparently exogenous variation in class sizes in Israeli public schools. The authors use it to obtain IV estimates of the effects of class size on children's scholastic achievement. They find that reducing class size causes a large and significant increase in test scores for fourth and fifth graders (though not for third graders).

THE GOLD STANDARD: RANDOMIZED TREATMENTS

Up to now, this chapter has pretty much followed the process any econometrician would follow trying to identify causal impacts of X on Y in a world where, more often than not, X is in some way endogenous. There is one situation in which X clearly *is* exogenous, though, and simple OLS can be used to make statements about the causal impacts of X on Y. This is the case when X is random, like in a drug test.

What if the amount of schooling each person got truly were random? If everyone were simply born with a given amount of schooling? Then we could simply compare the earnings of people with different schooling levels, regressing their earnings on schooling, and we'd have a BLU estimate of the impact of schooling on earnings.

When is X ever truly random like that, you might ask?

Randomized Control Trials

Having just seen some striking examples of endogenous right-hand-side variables, identification challenges, and clever IV strategies, let's consider the other extreme: an explanatory variable that we know is exogenous—because we create it to be so.

In 1962, the US Congress passed an act requiring that all new drugs be thoroughly tested on human subjects before they can be marketed. Drug manufacturers have to perform a *randomized control trial*, or RCT. You probably already know the formula to do an RCT: (1) devise a treatment; (2) identify your target population and from it randomly select a sample of people to run your experiment on; (3) split the sample randomly into two groups: a treatment group and a control group; (4) give the treatment group the treatment and the control group a "placebo" that looks like the treatment but isn't; (5) after enough time has elapsed for the treatment to take effect, gather new information on your treatment and control groups; (6) compare outcomes of interest between the treatment and control groups.

Think of Y_i as being the (bad) health outcome the new drug was designed to treat—for example, heart disease. T_i is the treatment variable, equal to 1 if person i gets the real drug and 0 if she gets the placebo. The equation to test whether the drug works looks like this:

$$Y_i = \rho_0 + \rho_1 T_i + \varepsilon_i.$$

With data on the health outcomes of N people as well as on whether or not each person got the real thing (T_i), we can estimate this equation using the simple regression tools we learned about in Chapter 2. A test of whether the drug is effective boils down to a test of the null hypothesis that $\rho_1 = 0$, versus the alternative hypothesis that $\rho_1 < 0$.

This is a clear case in which the right-hand-side variable, T_i, is exogenous. You can't get more exogenous than the toss of a coin, which is how the treatment variable is determined in a drug trial. People don't choose whether to get the real thing or the placebo. The researcher randomly chooses for them. (In fact, in a real-world drug trial, the researcher does not know who gets the real thing; a third party conducts the test.)

When it comes to testing for causation, you cannot do better than having a randomly determined right-hand-side variable. It is no wonder, then, that economists have embraced randomization in their efforts to model causation, producing a rich experimental economics literature. Here are a couple of examples of how experiments might be used to identify causation.

CONSUMER DEMAND Earlier in this chapter, we saw a novel IV approach to control for endogenous prices in a model of supply and demand. Can experiments offer an alternative way to estimate demand elasticities? How can we randomly hit some people with high prices and others with low prices for the same good?

We saw one example in Chapter 1. Katrina Jessoe and David Rapson estimated the elasticity of demand for residential electricity. They conducted an experiment in which they divided homes randomly into three groups. The first group faced electricity prices that jumped by 200–600% on certain days of the year. The second group faced the same price rises, but they also were given an electronic device that told them in real time how much electricity they were using. The third group was the control group: they experienced no change in their electricity prices. The researchers found that the first group had a price elasticity of demand close to zero, but the second group had an elasticity of −0.14. Having good information about the electricity we use matters.

The age of the internet and big data open up vast new possibilities to learn about consumer behavior using experimental methods. Scanner data from supermarkets allow researchers to estimate demand models with large data sets in ways that were not imaginable before. Big online retailers run their own experiments, targeting people online to estimate their sensitivity to prices, advertising, and other "treatments."

ECONOMIC DEVELOPMENT PROJECTS In 1997, Mexico launched a new poverty program called PROGRESA (Programa de Educación, Salud, y Alimentación), which gave cash to extremely poor women, conditional upon their kids being enrolled in school and the local health clinic. The government could not roll out this new program all at once, so it randomly chose which villages got the program in the first two years and which did not. The poor households in the villages that got the program were what we'd call the treatment group, and the poor households in the villages that did not get the program were the control group. By comparing the treatment and control villages, researchers were able to show that PROGRESA *caused* many favorable outcomes, from increased school attendance to improvements in children's nutrition and health. By comparing expenditures between treatment and control groups in cash transfer programs, we can come up with estimates of income elasticities of demand for specific goods. Randomization makes this possible: the flip of a coin determines whether poor people get the cash transfer or not. (You can learn about how RCTs have been used in a variety of development projects in Taylor and Lybbert.[11])

Sometimes economists spot "natural experiments," including historical accidents, which are arguably "as good as random." The weather in the civil conflict study we looked at earlier in this chapter is one example. Data before and after natural disasters, droughts, and unanticipated economic events like financial crises have been used to study how people and economies respond to exogenous shocks. Examples include David Card's study of the impacts of a surge in immigration (the Mariel Boatlift) on wages and employment in Miami; Dean Yang's study of the effects of the Asian financial crisis on households in the Philippines; Timothy Halliday's (2006) estimates of the impact of an earthquake on migration in El Salvador; and Richard Hornbeck's (2012) study of the impacts of the American Dust Bowl.[12] The biggest challenge in these "before and after" studies is making sure that other things that affect the outcome did not change at around the same time as the shock hit. For example, if large aid programs rush in after the disaster but before the "after" data can be collected, the impacts of the disaster may be confounded with the impacts of the aid; it will be difficult or impossible to separate the two.

Establishing causality is a complicated and messy science. In the past 20 years or so, many economists have become more skeptical of causality claims made from regression models. These economists believe that CR5 fails, or the chosen instruments fail IV1 or IV2. This skepticism is an important development. Business decisions or economic policies based on flawed causality analysis are likely to turn out badly. As we have learned in this class, regression models can be very informative about correlations in data. But we must be careful. Claims of causality should only be made when we have a watertight instrument or, even better, a truly randomized treatment variable.

A BRAVE NEW WORLD

We almost finished this book at the end of the last paragraph. But we could not help but add a glimpse of where we think the future of science, and especially economics, is headed, and how econometrics will fit into it.

It used to be that the image of science labs conjured up in vivo experiments, in which treatments were tested on living animals, often chimpanzees. An RCT is a sort of in vivo experiment, in which a treatment is given to one group but not to a control group. In November 2015, the US National Institutes of Health (NIH) ended the era of medical experiments on chimpanzees. Animal activists undoubtedly played a role in that decision, but the computer revolution is what really made it possible to phase out experiments on chimpanzees. Explaining the decision to stop using chimpanzees in medical research, NIH director Francis Collins said, "new scientific methods and technologies have rendered their use in research largely unnecessary."

Similarly, it is hard to overstate how technology companies like Google, Facebook, Apple, and Amazon have transformed the way we interact with each other and with the world around us. The answer to any question is at our fingertips at all times. New and old friends are just a screen tap away. This transformation is being driven by the heretofore unimaginable amounts of data collected by these companies, and the smart data analysts employed to comb through the data and figure out what people are doing, how they are behaving, and what they want to know.

What's happening out there? And does it affect economics, and in particular, the role of econometrics?

It's all about computing power.

Talk to any hip engineer and he or she will go on endlessly about the power of big data to improve our well-being. The sheer magnitude of the data allows analysts to tailor the research to individual groups. In the old days with limited data, we were stuck with averages and correlations across diverse observations. In the new era, we have vast data on subgroups of the population. Rather than estimating the average demand elasticity for the whole population, data scientists can estimate it for college students with a particular demographic profile living in a particular location.

Talk to almost any hip scientist, and he or she will tell you that the big new thing is not in vivo or in vitro (test tube) but in silico. In silico is a term used to describe scientific experiments or research conducted by means of computer modeling or computer simulation. Some scientists are now able to perform their research entirely by simulations, without performing physical experiments. Even old-school researchers are using in silico modeling to guide in vitro and in vivo research.

Here are three (among many) examples:

- *Rational drug design* (also called "computer-aided drug design"). Drug developers are using computer simulations to help design drugs to achieve specific health outcomes. Predicting the impacts of new drugs requires a good understanding of how drugs interact with human biological systems. Systems such as Molecular Dynamics, originally descended from the Monte Carlo simulations of the 1950s, are now frequently used to simulate atomic-scale molecular interactions between drugs and the biological systems they target.
- *Europe's human brain project* (HBP; a parallel project is underway in the United States). Is science ready to take on the challenges of simulating the workings of the human brain? The HBP thinks so: "Supercomputers make it possible to build and simulate brain models with unprecedented levels of biological detail."[13] Hundreds of scientists are performing experiments and statistical research to support this big new endeavor, and even the skeptics tend to agree it is a question of when, not if, it will succeed.
- *Climate modeling.* In an era of global climate change, the pressure is on to use quantitative methods to simulate the drivers of global climate change and predict future climate outcomes. Environmental scientists invest tremendous effort in creating climate models, and massive amounts of data are being gathered around the world to support this.

Economics, too, has a rich history of simulation modeling. Computable general equilibrium models simulate the workings of whole economies. Local economy-wide impact evaluation models simulate the impacts of government policies and programs on economic outcomes, like poverty. Economists team with climatologists to simulate impacts of climate change on the global economy. Any time we use an econometric model to predict, we are performing a kind of simulation.

These endeavors, as different as they may seem, have three important things in common. First, their goal is to understand how systems work, in order to predict outcomes. Second, they rely heavily on in silico computer simulations. Third, they depend on statistical methods applied to real-world data to estimate the relationships in their models.

Ultimately, the goal of science and social science is to understand how the world around us works and put this understanding to use to make the world a better place (however we may define that). Inevitably, we believe, economics will become more in silico, with greater reliance on simulation modeling and data analysis.

This will require putting the econometric tools in this book to new uses, constructing simulation models of economic systems from economic experiments and finding better ways to analyze data, including the "big data" made possible by the internet revolution. This brave new world presents many new challenges. But as you venture into it, you will find that the analysis of even the newest, biggest, data sets and the creation of the most cutting-edge simulation models relies on the very same econometric principles and tools that you have learned about in this book.

What We Learned

- Good instruments must satisfy two conditions in order to convincingly solve the endogeneity problem.
  - *IV1*: an instrument must be strongly correlated with the endogenous right-hand-side variable.
  - *IV2*: an instrument must not be correlated with the error term in the main equation of interest.

- In agriculture, this year's crop-yield shocks due to random weather are an instrument for prices in a demand model, and last year's crop-yield shocks are an instrument for prices in a supply model.
- In education, opening a new school nearby is an instrument for education in a wage model.
- In development economics, historical migration rates are an instrument for present migration rates in an inequality model, though not without some debate about the validity of IV2.
- In labor economics, the military draft lottery was a potential instrument for college attendance in a wage model, but it failed IV1.
- In development economics, rainfall is an instrument for local economic growth in a model of civil conflict in Africa.
- In growth economics, settler mortality risk is an instrument for extractive institutions in a model of economic growth, although researchers debate whether it satisfies IV2.
- In growth economics, distance from Mainz, Germany, is an instrument for adoption of the printing press in a model of income growth.
- In education, class size caps are an instrument for actual class size in a school performance model.

Critical Values for Commonly Used Tests in Econometrics

STUDENT'S *T*-DISTRIBUTION

Student's *t*- and *z*-Distributions

Student's *t*-distribution is symmetric and looks a lot like a normal distribution but with fatter tails, so it is more likely than the normal to generate values far from the mean.[1] However, as the degrees of freedom (df) become large, it converges to a normal distribution with a mean of zero and standard deviation of one. The critical values for a *t*-test thus depend on how many df we have.

Table A1 gives the critical *t* values for different df. The critical *t* tells us how many standard deviations your estimated parameter has to be away from whatever it is under the null hypothesis in order for the difference between the two to be statistically significant. If you compare (the absolute value of) your *t*-statistic to these critical *t* values, you can determine whether your result is statistically significant at different significance levels.

The three columns in Table A1 correspond to the three significance levels that are almost universally used in econometrics. Graphically, the significance levels are the areas in the tails of the *t*-distribution beyond the *t* values at which we reject the null hypothesis. The smaller the significance levels, the farther out in the tails you find yourself. This area is also the probability of rejecting the null hypothesis when in fact it is true (that is, the probability of a Type I error). The lower the significance levels you choose (see right-hand columns in the table), the lower the probability of a Type I error but the higher the probability of a Type II error (failing to reject when in fact the null hypothesis is false).

Econometricians pretty much uniformly consider as "insignificant" an outcome that does not pass the significance test at the 10% level ($\alpha = 0.10$). The lower the significance levels at which your result becomes significant, the farther out in the tail your result is, and the

Table A1   Student's *t*-Distribution

Degrees of Freedom	*p* Value (2-Tailed Test)		
	0.10	0.05	0.01
1	6.31	12.71	63.66
2	2.92	4.30	9.93
3	2.35	3.18	5.84
4	2.13	2.78	4.60
5	2.02	2.57	4.03
6	1.94	2.45	3.71
7	1.90	2.37	3.50
8	1.86	2.31	3.36
9	1.83	2.26	3.25
10	1.81	2.23	3.17
11	1.80	2.20	3.11
12	1.78	2.18	3.06
13	1.77	2.16	3.01
14	1.76	2.15	2.98
15	1.75	2.13	2.95
16	1.75	2.12	2.92
17	1.74	2.11	2.90
18	1.73	2.10	2.88
19	1.73	2.09	2.86
20	1.73	2.09	2.85
21	1.72	2.08	2.83
22	1.72	2.07	2.82
23	1.71	2.07	2.81
24	1.71	2.06	2.80
25	1.71	2.06	2.79

(continued)

Table A1 *continued*

Degrees of Freedom	p Value (2-Tailed Test)		
	0.10	0.05	0.01
26	1.71	2.06	2.78
27	1.70	2.05	2.77
28	1.70	2.05	2.76
29	1.70	2.05	2.76
30	1.70	2.04	2.75
40	1.68	2.02	2.70
50	1.68	2.01	2.68
60	1.67	2.00	2.66
80	1.66	1.99	2.64
100	1.66	1.98	2.63
150	1.66	1.98	2.61
∞(Z)	1.65	1.96	2.58

Table A2   Chi-Square Distribution

Degrees of Freedom	p Value		
	0.10	0.05	0.01
1	2.71	3.84	6.64
2	4.61	5.99	9.21
3	6.25	7.82	11.35
4	7.78	9.49	13.28
5	9.24	11.07	15.09
6	10.65	12.59	16.81
7	12.02	14.07	18.48
8	13.36	15.51	20.09
9	14.68	16.92	21.67
10	15.99	18.31	23.21
11	17.28	19.68	24.73
12	18.55	21.03	26.22
13	19.81	22.36	27.69
14	21.06	23.69	29.14
15	22.31	25.00	30.58
16	23.54	26.30	32.00
17	24.77	27.59	33.41
18	25.99	28.87	34.81
19	27.20	30.14	36.19
20	28.41	31.41	37.57

more confident you can be that what you got is, indeed, significantly different than whatever it is under your null hypothesis. If your t-statistic exceeds the critical t at a very low significance levels, you can conclude that what you got would be very unlikely if the null hypothesis were true. Thus, you'll reject the null hypothesis.

Towards the bottom of the table, you will see that the critical t values do not change much as the df increase. The bottom row gives the critical t values for df = ∞. They are the same as the critical z values you would find in any z table.

THE CHI-SQUARED DISTRIBUTION

Chi-square (χ^2) statistics are used in this book for tests in which the df equal the number of restrictions in a regression (e.g., variables in White's auxiliary regression, lags in a Breusch-Godfrey or Lagrange multiplier test, or restrictions in a Wald test). In most cases, this number will not be very large. Unlike Student's t-distribution, the critical value increases with the number of df in these χ^2 tests.

THE F-DISTRIBUTION

The F-distribution is asymmetric: it has a minimum value of zero but no maximum value. It is used for many different tests in econometrics. The ratio of two χ^2 variables divided by their df is distributed as an F. That's why we use the F table for some tests involving multiple parameters (Chapter 6). The sum of squared errors (SSEs) and the difference between SSEs are distributed as χ^2; thus, the test statistic we derive for tests involving multiple parameters has a χ^2 (divided by its df) in both the numerator and the denominator. So does the Gold-feld-Quandt test for heteroskedasticity.

The F-test has two df, one for the numerator and one for the denominator. There is a different critical F value

Table A3 *F*-Distribution

$p = 0.10$

Denominator df	\ Numerator df 1	2	3	4	5	6	7	8	9	10	20	40	60	120	∞
1	39.86	49.50	53.59	55.83	57.24	58.20	58.91	59.44	59.86	60.19	61.74	62.53	62.79	63.06	63.33
2	8.53	9.00	9.16	9.24	9.29	9.33	9.35	9.37	9.38	9.39	9.44	9.47	9.47	9.48	9.49
3	5.54	5.46	5.39	5.34	5.31	5.28	5.27	5.25	5.24	5.23	5.18	5.16	5.15	5.14	5.13
4	4.54	4.32	4.19	4.11	4.05	4.01	3.98	3.95	3.94	3.92	3.84	3.80	3.79	3.78	3.76
5	4.06	3.78	3.62	3.52	3.45	3.40	3.37	3.34	3.32	3.30	3.21	3.16	3.14	3.12	3.10
6	3.78	3.46	3.29	3.18	3.11	3.05	3.01	2.98	2.96	2.94	2.84	2.78	2.76	2.74	2.72
7	3.59	3.26	3.07	2.96	2.88	2.83	2.78	2.75	2.72	2.70	2.59	2.54	2.51	2.49	2.47
8	3.46	3.11	2.92	2.81	2.73	2.67	2.62	2.59	2.56	2.54	2.42	2.36	2.34	2.32	2.29
9	3.36	3.01	2.81	2.69	2.61	2.55	2.51	2.47	2.44	2.42	2.30	2.23	2.21	2.18	2.16
10	3.29	2.92	2.73	2.61	2.52	2.46	2.41	2.38	2.35	2.32	2.20	2.13	2.11	2.08	2.06
15	3.07	2.70	2.49	2.36	2.27	2.21	2.16	2.12	2.09	2.06	1.92	1.85	1.82	1.79	1.76
20	2.97	2.59	2.38	2.25	2.16	2.09	2.04	2.00	1.96	1.94	1.79	1.71	1.68	1.64	1.61
40	2.84	2.44	2.23	2.09	2.00	1.93	1.87	1.83	1.79	1.76	1.61	1.51	1.47	1.42	1.38
60	2.79	2.39	2.18	2.04	1.95	1.87	1.82	1.77	1.74	1.71	1.54	1.44	1.40	1.35	1.29
120	2.75	2.35	2.13	1.99	1.90	1.82	1.77	1.72	1.68	1.65	1.48	1.37	1.32	1.26	1.19
∞	2.71	2.30	2.08	1.94	1.85	1.77	1.72	1.67	1.63	1.60	1.42	1.30	1.24	1.17	1.00

$p = 0.05$

Denominator df	\ Numerator df 1	2	3	4	5	6	7	8	9	10	20	40	60	120	∞
1	161.40	199.50	215.70	224.60	230.20	234.00	236.80	238.90	240.50	241.90	248.00	251.10	252.20	253.30	254.30
2	18.51	19.00	19.16	19.25	19.30	19.33	19.35	19.37	19.38	19.40	19.45	19.47	19.48	19.49	19.50
3	10.13	9.55	9.28	9.12	9.01	8.94	8.89	8.85	8.81	8.79	8.66	8.59	8.57	8.55	8.53
4	7.71	6.94	6.59	6.39	6.26	6.16	6.09	6.04	6.00	5.96	5.80	5.72	5.69	5.66	5.63
5	6.61	5.79	5.41	5.19	5.05	4.95	4.88	4.82	4.77	4.74	4.56	4.46	4.43	4.40	4.36
6	5.99	5.14	4.76	4.53	4.39	4.28	4.21	4.15	4.10	4.06	3.87	3.77	3.74	3.70	3.67
7	5.59	4.74	4.35	4.12	3.97	3.87	3.79	3.73	3.68	3.64	3.44	3.34	3.30	3.27	3.23
8	5.32	4.46	4.07	3.84	3.69	3.58	3.50	3.44	3.39	3.35	3.15	3.04	3.01	2.97	2.93

Denominator df	1	2	3	4	5	6	7	8	9	10	20	40	60	120	∞
9	5.12	4.26	3.86	3.63	3.48	3.37	3.29	3.23	3.18	3.14	2.94	2.83	2.79	2.75	2.71
10	4.96	4.10	3.71	3.48	3.33	3.22	3.14	3.07	3.02	2.98	2.77	2.66	2.62	2.58	2.54
15	4.54	3.68	3.29	3.06	2.90	2.79	2.71	2.64	2.59	2.54	2.33	2.20	2.16	2.11	2.07
20	4.35	3.49	3.10	2.87	2.71	2.60	2.51	2.45	2.39	2.35	2.12	1.99	1.95	1.90	1.84
40	4.08	3.23	2.84	2.61	2.45	2.34	2.25	2.18	2.12	2.08	1.84	1.69	1.64	1.58	1.51
60	4.00	3.15	2.76	2.53	2.37	2.25	2.17	2.10	2.04	1.99	1.75	1.59	1.53	1.47	1.39
120	3.92	3.07	2.68	2.45	2.29	2.17	2.09	2.02	1.96	1.91	1.66	1.50	1.43	1.35	1.25
∞	3.84	3.00	2.60	2.37	2.21	2.10	2.01	1.94	1.88	1.83	1.57	1.39	1.32	1.22	1.00

$p = 0.01$

Numerator df

Denominator df	1	2	3	4	5	6	7	8	9	10	20	40	60	120	∞
1	4,052.00	4,999.50	5,403.00	5,625.00	5,764.00	5,859.00	5,928.00	5,982.00	6,022.00	6,056.00	6,209.00	6,287.00	6,313.00	6,339.00	6,366.00
2	98.50	99.00	99.17	99.25	99.30	99.33	99.36	99.37	99.39	99.40	99.45	99.47	99.48	99.49	99.50
3	34.12	30.82	29.46	28.71	28.24	27.91	27.67	27.49	27.35	27.23	26.69	26.41	26.32	26.22	26.13
4	21.20	18.00	16.69	15.98	15.52	15.21	14.98	14.80	14.66	14.55	14.02	13.75	13.65	13.56	13.46
5	16.26	13.27	12.06	11.39	10.97	10.67	10.46	10.29	10.16	10.05	9.55	9.29	9.20	9.11	9.02
6	13.75	10.92	9.78	9.15	8.75	8.47	8.26	8.10	7.98	7.87	7.40	7.14	7.06	6.97	6.88
7	12.25	9.55	8.45	7.85	7.46	7.19	6.99	6.84	6.72	6.62	6.16	5.91	5.82	5.74	5.65
8	11.26	8.65	7.59	7.01	6.63	6.37	6.18	6.03	5.91	5.81	5.36	5.12	5.03	4.95	4.86
9	10.56	8.02	6.99	6.42	6.06	5.80	5.61	5.47	5.35	5.26	4.81	4.57	4.48	4.40	4.31
10	10.04	7.56	6.55	5.99	5.64	5.39	5.20	5.06	4.94	4.85	4.41	4.17	4.08	4.00	3.91
15	8.68	6.36	5.42	4.89	4.56	4.32	4.14	4.00	3.89	3.80	3.37	3.13	3.05	2.96	2.87
20	8.10	5.85	4.94	4.43	4.10	3.87	3.70	3.56	3.46	3.37	2.94	2.69	2.61	2.52	2.42
40	7.31	5.18	4.31	3.83	3.51	3.29	3.12	2.99	2.89	2.80	2.37	2.11	2.02	1.92	1.80
60	7.08	4.98	4.13	3.65	3.34	3.12	2.95	2.82	2.72	2.63	2.20	1.94	1.84	1.73	1.60
120	6.85	4.79	3.95	3.48	3.17	2.96	2.79	2.66	2.56	2.47	2.03	1.76	1.66	1.53	1.38
∞	6.63	4.61	3.78	3.32	3.02	2.80	2.64	2.51	2.41	2.32	1.88	1.59	1.47	1.32	1.00

NOTE
1. If you ever wondered why it's called "Student's t," it's because the inventor of this distribution, William Gosset, published his paper about it in 1908, but his employer, Guinness Breweries, would not let him publish it under his real name. He chose the assumed name "Student." Think about that the next time you pop open a Guinness!

for each combination of numerator and denominator df and also for every significance levels. Every significance levels thus requires its own F table. In an F table for a particular significance levels, the numerator df are typically in columns and the denominator df are in rows.

In significance tests involving multiple parameters, the numerator df is the difference in the number of parameters to be estimated between the unconstrained and constrained models. This difference is usually not very large. However, the denominator df can be very large: it is the df in the unrestricted regression. For this type of test, we could get by with F tables that have a few columns but many rows. This is not always the case, though. In the Goldfeld-Quandt test, the numerator df is the df in the subsample of data used to estimate the regression variance appearing in the numerator of the test statistic. This number can be very large indeed.

It would take a tome to present F tables for many significance levels and large numerator and denominator df. The best way to find critical F values these days is to use an online F calculator: you simply enter the numerator and denominator df and the p value you choose, and the calculator gives you the corresponding critical F value. There are several of these out there; one example is at http://stattrek.com/online-calculator/f-distribution .aspx.

In the spirit of saving space, we've provided abbreviated F tables here (Table A3). They have plenty of gaps in them, but you can interpolate to get a pretty good approximation for any numerator and denominator df ranging from 1 to ∞.

Notes

CHAPTER 1

1. "Measuring the Impacts of Teachers I: Evaluating Bias in Teacher Value-Added Estimates." *American Economic Review* 104, no. 9 (2014a): 2593–2632 and "Measuring the Impacts of Teachers II: Teacher Value-Added and Student Outcomes in Adulthood." *American Economic Review* 104, no. 9 (2014b): 2633–2679.
2. Present value of lifetime earnings in 2010 dollars (see Chetty et al. 2014b).
3. "Knowledge Is (Less) Power: Experimental Evidence from Residential Energy Use." *American Economic Review* 104, no. 4 (2014): 1417–1438.
4. The book *The Big Short* by Michael Lewis tells one interesting such story.
5. "A Comprehensive Look at the Empirical Performance of Equity Premium Prediction." *Review of Financial Studies* 21, no. 4 (2008): 1455–1508.
6. Jacob Mincer introduced human capital theory to modern economics in what has become a seminal article: Mincer, Jacob. "Investment in Human Capital and Personal Income Distribution." *The Journal of Political Economy* 66, no. 4 (1958): 281–302.
7. These authors were not the first to develop VA measures, but their method is significantly better than previous methods.
8. Most residential consumers do not face electricity prices that depend on temperature, although that may change soon. At present, hot weather causes wholesale electricity prices to increase, but regulation prevents those increases from being passed along to residential customers.

CHAPTER 2

1. To simplify things, we do not replicate all of the columns of the original table, but we keep the column labels.

CHAPTER 4

1. Dubner, Stephen J., and Steven D. Levitt. *Freakonomics: A Rogue Economist Explores the Hidden Side of Everything*. New York: William Morrow and Co., 2005, p.8.

CHAPTER 7

1. Purchasing power parity: this adjusts income to account for differences in prices across countries, so that income can be compared in terms of purchasing power.

2. Answer: e^{ε_i}, since the natural logarithm is the inverse of the exponential function: $\ln(e^{\varepsilon_i}) = \varepsilon_i$.
3. Potential experience is what economists use when we don't really know how many years a person has worked. Usually it is defined as $AGE - S - 6$, on the assumption that kids begin school at age 6, and any years a person was not in school she could have been working. A 24-year-old with 12 years of schooling, then, has $24 - 12 - 6 = 6$ years of potential work experience.
4. Moss-Racusin, Corinne A., John F. Dovidio, Victoria L. Brescoll, Mark J. Graham, and Jo Handelsman. "Science Faculty's Subtle Gender Biases Favor Male Students." *Proceedings of the National Academy of Sciences of the United States of America* 109, no. 41 (2012):16474–16479.

CHAPTER 9

1. The general form of the equilibrium or long-run relationship is

$$C = \frac{\beta_0}{(1 - \beta_1)} + \frac{(\beta_2 + \beta_3)}{(1 - \beta_1)} X$$

2. Here is the exact formula for the error correction model:

$$C_t - C_{t-1} = -(1 - \beta_1)\left[C_{t-1} - \left(\frac{\beta_0}{(1 - \beta_1)} + \frac{(\beta_2 + \beta_3)}{(1 - \beta_1)} X_t \right) \right] - \beta_3 (X_t - X_{t-1}) + e_t.$$

You can see that it contains the equilibrium or long-term relationship.
3. "An Illustration of a Pitfall in Estimating the Effects of Aggregate Variables on Micro Units." *The Review of Economics and Statistics* 72, no. 2 (1990): 334–338.

CHAPTER 10

1. Taylor, J. Edward, and Antonio Yúnez-Naude. "The Returns from Schooling in a Diversified Rural Economy." *American Journal of Agricultural Economics* 82, no. 2 (2000): 287–297.
2. "Site Selection Bias in Program Evaluation." *The Quarterly Journal of Economics* 130, no. 3 (2015): 1117–1165.

CHAPTER 11

1. "Mismeasured Variables in Econometric Analysis: Problems from the Right and Problems from the Left." *The Journal of Economic Perspectives* 15, no. 4 (2001): 57–67. doi:10.1257/jep.15.4.57.

CHAPTER 12

1. "Identifying Supply and Demand Elasticities of Agricultural Commodities: Implications for the US Ethanol Mandate." *American Economic Review* 103, no. 6 (2013): 2265–2295.

2. "Schooling and Labor Market Consequences of School Construction in Indonesia: Evidence from an Unusual Policy Experiment." *American Economic Review*, 91, no. 4 (2001): 795–813.

3. "Network Effects and the Dynamics of Migration and Inequality: Theory and Evidence from Mexico." *Journal of Development Economics* 84, no. 1 (2007): 1–24.

4. You can learn about the Gini coefficient in J. Edward Taylor and Travis J. Lybbert. *Essentials of Development Economics.* Oakland: University of California Press, 2015.

5. *Estimating the Payoff to Schooling Using the Vietnam-Era Draft Lottery.* Working Paper No. 4067. Washington, DC: NBER, 1992. Available online at: http://www.nber.org/papers/w4067.

6. "Economic Shocks and Civil Conflict: An Instrumental Variables Approach." *Journal of Political Economy* 112, no. 4 (2004): 725–753.

7. From Taylor and Lybbert (2015, Chapter 8).

8. "The Colonial Origins of Comparative Development: An Empirical Investigation." *The American Economic Review* 91, no. 5 (2001): 1369–1401.

9. "Information Technology and Economic Change: The Impact of the Printing Press." *The Quarterly Journal of Economics* 126, no. 3 (2011): 1133–1172.

10. "Using Maimonides' Rule to Estimate the Effect of Class Size on Scholastic Achievement." *The Quarterly Journal of Economics* 114, no. 2 (1999): 533–575.

11. Taylor and Lybbert (2015).

12. "The Impact of the Mariel Boatlift on the Miami Labor Market." *Industrial and Labor Relations Review* 43, no. 2 (1990): 245–257; "International Migration, Remittances, and Household Investment: Evidence from Philippine Migrants' Exchange Rate Shocks." *Economic Journal* 118, no. 528 (2008): 591–630; "Migration, Risk, and Liquidity Constraints in El Salvador." *Economic Development and Cultural Change* 54, no. 4 (2006): 893–925; "The Enduring Impact of the American Dust Bowl: Short- and Long-Run Adjustments to Environmental Catastrophe." *American Economic Review* 102, no. 4 (2012): 1477–1507.

13. *The Human Brain Project.* A Report to the European Commission, 2015. Available online at: http://tierra.aslab.upm.es /documents/projects/HBP_flagship_report_for_Europe.pdf.

Index

Note: Page number followed by (f) and (t) indicates figure and table, respectively.